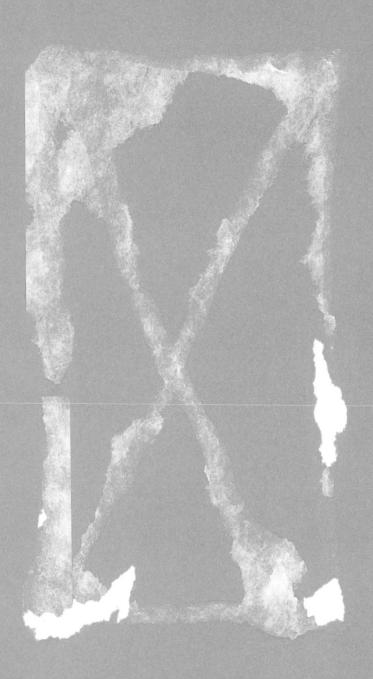

MYTHOLOGY

Tales of Ancient Civilizations

MYTHOLOGY

Tales of Ancient Civilizations

TIMOTHY R. ROBERTS ❧ MORGAN J. ROBERTS
BRIAN P. KATZ

MetroBooks

AN IMPRINT OF FRIEDMAN/FAIRFAX PUBLISHERS

©1997 by Michael Friedman Publishing Group, Inc.

Library of Congress Cataloging-in-Publication Data available upon request.

Editors: Nathaniel Marunas, Benjamin Boyington

Art Director: Jeff Batzli

Designer: Susan E. Livingston

Layout: Lynne Yeamans, Charles Donahue

Photography Editors: Susan Mettler, Wendy Missan

Color separations by HBM Print Ltd.

Printed in Singapore by Tien Wah Press (Pte) Limited

For bulk purchases and special sales, please contact:

Friedman/Fairfax Publishers

Attention: Sales Department

15 West 26th Street

New York, NY 10010

212/685-6610 FAX 212/685-1307

Visit our website:

http://www.metrobooks.com

CONTENTS

8   INTRODUCTION

14   PART 1: CLASSICAL DEITIES & HEROES

118   PART 2: NORSE GODS & HEROES

222   PART 3: THE CELTS IN MYTH & LEGEND

326   PART 4: DEITIES & DEMONS OF THE FAR EAST

432   BIBLIOGRAPHY

434   A GUIDE TO GREEK AND ROMAN NAMES

435   PRONUNCIATION OF CELTIC WORDS AND NAMES

436   INDEX

THE COMMONALITY
OF MYTHS

Myths mirror the innermost stirrings of the people who created them, helping later generations to understand the minds of their preliterate ancestors. Archaeologists excavate ruins and tombs, which reveal many of the details about the day-to-day lives of the peoples of early civilizations as well as details of the myths that helped shape their worlds. Perhaps the most penetrating way to investigate how our predecessors thought and how they viewed the world is by studying these myths. The heroes, the creatures, and the events that live on in the mythologies of the world are reflections of how ancient peoples viewed their physical and cultural environments. The ways in which these views resonate with our own experiences give us invaluable insight into the pressures our ancient forebears faced and the triumphs they enjoyed.

While certain forces, such as different physical environments, had varying effects upon the unfolding of myths in different cultures, intriguing questions arise when one ponders how the myths of seemingly diverse peoples can be so similar. Cultures as separated as the Norse and Chinese or the Greek and Japanese, for example, share a surprising number of mythological parallels. The Norse explain the creation of the world with the myth of how the gods Odin, Vili, and Ve cut up the giant Ymir to use his hair to make vegetation and his flesh to make the earth; similarly, the Chinese god P'an Ku sacrifices his hair and flesh to make vegetation and soil. The Greek hero Orpheus descends into Hades in an unsuccessful attempt to reclaim Eurydice, his lost bride, just as the Japanese god Izanagi attempts an equally unsuccessful rescue of his bride, Izanami, from the underworld. While some details may differ, the similarities between these myths are too striking to be coincidental, especially when one finds numerous other similarities scattered throughout the mythologies. The myths of the world seem to come from a few common sources, and uncovering these common sources is one of the most intriguing things about studying mythology, for it suggests, in a very real way, that humankind comprises a demonstrably unified family.

Heroes from widely diverse mythologies often share a remarkable number of characteristics, leading those familiar with stories from different cultures to suspect that they share antecedents. The Celtic hero portrayed in bas-relief on this stone obelisk may have counterparts in the legends of the Greeks, Romans, Norse, Japanese, Chinese, or Indians, to name just a few.

CELTIC AND NORSE MYTHS

Often such similarities among myths are easy to explain because archaeology and history show that the cultures that produced the myths directly interacted. For instance, the similarities between Norse and Celtic myths make perfect sense because the Celts and the Germanic ancestors of the Norse lived side by side—though seldom peacefully—for centuries in northern Europe. Thus it is no coincidence that Odin, the king of the Norse gods, and Lugh, the ruler of the Celtic gods, each has a single eye, carries a huge spear, and is always accompanied by two ravens that sit on the back of his throne giving advice and occasionally flying high over the world to gather intelligence for their masters.

Other similarities exist as well. Both Norse and Celtic mythologies preserve legends of trickster gods who have much in common. Neither the Norse trickster god, Loki, nor the Irish Celtic trickster, Bricriu, derives any special benefit from creating trouble; instead, both regard mischief as an end in itself. Another mythic motif that the Norse and Celts share is a hero who must prove himself before he can gain entrance into a king's hall. When the Norse gods Thor, Loki, and Hugi ask the gatekeeper at Jotunheim, the palace of the giant king Utgard-Loki, for admittance, the gatekeeper tells them that no one may enter unless he possesses a special skill. This is exactly the same challenge that Lugh, the Celtic hero, faces when he seeks entrance to the palace of Tara, where King Nuadha rules the Tuatha de Danu. Of course the gods of both groups deftly display a host of talents and gain admittance.

Both Norse and Celtic canons recount victories over giants, demons, or cruel enemies using magical spears that never miss their mark, swords that always strike true, and strange and magical practices involving huge cauldrons that return dead warriors to life. Finally, in both mythologies, battles between gods and their enemies do not end simply in complete victory; instead, they end in alliances between the heroes and their enemies—the Norse gods make an alliance with the Vanir, who are gods of the natural world and of magic, while the Irish Celts make a similar peace with the Tuatha de Danu, who are also nature gods and mighty magicians.

We know that the Norse canon borrowed heavily from the Celtic myths because Celtic residence in northern and central Europe predated the arrival of the German ancestors of the Norse by a thousand years, and archaeological and linguistic studies firmly identify Celtic deities long before the arrival of German tribes. It is most probable that the majority of mythological influences flowed from the Celts to the Norse through the continental Germans.

THE ROMAN INFLUENCE

While the Celts influenced the Germans, the Romans influenced both. The Romans borrowed their mythology wholesale from the Greeks and then passed these myths along to their less civilized northern European neighbors. Indeed, the Celtic, and later the German, greed for all things Roman was the chief reason both groups waged war so frequently against the Romans. Neither gold nor silver attracted

the barbarians to Rome, however, for both the Celts and the Germans had precious metals of their own. It was the cultural fruits of the mighty civilization that the northerners wanted. According to the Roman historian Titus Livius, when the Celts invaded Italy in 391 B.C., they came for wine, which they could not make themselves. Once the Celts arrived in Italy, however, they found much more to interest them than wine.

Perhaps the Celts sought to tap the power of their Roman enemies by adapting the classical gods to fit the Celtic pantheon, because at this time, many of the heretofore purely Celtic deities took on characteristics of the Greek and Roman gods. Ogmios, a powerful Celtic god, assumed the attributes of Hercules; the Celtic god of healing, Belenus, acquired the medical reputation of Apollo; Sulevia, or Sulis, a female healing deity, became identified in the Celtic mind with the Roman goddess Minerva (herself a Roman adaptation of the Greek goddess Athena); and finally Cernunnos, the dreaded Celtic god of the underworld, assumed many of the characteristics of Pluto, his Roman counterpart.

Fresh from their dark northern forests, the German barbarians probably not only aped the earlier Celts but also gazed with wondrous envy at the works of the Roman Empire. It is not surprising, then, that the Germans drew so largely from Roman mythology and made much of it their own. Dozens of German-influenced Norse myths show this slavish imitation: the Norse world was formed out of chaos just as the Greco-Roman world had been; the Norse gods, like their classical counterparts, initially had to battle giants in order to gain possession of the world. Just as some of the classical giants were huge and grotesque, so too were the Norse giants; just as the Romans believed that the sun was pulled across the sky every day by a horse-drawn chariot, so did the Norse believe that their god Sol (which is the Latin word for sun) did the same in his chariot, which was drawn by wolves. As the classical world believed that everything was predetermined by the three goddesses of fate—Cloth, Lachesis, and Atropos—the Norse also had three goddesses of destiny—Urd, Verdandi, and Skuld, known collectively as the Norns. Even the central edifice of Norse mythology, the great hall of Valhalla, where the spirits of departed warriors met daily to fight and feast, seems to have been inspired by the huge Roman Coliseum, with its hundreds of gates and openings, where gladiators feasted together before joining in fierce combat.

THE INDO-EUROPEANS

The similarities among Greco-Roman, Celtic, and Germanic myths are obvious and easily explained because of their geographic and temporal proximity and the awe with which these northern barbarians must have viewed Rome. Yet, behind these three mythologies lies an older body of myths that suggests another reason that the Romans, Celts, and Norse had similar myths—and that once, long before, they were part of the same people. Based on archaeology, linguistics, and myths, we know that the ancestors of all three groups were once part of the great Indo-European culture that flourished before 2000 B.C. on the Russian steppes between the Caspian Sea and the Black Sea. The ancestors of the subcontinental Indians came from that same area and culture, and their legends and myths would influence even the

myths of the non-Indo-European people of China and Japan.

One branch of these Indo-Europeans moved into Europe and produced the myths about Odin, Cuchulainn, Zeus, and Venus, while another branch was responsible for the myths that tell of the deeds of the Indian gods Indra, Vishnu, Vivasvat, Sarasvati, and Yakshini. By the time that all of these myths had developed into their individual forms, no Greek, Celt, German, or Indian would suspect that they had once shared a common origin. Only in the last two hundred years have scholars pieced that story together.

LINGUISTIC CONNECTIONS

The realization that Germans, Celts, Greeks, Romans, and Indians shared common cultures came about when Sir William Jones, a supreme court judge serving in India with the British East India Company in 1786, published, with the Bengal Asiatic Society, a study of Sanskrit, the sacred language of Hinduism. He concluded that there was solid linguistic evidence that Sanskrit, Latin, Greek, Celtic, German, and Slavic all evolved from a single but extinct language that he termed Indo-European. Proof of this, he asserted, lay in the similarities between hundreds of key words in each language. For instance, in Sanskrit and in Latin, the word for mother is *mater*. In Greek, it is *meter*; in Anglo-Saxon, *moder*; in German, *mutter*; and in Celtic, *mathir*. Similar close relationships between other words exist. Ten in Sanskrit is *daca*; in Latin, *decem*; in Greek, *deka*; in Anglo-Saxon, *tien*; in German, *zehn*; and in Celtic,

deich. (D, Z, and T are interchangeable in liguistics; over time, the D, Z, or T in one language can evolve into either of the two other letters.)

Other scholars continued to reinforce Jones' pioneer study, and many extended his work. By 1859, a Swiss linguist, Adolphe Pictet, quipped, "Words last as long as bones," and supported Jones' contention that similar languages imply that the people who speak them ultimately can trace their ancestry back to a common source. With the work of Jones and Pictet, the science of protolinguistics, or linguistic paleontology, was born. These studies point to the relatedness of the Germans, Irish, English, Swedes, and Italians, along with Russians, Poles, Persians, and subcontinental Indians, which made all these peoples realize that they were all related—one large, often unhappy family. In Europe the only linguistic "outsiders" seem to be the Finns, Basques, Hungarians, Estonians, and Lapps.

THE VEDIC MYTHS

Many Indo-European myths in India are preserved in the *Rig Veda*, a collection of poems written down about 600 B.C., but composed orally much earlier. The gods and heroes in this compilation, collectively called the Vedic gods, have much in common with their divine western European counterparts: Indra, the chief god, is, like Zeus, a rake who delights in the seduction of numerous women and, like Zeus, transforms himself to achieve his purpose. Just as Zeus assumed the appearance of her husband, Amphitryon, to seduce the beautiful and virtuous

Alcmene, so Indra, the most powerful of the Vedic gods, changed himself into the image of the sage Gautama in order to seduce the maiden Ahalya. This tale has a unique and gruesome twist, however, for Gautama discovers the lovemaking in progress and slices off Indra's testicles. Only an appeal to the collective healing arts of all the gods allows Indra to replace his testicles with those of a ram and so increase his virility sevenfold. Except for the testicles, the Indra and Amphitryon legends are also reminiscent of the Celtic myth in which Merlin assists Uther Pendragon in a metamorphic change to accomplish the seduction of Igerna, the wife of Gorlois.

Other similarities exist. The Vedic god Vivasvat shines like the sun and every day illuminates the world by driving his chariot drawn by seven white horses across the sky. It is not difficult to see this as the origin of the myth of Helios (or in other accounts, Apollo) who draws the sun across the sky in a chariot led by four white horses, or of the tale of the German and Norse god Sol who draws the sun across the sky in a chariot led by wolves. In Celtic mythology the shining face of Lugh is often mistaken for the sun when the god rises in the morning and uncovers his face.

Severed heads also play a role in all four mythologies. The Vedic god Shiva had a wife who gave birth to a son, Ganesha, during one of Shiva's frequent absences. When Shiva returned, he did not recognize Ganesha, who was guarding his mother's house, and so he struck off Ganesha's head. When Shiva realized his mistake, he beheaded a young elephant and placed that head on Ganesha's body. Since the elephant was known for its wisdom, Ganesha quickly became a sage to whom people came when seeking advice. It is not too

much of a mental stretch to see a similarity between this legend and that of the severed head of the Norse giant Mimur that the god Vanir cut off and placed beside the great well at the base of the World Tree that stands at the center of the earth. Norse gods and heroes often visited the head to ask it questions, for Mimur had a reputation for wisdom. Similarly, in Greek mythology, Orpheus' severed head is reputed to be the source of both wisdom and song for the people of the island of Lesbos. Welsh mythology records that the Welsh Celts similarly revered the head of King Bran of Wales.

The similarities continue: the Roman hero Perseus was born to the imprisoned Danaë, and the Indian god Krishna was born to Vasudeva under similar circumstances. The beautiful Sarasvati, the Indian goddess of music and poetry, who was also noted for her wisdom, is an early prototype of Athena, who presided over the same spheres for the ancient Greeks. The Vedic goddess of healing and wisdom, Yakshina, is likely the origin of Artemis, because they both presided over wild animals and the forests. It is not hard to see in Yakshina the origins of the Celtic goddess Brigantia, or Sulevia, who in turn would later evolve into Christianity's St. Brigid. Finally, the Vedic deities even ate a special food called soma that seems suspiciously like ambrosia, the magical food of the Olympians.

CHINESE
MYTHS

The ancient Chinese were not from the same cultural line as the Indo-Europeans, but surprisingly some of their myths reflect the influence of this prehistoric Indo-European culture. In fact, while

an indigenous Chinese mythology does exist, most Chinese myths were imported from India after much Chinese mythology had been intentionally destroyed. In 213 B.C. the Emperor Shih huang-ti (259–210), a brilliant and powerful egomaniac, ordered all books in the land burned except for those on agriculture, medicine, and fortune-telling. Included in this destruction were books of the centuries-old myths of the Chinese people.

After Shih huang-ti died, the Chinese were left to recreate a new mythology for themselves. Scholars throughout the following Han Dynasty attempted to reconstruct the lost mythology out of a few surviving fragments and some stray bits of history. Mainly, however, they seem to have relied on imported myths from India.

The Chinese creation myth is clearly an Indian import. Just as the *Rig Veda* tells how the world emerged from a giant egg— the lower half became the earth and the upper part became the sky—so the Chinese myth relates that the world was created from an egg: the shell of a great egg became the sky and the yolk became the earth. The Indian myth recounts how the god Brahma emerged from this egg to hold the sky apart from the earth. Likewise, the Chinese myth records that the god P'an Ku emerged from a giant cosmic egg to become a giant pillar that holds the sky and earth apart.

Later, when the sky was firmly in place, P'an Ku selflessly sacrificed his body, and its parts became the distinctive features of the earth. His left eye became the sun and his right eye the moon; his blood became the rivers; his sweat, the rain; his hair, the stars; his body and body hair, grass and flowers; and his body lice, mankind. The myth is obviously derived from the Indian myth about the giant Pursha, whose body is dismembered to create the physical features of the world.

The Chinese also borrowed the Indian myths about the underworld—a concept they did not originally have in their older mythology. Yen-lo, the god of Ti Yu, the Chinese underworld, is the exact counterpart of Yama the lord of Yamapua, the Indian underworld. A river surrounds these worlds and both have gatekeepers—the Chinese have P'an Kuan and the Indians have Chitragupta—both of whom judge a person's sins upon arrival in the underworld and assign each soul a place within the vast complex. Further proof of an earlier Indo-European link between P'an Kuan and Chitragupta is the Greco-Roman Rhadamanthys, who oversees admission into the Greco-Roman underworld, Hades, which is also surrounded by a river, the Styx.

Another Chinese myth that clearly traces back to India is about Chun-T'i, the goddess of light, who travels through the sky in a chariot drawn by seven pigs. She has eight arms, two of which hold the sun and moon. It is hard to escape the notion that Chun T'i is a form of the Vedic god of light, Vivasvat, who rides through the sky in a brightly polished copper chariot drawn by seven horses. Chun T'i's multiple arms also suggest an Indian origin, for Shiva, Vishnu, and Krishna, the most important gods of the Vedic religious hierarchy, are also multilimbed.

JAPANESE
MYTHS

The Japanese have borrowed myths from everywhere and blended them all into a unique canon of their own. Only a few Japanese myths appear to be based on those of the Japanese Mongol ancestors.

Most Japanese myths seem to have definite Indo-European roots, although the path by which these reached Japan is not known. Still other Japanese myths have Polynesian elements that drifted into the island kingdom from the Pacific, while a few minor gods and myths were imported directly from China during the great Buddhist missionary venture from that country in the sixth century A.D.

The legend of Izanagi and Izanami is a Japanese myth that contains both Indo-European influences and some distinctive Japanese elements. Grief-stricken over the death of his wife, Izanami, Izanagi descended into Yomi, the Japanese underworld, to bring her back. When he found he could not because she had already eaten food there, Izanagi wept for his wife; the tears from his left eye gave birth to the sun goddess, Amaterasu, and those of his right eye gave birth to the moon and to the moon god, Tsuklyomi.

The story of Izanagi and Izagami has always reminded researchers of Greek myths about Orpheus and Eurydice and Hades and Persephone. Izanagi's descent into the underworld to retrieve his wife clearly parallels Orpheus' attempt to bring back his wife, Eurydice. Izanami's inability to leave the underworld because she has eaten food there is similar to Persephone's six-month yearly tenure in the underworld because she ate six pomegranate seeds there. The creation of the sun goddess, Amaterasu, and the moon god, Tsuklyomi, from the eyes of Izanagi is also similar to the myth of P'an Ku.

The most remarkable feature of Japanese mythology is its durability. While many polytheistic myths and religions throughout the world gave way to monotheism, the Japanese continued to worship a huge pantheon of gods through-

out much of the twentieth century A.D. Japanese mythology, complete with gods, goddesses, demons, fantastic monsters, and miraculous and unscientific explanations for creation fueled the fierce nationalistic spirit that motivated the Japanese during World War II. The Japanese government ordered mythology taught in the schools, and the same government forbade the scholarly and critical study of myths—myth was taught as historic fact. Japanese soldiers believed that Emperor Hirohito was the direct descendent of the sun goddess, Amaterasu, who in turn had descended from the first divine couple, Izanagi and Izanami. The fierce fighting spirit of the Japanese that the allied nations encountered was at least partially due to Japan's ancient religion. It was also an eloquent testimony to the power of myth.

Timothy R. Roberts
June 15, 1997

PART 1
CLASSICAL DEITIES
& HEROES

THE CREATION OF THE UNIVERSE

According to Greek mythology, the universe was spawned from a great, limitless abyss devoid of form or content, an area of continual confusion and unrelenting darkness. This was Chaos, the progenitor of all things. Out of it came all aspects of the classical universe: the gods, the monsters, the earth, and man.

Chaos gave birth to, and subsequently was lord over, three entities: Erebus, the primeval darkness; Nox, the deepest night; and Eros, the unbridled

Detail from Greek sculpture, second century
B.C., showing Athena (left) fighting Gaea's
sons while Gaea (bottom right) emerges from
below to tend to her fallen children.

reproductive urge. Along with Chaos, these entities were the only things to exist in the universe for untold ages.

The next entity to come into being was Love, the child of Erebus and Nox. Without question, Eros had a hand in Love's creation, for without Eros, the urge to reproduce would never have overtaken Erebus and Nox. (In later myths there is another character named Eros who is a more anthropomorphic version, a more limited and understandable characterization of this primordial reproductive force.) Once Love had been created, there was no way that Chaos could continue its reign—Love began to order and harmonize the haphazard nature of the universe.

Eventually Love gave birth to the primary forces of Light and Day. These two siblings were able to vanquish disorder and create an environment ripe for the spontaneous creation of Gaea (Earth) and Uranus (Heaven).

With the advent of Gaea and Uranus, we begin to see the emergence of the first true characters of classical mythology. During their reign, Uranus and Gaea had five distinct types of children, all of whom Uranus treated rather poorly. It was Uranus' mistreatment of his offspring that eventually led to his downfall.

Their first three children were extremely strong, gargantuan monsters with a hundred hands and fifty heads each. These creatures were called the Hekatoncheires, or the Hundred-handed Ones. As soon as they were born, Uranus, filled with disgust, imprisoned them beneath the earth. Next to emerge from Gaea were the Cyclopes, another hideous race, easily recognizable by the one large eye in the center of their heads. Like the Hekatoncheires, these creatures were mountainous in size and possessed terrifying power. Unlike the Hundred-handed Ones, however, they were allowed to roam the earth as they pleased.

The last intentional children to come from Gaea and Uranus were the Titans, who, apart from their tremendous size and strength, were not the monsters their brethren were. They were twelve in number, consisting of six males—Coeus, Hyperion, Iapetus, Krios, Kronos, and Oceanus—and six females—Mnemosyne, Phoebe, Rhea, Theia, Themis, and Tethys. As he did with the Cyclopes, Uranus allowed the Titans to wander the earth at will.

Gaea was outraged that her husband would punish the Hekatoncheires simply because of their appearance. In her matriarchal fury she convinced the Titans that justice was due and that they should rebel against their father. Kronos, the leader of the Titans, ambushed Uranus and castrated him, stripping

The Castration of Uranus by Kronos, Georgio Vasari, c. 1555–1559.

him of his power. The blood from Uranus' wounds fell upon Gaea and was transformed into the last two pre-Olympian races: the Giants and the Erinnyes.

The Giants would prove to be continual adversaries for the race of gods still to come, the Olympians, although their attacks never gained them anything more than numerous wounds and the shame of defeat. The three Erinnyes (or Furies) were, for mortal man at least, the most terrible of all the pre-Olympians. It was the job of these blind, winged, birdlike sisters to torment those guilty of crimes against the social order, particularly blood-crimes against the family and murder. The Erinnyes were horrible creatures with their hair entwined with countless serpents. They wielded whips and hurled fire against their enemies. Because of their blindness, the Erinnyes couldn't tell when their victims had been suitably punished, and the victims often went insane because of this continual torture and were driven to kill again.

With the castration of Uranus, and Kronos' subsequent ascension to the throne, the reign of the first cycle of gods came to an end, and the stage was set for Kronos (Time) to rule the world with his wife and sister, Rhea.

The Fall of the Giants, fresco, Giulio Romano, c. 1532–1534.

THE
REIGN OF KRONOS

Some time after his reign began, Kronos learned of a prophecy that one of his children would overthrow him in much the same way he had overthrown his father. In an attempt to forestall this, he devised a simple plan: He would eat each of his children the moment they were born. Although she was overwhelmed with grief, Rhea was powerless to stop her husband and could only stand by and watch while Kronos devoured their first five children, the gods Demeter, Hades, Hera, Hestia, and Poseidon. Before their sixth child—

Relief of seventh century B.C. sculpture from
the Temple of Artemis in Corfu, Greece,
depicting Zeus fighting Kronos.

the infant Zeus—was born, however, Rhea had devised a plan that would save him. Immediately after his birth, she wrapped a stone in swaddling clothes and gave this to Kronos in place of the child. The Titan swallowed the bundle, thinking he had once again averted his deposal. Meanwhile, Rhea carried the infant to Mount Ida, on the island of Crete, where she placed him in the care of the Curetes (spirits of indeterminate origin).

The Curetes were a warrior race who were masters of bronze weaponry. In order to hide the cries of the infant Zeus from Kronos' ears, they continuously danced a wild war dance, clashing their swords and shields together,

creating a furious cacophony. In later myths, the Curetes were credited with endowing the Cretans with the knowledge of both metallurgy and agriculture.

Since Rhea could not come to Crete regularly to feed her young son, the she-goat Amaltheia nourished the young god in her stead. It was Amaltheia's hide that eventually covered the Aegis, Zeus' all-protective shield, and it was one of her horns, after it broke off, that was transformed by Zeus into the Cornucopia—a magical horn that would become filled with whatever its possessor wished.

During the time Zeus was on Crete, his companion and teacher was Metis, a daughter of the Titans Oceanus and Tethis. The word *metis* means "wisdom," and wisdom is exactly what Metis brought to the young Zeus. As his teacher, she taught him the ways of the world and provided him with the means to overthrow his father. Later, as Zeus' first consort, she literally filled him with all the wisdom she herself personified.

When Zeus was fully grown, he decided that it was time he replaced Kronos as the lord of the heavens. Unfortunately, although he was full of desire, he had no concrete plans. Metis gave him a potion that, she said, would force Kronos to vomit up the five swallowed children still living in his stomach. With the help of Rhea, Zeus was able to trick Kronos into drinking the elixir, and Zeus' five brothers and sisters were soon free. When they came back into the world, they were furious at their father, and Zeus had no trouble convincing them to combine their forces and help Zeus to achieve Kronos' overthrow.

Thus began the war between the Titans and the Olympians. Of all wars, there is none so destructive as that between immortals, for in a conflict of this kind there can be no casualties—the fallen will quickly rise again, completely healed, to continue the battle. Such was the war between the Titans and the Olympians; had not Zeus enlisted the aid of some formidable allies, this war might have caused the destruction of the earth itself.

Hoping to turn the tide of battle to his advantage, Zeus freed the Hundred-handed Ones from their prison in Tartarus. Indebted to the young god, these monsters gladly agreed to add their earthshaking power to the forces assembled against the Titans. The Cyclopes also allied themselves with Zeus, supplying him with the arsenal of thunder and lightning that would later become his

trademark weapons. With the ranks of their relatively young army now bolstered, Zeus and the Olympians soon defeated the Titans. Much as Kronos had done to Uranus countless ages before, Zeus castrated his father. He then imprisoned the Titans in the bowels of the earth.

With the Titans now vanquished, the question of leadership arose, with each of the three male Olympians—Hades, Poseidon, and Zeus—vying for the position. Even though Zeus had freed them from their father's stomach and masterminded his overthrow, Hades and Poseidon still thought of him as their younger brother, and therefore not suited to the position of supreme ruler. Since there were two other areas in need of rulers, the oceans and the underworld, the three decided to draw lots. Hades became ruler of the underworld; Poseidon was made sovereign over the oceans; and Zeus was granted reign over all else, becoming the king of the gods. The age of the Olympians had begun.

LEFT: Bronze statuette of Jupiter (the Roman name for Zeus), Hellenistic period.

BELOW: Poseidon, the ruler of the oceans, holding his trademark trident.

THE
CREATION OF MAN

After all of the original Olympians were born and Zeus usurped the throne, it was time for man to come into being. In the classical canon there are two versions of the ascent of mankind; in both versions, the Titan Prometheus plays an important role.

In the first version, men were said to grow from the earth like grain. In this account, the gods oversaw five different generations, or ages, of man that became less perfect with each successive age.

Prometheus Carrying Fire, Jan Crossiers,
seventeenth century.

The first generation was called the Golden Age. Although mortal, the men of this age lived as carefree a life as the gods: Food and drink were abundant; hardship and strife were unknown; and when death finally took them, they became the guardian angels of mankind. The men of the Golden Age lived in harmony with the gods, with the two races at times even sharing the same table. It was during one of these banquets that Prometheus played a trick on Zeus that the king of the gods did not appreciate—his resultant wrath led to the end of the Golden Age.

As the table was being prepared, Prometheus slew an ox and divided it into two portions, of which the gods were to have first pick. One portion contained the tender meat, but Prometheus covered this share with the hide of the ox, making it appear unappetizing and stringy. The other portion contained nothing more than bones, but was covered with tantalizing layers of rich fat. Zeus immediately chose the fat-covered, tasty portion, thus giving the fulfilling meat to the mortals. When Zeus, who was never known for his cool head, discovered this deception, he became enraged and decreed that from that point on man would no longer be free of hunger and would no longer be permitted to use fire, which cooked the meat and made it edible. From now on, man would have to toil furiously in the fields, spending all his time planting and harvesting the grain that until then had grown without aid.

Feeling guilty, Prometheus flew to the sun and stole some of its fire, which he brought

RIGHT: **Black-figured kylix, c. 555 B.C., depicting two of the early punishments of Zeus: Atlas supporting the world, in retaliation for leading an unsuccessful coup against Zeus, and Prometheus having his liver eaten by the eagle.**

OPPOSITE: **Marble relief from a Roman sarcophagus, A.D. 3rd century, showing Prometheus creating man. Behind the Titan stands Minerva (the Roman version of Athena) guiding him in this endeavor.**

to earth, hid in the stem of the fennel plant, and gave to man. This fire, however, was not as perfect as the fire of the Golden Age—it had as delicate a life as man, and would die if not attended constantly.

Zeus soon learned of Prometheus' transgression. Always prone to violent retaliation, Zeus decided to punish not only Prometheus but man as well. Prometheus was chained to a rock in the Caucasus Mountains where every day a ravenous eagle would tear open his belly and devour his liver. This ghastly wound would heal overnight, just in time for the eagle's next visit. Man's punishment, though less violent, was no less painful. Up to this point, man had lived without women; new men grew from the ground, much like wheat, and when they died, they died peacefully, without pain. Sickness, plague, feebleness—all these things were unknown to them, as were heartbreak, lust, and deception.

Eva Prima Pandora, Jean Cousin, c. 1530–1560.

Zeus ordered that a "gift" be made for man. This gift had the form of the goddesses and was endowed by different deities with different traits. Aphrodite, the goddess of physical love, graced the creation with a beauty that would instill lust in the hearts of man. Athena, the goddess of wisdom, gave the gift the knowledge of how to care for man. Hermes, the god of thievery and cunning, granted the creation the ability to lie. Zeus' gift was named Pandora, and she was the first woman.

Zeus sent Pandora to earth. Upon her arrival, men became helplessly enthralled by her beauty. From this point on, man was not alone on the earth; there was now something that would arouse his desires and make his mind stray from whatever he was doing. In order to have children, he would have to take time away from his crops and his animals to woo her and convince her that he was worthy of her affections.

EVA PRIMA PANDORA

Pandora also brought with her an infamous piece of luggage: a box that Zeus had ordered her never to open. Curiosity soon got the better of her and she lifted the lid just a little. Out of the tiny crack flew all the evils and pestilence that contaminate the world; Painful Death, Suffering, Disease, Plague, Jealousy, Hatred, Envy, Crime—all these demons and more flew from the box. Terrified, she slammed the lid back down, but it was too late. She'd been able to keep only one of the box's residents inside; if Hope had escaped as well, mankind would have nothing to believe in during times of hardship. Thus the Golden Age of man came to an end.

The men of the Silver Age were decidedly less intelligent than those of the Golden Age. This lack of intelligence, coupled with all the pain and suffering released by Pandora, made the Silver Age a time of great hardship. Men would fight each other over trifles. But because their intelligence was so low, or perhaps their worries so great, they were never able to do anything more than fight small battles among themselves.

Such was not the case with the Brass Age. The men of this age had had the time to grow accustomed to the evils released by Pandora and hence were of a sturdier stock. This proved to be their downfall. They banded together into groups and waged war against others of their own kind. The Brass Age was an age of brutality, a time during which men forgot that they were brothers. This generation soon killed itself off with countless violent wars and blood feuds.

The next era was the Bronze Age, the age of the greatest heroes of classical mythology. This was the age that supplied the stories that poets and storytellers would recount throughout the ages—in *The Iliad* and *The Odyssey*, the great poet Homer would tell of the famous Bronze Age heroes Achilles and Odysseus. The Bronze Age was the time of Jason and the Argonauts and the demigod Heracles. It was a time of legend and greatness.

The last age, the Iron Age, was the time during which ancient Greek civilization as we know it flourished. It was an age dominated by the seductiveness of power, a corrupt age during which good was easily put aside for personal gain, and a time when the lines between good and evil were blurred and confused.

The second version of the creation of man again has Prometheus, this time with his brother Epimetheus, playing an important role.

The two brothers were complete opposites. Prometheus, whose name means "foresight," was level-headed, while Epimetheus, whose name means "afterthought," was prone to acting without thinking.

After the war with the Titans, the job of creating the earth's inhabitants was entrusted to these two brothers. Epimetheus was the first to act, diving into the act of creation without much preparation. He created the animals first, endowing them with the qualities needed to survive in a harsh, unforgiving environment, such as speed, agility, and strength. He also gave the animals their hides, wings, fins, and shells, but left nothing to protect man, his final creation. Being true to his name, Epimetheus looked back on what he had done and realized he'd made a terrible mistake. He went to his brother for help.

Prometheus, taking stock of the situation, believed that man could be salvaged. He made man stand upright, in the posture of the gods, making him tower over the animals. He also gave man fire from the sun, which not only would provide protection from all the beasts, but would enable him to warm his furless body, even on the coldest of nights.

In both versions, with the aid of Prometheus, man came to master fire, and he subsequently became the master of the tiny globe he called home.

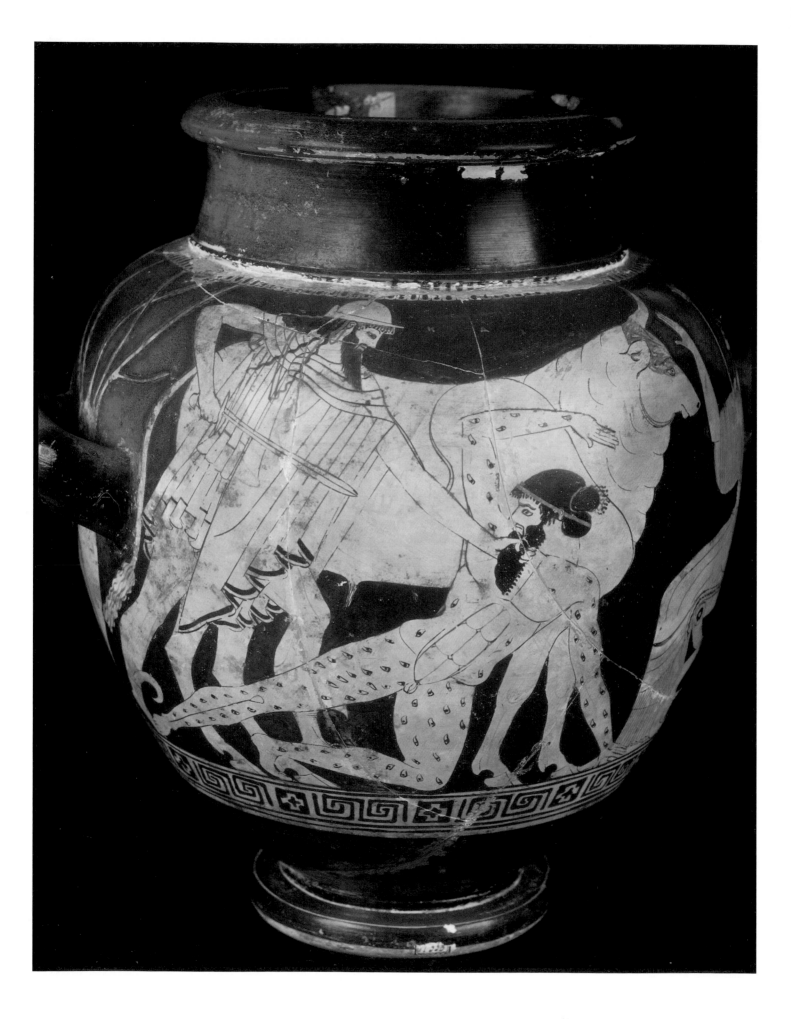

ZEUS
AND HERA

ZEUS—KING OF THE GODS

As supreme ruler of both Olympus and the world beneath it, Zeus was the most powerful god in classical mythology. He controlled such primal forces as thunder and lightning, and had the power to squeeze the clouds together, forcing them to feed the earth with nourishing rain.

Besides his terrible power, Zeus possessed the Aegis, an impervious piece of armor. In different myths, the Aegis appears in different forms, the most com-

Red-figured stamnos, fifth century B.C., depicting Hermes slaying Argus, the hundred-eyed guardian of Io. On the far right, the arm and leg of Zeus are visible.

mon being that of a shield or breastplate covered with Almaltheia's hide. In some myths, the Aegis is a thundercloud. Whatever its form, the Aegis always has the same purpose: to protect Zeus from any foe, mortal or otherwise. When shaken, it produces a mighty thunderstorm, sending terror and fear into the hearts of Zeus' enemies. Of all his attributes, the Aegis most clearly depicts Zeus' unparalleled power.

Despite Zeus' status as the most powerful Olympian, he also had his share of human characteristics. The ancient Greeks believed Zeus to be a rather promiscuous god. The exact number of his lovers would be staggering if it could be calculated. It seems he was always either in the middle of an affair or calculating his next seduction. Most of his children were conceived not with his wife, Hera, but with the women with whom he had his countless affairs.

Bust of Juno, Roman copy after Greek original. Juno was the Roman name for Hera.

Even as a young god on the island of Crete, his desires had a strong hold on him. His first conquest was Metis, the daughter of Oceanus and Tethys and the personification of wisdom. When Metis became pregnant, Uranus and Gaea warned their grandson that the child born to Metis might grow to be greater than Zeus in both power and wisdom. Zeus felt he had no choice but to swallow both Metis and her unborn child, ending the possible threat to his future rule. As a result, Zeus was literally filled with wisdom, a trait the king of the gods must possess, and was made "pregnant" with the goddess Athena, who, some time later, emerged fully armed and fully grown from the head of Zeus.

By other "companions," Zeus fathered such gods and demigods as Apollo, Artemis, Hermes, Aphrodite (in some versions), Dionysus, Heracles, Helen of Troy, and Persephone. Many of the most famous Greek heroes were illegitimate children of Zeus, and many of the great families of ancient times claimed to have at least one direct descendant of Zeus somewhere on their family trees.

HERA—
QUEEN OF THE GODS

Wife and sister of Zeus, and daughter of Kronos and Rhea, Hera was the goddess of the family, of familial love, and of legitimate childbirth. Since Hera was the personification of marital fidelity, Zeus' constant philandering angered her to no end. Her jealousy was so great that she kept a continual eye on her husband. When she discovered an infidelity, she would become so enraged that Zeus' lover, and at times the offspring of their coupling, would soon suffer her wrath.

THE MYTH OF IO—
CONSEQUENCES OF
OLYMPIAN INFIDELITY

There was a time when Zeus became enamored of Io, a princess of Argos. Patiently, he waited for a moment when Hera's hawklike eyes would stray. When the opportunity finally presented itself, he flew down to Io's bedchamber, where he seduced her by whispering sweet nothings in her ears while she slept, thus convincing her to let him inside her dreams, where he would make love to her.

While Zeus normally planned ways to conceal his affairs from Hera, it was not until late in the act that he realized that Hera might see this infidelity. Zeus quickly wrapped the earth in a blanket of dark clouds, hoping to hide his adultery. Hera, however, immediately saw through this feeble deception and flew down to earth, her eyes blazing with anger. But instead of catching Zeus in the act, she came across her husband standing calmly next to a white heifer. When she asked him what he was doing standing next to a cow, he replied that he'd been standing there when the cow had suddenly sprung from the earth.

Hera, however, was not to be fooled; she knew the cow must be the illicit lover, transformed by her husband at the last possible moment. No matter how hard Hera pressed, Zeus stuck to his story. In order to catch her husband in his lie, Hera asked Argus, a hundred-eyed herdsman, to watch over the supposed heifer. She was sure Zeus would turn the cow back into a human the next time he desired her, and when he did, Argus would alert Hera to the indiscretion.

Not to be bested, Zeus sent Hermes, the god of trickery, to slay the watchman. This was no easy task since Argus never closed all of his one hundred eyes at the same time. But the god of thieves had a plan. He pretended to be a simple country fellow who was adept at playing the pipes and telling stories. Hermes interested Argus in his melodic tales, and soon the monster was captivated by the yarns, yet not enough to take his eyes off Io. Hermes gradually told duller stories and played less melodic music until he told a story so dull and played music so boring that Argus fell asleep. The second all one hundred eyes were closed, Hermes quickly killed the herdsman. (Feeling it a shame to waste Argus' odd appearance, Hermes quickly placed all one hundred eyes in the tail of the peacock.)

Although Io was now free of Argus, Hera had been expecting this. She ordered a gadfly to torment and bite Io, who was still in cow form. The merciless little fly did its job well,

sending Io into such fits of pain that she eventually tried to rid herself of the torturous little insect by running great distances and swimming great oceans. The Ionian Sea and the Bosphorus Strait, meaning "channel of the cow," are both named after her. Eventually she ran to Egypt, to the banks of the Nile, where the fly lost interest in her and flew away. Zeus then transformed her back into the lovely woman she had been.

By this time Hera figured that Io had been killed during her insane frenzy, and she forgot about her. Zeus used this to his advantage and quickly made love to Io once again, this time conceiving with her a son, Ephastus, a forefather of the mighty Heracles.

Bust of Jupiter, Roman copy after Greek original.

POSEIDON—GOD OF THE OCEANS

T he son of Kronos and the brother of Zeus and Hades, Poseidon (or Neptune, as he was called by the Romans) was the god of the oceans. He ruled the waves as completely as Zeus ruled the heavens and Hades ruled the land of the dead. The three-pronged trident was his symbol—the equivalent of Zeus' thunderbolts—and it signified his control over the seas and both the beneficent (as when it was used to spear fish) and malevolent (as when it was used against man) natures of the world's waters.

Head of bronze figure, c. 460 B.C. The identity of this figure—whether he is meant to be Zeus or Poseidon—is still a matter of debate among classical scholars.

gle glance, he fathered the Giant Chrysaor. The Cyclops Polyphemus, who caused so much trouble for Odysseus on his return from Troy, was also a son of the sea god. Two of his other sons, Otus and Ephialtes, known collectively as the Aloidae, imprisoned Ares, the god of war, in a bronze cask for thirteen months and pursued Artemis and Hera, intent on rape. (They were defeated by the gods and given eternal punishment in Tartarus.) In fact, so many of Poseidon's children invoked the wrath of both god and man, either for their physical ugliness or the ugliness of their deeds, that Poseidon soon found it easier to bury his vile offspring under the earth than to watch over them and make sure they kept out of trouble.

Besides being god of the seas, Poseidon was also the god of both horses and earthquakes. He was believed to have been the god that first gave the tamed horse to man to be used to plow fields, to carry heavy loads, and as transportation. The ancient Greeks believed that the manes of Poseidon's aquatic steeds could be seen in the waves of the sea.

The earthquake was also attributed to Poseidon. In *The Iliad*, Homer often refers to Poseidon as the "Shaker of the Earth," a title he richly deserved.

When the reign of the Olympians was young, each of the gods selected earthly regions that would be sacred specifically to him or her alone. Naturally, some arguments arose

Poseidon took for his wife the Nereid, or water nymph, Amphitrite. Like his younger brother Zeus, however, Poseidon possessed a voracious sexual appetite and was often unfaithful. But whereas Zeus seemed to have an eye for the lovely and beguiling, Poseidon seemed indifferent to the physical characteristics of his concubines. This indifference occasionally resulted in his offspring being some of the vilest and most terrifying creatures in the classical canon.

By the Gorgon Medusa, a terrifying creature with snakes for hair and the ability to turn men to stone with a sin-

when several gods desired reign over the same area. Poseidon always ended up getting the worst of the deal. In the end, all he could lay claim to was the legendary island of Atlantis, which according to some stories, eventually lost favor in his eyes. He brought upon the island an earthquake of such magnitude that Atlantis was literally torn apart, disappearing forever into the depths of the sea.

Along with his brothers Zeus and Hades and his sister Demeter, the goddess of vegetation, Poseidon was one of the four chthonic gods, that is, those deities who had control over the powerful forces of nature. To the ancient Greeks, the oceans were a limitless source of wonder. Why is the sea covered with waves, they wondered. Why do the waters sometimes turn destructive, ruining crops and flooding and eroding the coastline? How can something that supplies a man with food also be able to quickly kill the same man if he falls out of his boat?

To this day, the ocean continues to be an extremely powerful force over which humans have little control. It is doubtful that we will ever be able to understand the seas or to bring them under our control. The oceans of the world seem petulant, responding to whatever whim takes them, and capable of terrible vindictiveness and violence, as in the case of hurricanes and coastal storms.

Such a character fits Poseidon perfectly. Just as when man is dealing with the sea, caution should be exercised at all times when dealing with the god of the oceans—all it takes is one slip or mistake and the waters will be one's doom.

HADES
AND DEMETER

HADES—KING OF THE DEAD

The brother of Zeus and Poseidon, Hades (or Pluto as the Romans referred to him) was the lord of the underworld and the god of wealth. He is often perceived as an evil god simply because he rules over a particularly unpleasant realm. Occasionally, he is even mistaken for Death himself. Neither of these characterizations is correct. Hades is not the god of death. That role belongs to Thanatos, who, with his brother Sleep, resides in Hades'

Relief of the face of Hades from a Greek
krater, fourth century B.C.

kingdom. Hades is not an evil god; he simply has a rather unpleasant job that by association colors his reputation.

Hades was always a just and fair god. He had a strict set of rules by which he governed the underworld, and he rarely—and then usually only against his will—broke those rules. He is generally portrayed as a god with a dark visage who is cloaked in shadows and rarely, if ever, shows himself. During the war with the Titans, the Cyclopes fashioned for him a magical helmet that rendered him invisible. He wore this helmet whenever he ventured forth from his shadowy realm.

Of all the gods, Hades alone was not welcome on Mount Olympus. It may be that the Olympians, all of whom possessed human prejudices and character flaws, were as put off by Hades as were the mortals who feared him.

GEOGRAPHY
OF THE
UNDERWORLD

In many Homeric and pre-Homeric Greek myths, Hades' kingdom is described simply as a shadowy realm where spirits wander aimlessly back and forth, bemoaning the fact that their lives are over. It was the Roman imagination that created a distinct geography for his dark world.

The underworld as imagined by the Romans consisted of four separate regions. Tartarus, the area that most people would consider "hell," was the blackest and most vile of the four, the place where those mortals who had committed evil during their lives were sent for all eternity. Like the Christian hell, Tartarus was the place of eternal punishment.

The opposite of Tartarus, the "heaven" of the underworld, was Elysium (which is some-

times referred to as the Elysian Fields). Ruled by the dethroned Kronos, this region was an area of light and perpetual day, a realm of eternal happiness where music played continuously and good cheer was always in the air. The inhabitants of Elysium, those souls who had led honest and virtuous lives, were able to wish themselves back to life whenever they grew weary of the afterlife.

The third area of Hades was the Asphodel Fields, so named for the Asphodel, the pale flowers that blanketed the mournful ground. This was where most departed souls resided.

The fourth area of the underworld was Erebus, and this was where Hades' palace was located. Occasionally, Erebus was depicted as the first area the dead must pass through on their way to the underworld.

The underworld was also home to five rivers, all of which had specific symbolic functions. The Acheron and the Styx often served the same function, and hence often were interchangeable. These were the first rivers the newly dead had to cross. The Styx was considered so holy that an oath sworn by it could never be broken, not even by Zeus himself. Upon reaching the underworld, the newly

RIGHT: Marble relief from a Roman sarcophagus, c. A.D. 1st–2nd century, showing Charon, the ferryman of the river Styx, demanding payment from recently dead souls before transporting them to the gates of the underworld.

BELOW: Hades upon his throne in Erebus. Cerberus, the three-headed watchdog of the underworld's gates, stands faithfully at his side.

dead would wait on the shore of the Styx until Charon, the ferryman, appeared. The ancient Greek custom of burying loved ones with a small coin in their mouths was the result of the Greek belief that Charon required payment in return for safe passage to the gates of Hades. Without payment, Charon would refuse his service and the dead would be stranded for all time on the banks of the Styx, forever denied their eternal rest.

Three other rivers also lay inside Hades' gates. The river Cocytus was the river of la-

mentation; it was by drinking the waters of this river that souls fully realized the wonder of life and came to understand all that they had lost by dying. The river Phlegethon was the river of fire; its services were put to use mainly in Tartarus, where its painful, undying flames were used to torture the evil. The river Lethe provided the most merciful service of all five Hadean rivers; once the spirits of the dead drank from its waters, they would blissfully forget their past lives and become content with their new existence.

After being ferried across the Styx (or the Acheron) by Charon, the dead arrived at the gates to Hades, which were guarded by Cerberus, a three-headed demon watchdog with the tail of a serpent. His job, which he performed with unerring fidelity, was simple: to make sure that every soul that went in never came back out again.

Once inside, the dead were faced with judgment. There was a trio of judges who heard and reviewed each spirit's life story, then determined whether the soul deserved to go to Tartarus, Elysium, or the Asphodel Fields. The first of these judges was Aeacus, who in life had been a kind, fair, and pious king of Aegina. The second judge was King Minos, who had ruled the island of Crete with a fair and just hand. Rhadamanthys, the brother of Minos, was the last of the three. Although he had never been a king, he had a sense of justice noble enough to earn him a position as judge of the dead. All three were mortal sons of Zeus.

According to some myths, the Erinnyes, or the Furies, as they were sometimes called, also inhabited the underworld, forever torturing murderers and those individuals who had directly or indirectly shed the blood of their own kind.

DEMETER— GODDESS OF VEGETATION

The daughter of Kronos and Rhea and the sister of Zeus, Poseidon, and Hades, Demeter was one of the original Olympians. She was the goddess of the earth's vegetation—its plants, flowers, and grains. She is paired with Hades in this chapter because the most prominent myth concerning her also involves Hades.

THE MYTH OF PERSEPHONE

Demeter had a single daughter, Persephone, by her brother Zeus. Hades took notice of the young goddess one day while she was lying in a field admiring a flower. He fell in love with her at first sight. Using his godly powers, Hades caused the earth near Persephone to split open. He flew out, grabbed the surprised Persephone, and dragged her down into the depths of his murky kingdom.

Roman statue, c. A.D. 420, of Ceres, the goddess of vegetation and the mother of Proserpïna. Ceres was the Roman name for Demeter; Proserpïna was what the Romans called Persephone.

The Rape of Proserpīna, Niccolo dell'Abate, sixteenth century.

When Persephone failed to return from her afternoon stroll, Demeter became extremely worried and set out to find her. After a long search, she discovered what had happened, who had taken her daughter, and why. Enraged, she swore that the earth would not receive the gifts she usually bestowed upon it until her daughter was returned—it would become a barren, dead world without flower, tree, or field of grain.

She renounced her seat on Olympus and exiled herself to the earth, angered that her fellow gods did nothing to aid her. Roaming the earth as an old woman, Demeter came to the kingdom of Eleusis, where she was be-

friended by a kind woman named Metaneira. In return for the woman's hospitality, Demeter bestowed upon Demophoön, the woman's infant son, the innate knowledge of growing and harvesting corn, which, when the boy grew to manhood, would prove invaluable to the whole of humanity. Still Demeter refused to return to the earth its bounty. With every day that passed, the earth grew more desolate.

After a time, Zeus decided that this had to stop. He asked each of the Olympians to try to convince Demeter to lift her curse. The gods pleaded with her, but Demeter's outrage and sorrow were too great and she refused even to listen to her fellow gods. Having no other option, Zeus knew he must either convince Hades to let Persephone leave the underworld to see her mother or resolve himself to reigning over a barren husk of a world.

Hades couldn't refuse his brother, so he granted Persephone a temporary freedom. Before she left, he tricked her into eating three seeds from a pomegranate, a traditional symbol of fertility and marital obligations. As a result, Persephone was bound to return to him every year. It was soon decided that Persephone would stay with her mother on Mount Olympus for nine months out of every year—

spring through autumn, the growing season. As soon as harvesting had begun across the earth, she would return to Hades and rule as queen of the underworld. During this time nothing would grow on the earth.

In the myth of Persephone we see an interesting interaction between the forces of life and growth and the forces of death. We are presented with an example of how ancient man characterized the cyclical aspect of nature. It is stories like this one that make the study of myth much more than simply the investigation of tales of gods and heroes.

Greek vase, c. 330 B.C., showing Hades and his wife, Persephone, at their palace in the underworld. Since Persephone is with her husband, it must be winter on the earth.

CHAPTER VII

APHRODITE
AND ARES

APHRODITE—GODDESS OF ROMANTIC AND SEXUAL LOVE

Aphrodite (or Venus, as the Romans called her) was the goddess of both sexual and romantic love. The Greek personification of physical beauty, she represented both raw lust and gentle affection, and it was she who caused young, single people to fall in love and older, married folks to commit adultery.

The Birth of Venus, Eugene Amaury-Duval, nineteenth century.

47

Physically, Aphrodite was the most beautiful of all the Olympians. There are two different stories concerning Aphrodite's birth. In *The Iliad* she is the daughter of Zeus and the Titaness Dione. The majority of post-Homeric poets, however, tell how the goddess was born from the combination of the sea and Uranus' castrated genitalia. After Kronos hurled his father's privates into the sea, the waves swirled around them, creating a mass of foam that became the goddess.

If Aphrodite were created as recounted in the latter version, she would be older than the rest of the Olympians. This is somehow more sensible than Homer's version, since without the qualities and temperaments Aphrodite instills in others, Kronos and Rhea may not have had six children. Maybe they wouldn't have had any children. Maybe they would have grown bored with each other and not had Zeus. Of course, this speculation is all in fun, but it makes sense that the goddess of sexual love and desire should predate the core Olympians.

The philosopher Plato reconciled the issue by saying that there were in fact two goddesses of love. The one born of the sea foam he called Urania. She was the goddess of romantic, pure love. The other, the daughter of Zeus and Dione, he dubbed Pandemos. She represented the base, earthly sexual desires. But Plato came up with that idea long after many of the Greek religious beliefs were cemented in the culture. And in those myths, there was one goddess of love, both sexual and romantic, the epitome of physical beauty, who was incredibly jealous of competition and vindictive when opposed.

Aphrodite is usually said to be the wife of Hephaestus, the god of fire and blacksmiths, and the mother of the Eros of the later myths, the cherubic archer whose arrows are love.

Red-figured skyphos, c. 420–410 B.C., showing Aphrodite and her son Eros. It is unclear whether the child's father was Ares or Hermes, and it is doubtful whether Aphrodite herself knew which god was the true father.

Some of Aphrodite's children bore the unmistakable stigma of bizarre genital aberration. After seducing Hermes, Aphrodite gave birth to Hermaphroditus, a being with both male and female genitalia. Her union with Dionysus, the god of wine, resulted in the birth of Priapus, an ugly but talented child who would go on to become a woodland deity, famous for both his skills in gardening and his elephantine phallus.

Although she was married, Aphrodite never held her vows of fidelity too close to her heart. She was, after all, the goddess of lust, and unbridled desire seldom abides by the rules of marriage. One of her favorite and most powerful lovers was Ares, the god of war, with whom she conceived three children. This relationship is interesting in that the other gods never cared a great deal for Ares.

ARES—GOD OF WAR

The son of Zeus and Hera (and perhaps Zeus' only legitimate son), Ares was a thick-headed, temperamental, violent god. Since he, like Aphrodite, is the personification of one of man's base qualities, it is only fitting that his actions and attitudes should betray a rather primitive and thoughtless mentality.

Ares loved battle for its own sake. He rarely cared for the reason behind war; his passion was the shriek of metal on metal, sweat and dust, the bloodlust of battle, the thrill of victory. This shallow attitude made him quite unpopular on Olympus. The only gods who cared for him were Aphrodite; Hades, who was always happy to receive new

souls; and his sister Eris, the goddess of discord. The other Olympians found him to be a bore because all he did was swagger around Olympus talking about battle. Like their gods, the Greeks wanted little to do with Ares. They recognized but did not respect the god of war. They realized there was a bit of Ares in all of them but were rather ashamed of that fact. This being the case, Ares never figured prominently in the Greek canon.

It was the Romans who gave Mars (the Roman name for Ares) the character he is famous for, that of a brave, cunning, and brilliant warlord. This makes sense when one considers the different cultural mindsets of Greece and Rome. The Greeks, though they had large, well-trained armies, were generally more concerned with peaceful endeavors such as philosophy and the arts, while the Romans concerned themselves more with waging war and expanding an empire.

CAUGHT IN THE ACT

Ares and Aphrodite were rather careless when it came to their liaisons—it was no secret to any of the Olympians that they were romantically involved.

During one of their trysts, Helios, the driver of the sun-chariot, spied the two in bed as he began his ascent across the morning sky. He immediately sent word to Hephaestus, who devised a plan to catch the lovers in the act. After fashioning a net of bronze, which he hammered so thin as to be invisible, the god of blacksmiths crept into Aphrodite's bed-

While it is generally said that Hermaphroditus was the result of a union between Hermes and Aphrodite, in an alternate myth concerning Hermaphroditus' origin, the double-sexed being is the result of the nymph of the Carian fountain praying to be united with a male named Hermaphroditus.

Roman statue of Mars, Hellenistic period. The Romans, being extremely fond of the god of war, created many artworks honoring him, while the Greeks rarely depicted him.

chamber while the illicit lovers were away and affixed the corners of the net to the four posts of the bed, then went to Aphrodite and told her that, as he needed a holiday, he would be going away for a while.

As soon as Hephaestus was out the door, Aphrodite quickly called on Ares, informing him that as long as her husband was away, the palace would be theirs. The god of war soon arrived and the lovers fell on the bed, where their smiles and laughs quickly changed to curses and vain struggles—Hephaestus' net was too strong, even in the face of the mighty god of war. In order to embarrass and discredit the two adulterers, Hephaestus, who had not left at all, called all the Olympians to gather as witnesses and judges.

The goddesses, out of modesty, refused to set eyes on the spectacle, but the male gods all huddled around the bed, nudging and winking at each other. Hermes even ventured to say that he wouldn't mind being in Ares' predicament even with three nets and the goddesses looking on. This crassness met with a good-natured round of laughter from all. Shamed and disgraced, Ares and Aphrodite fled to different parts of the earth to lie low for a while and allow everyone to cool down.

CHAPTER VIII

APOLLO AND ARTEMIS—
THE TWINS OF JUSTICE

THE BIRTH OF THE TWINS

After an affair with Zeus, the Titaness Leto was forced to wander the earth in an effort to escape the wrath of the jealous Hera. The queen of the gods sent the monstrous Python, a large and vicious serpent, to hunt Leto, thinking that as the object of Python's hunt, Leto would never have time to rest or be safe long enough to deliver her children. The Titaness seemed doomed to wander the earth forever, but Poseidon soon took pity on her

Terra-cotta plaque, Hellenistic period, from
the Temple of Apollo on the Palatine in Rome
depicting Apollo and Diana decorating
a sacred pillar.

53

and granted her sanctuary on the island of Delos. Here, Leto finally gave birth to Apollo and Artemis.

APOLLO— GOD OF LIGHT AND TRUTH

Apollo, the younger of the twins, represented everything that the Greeks themselves strove for; he was *the* male archetype. As Aphrodite was the epitome of female beauty, Apollo was the paragon of male beauty. His clarity and stability of mind were the greatest of any member of the pantheon. His talents in the artistic and medicinal fields were unmatched by god or man.

Also, it was believed that it went against Apollo's grain to lie, that he was in fact incapable of falsehood or misrepresentation. As a result, Apollo's oracles were by far the most trusted in all of Greece. The most famous of these was the Oracle at Delphi on the island of Delos, said to be near the area where Apollo slew Python a mere four days after being born. This particular temple of Apollo grew in renown until it was famous throughout the ancient world. Pilgrimages to Apollo's Oracle at Delphi were made from the farthest reaches of Greece and beyond to pay tribute to the god of light and to ask Pythia, his priestess, for guidance.

Another of Apollo's godly aspects was his complete knowledge of all evil existing in the world. He could see and hear any malicious act, and he knew how such an act could be stopped. It is for this reason that his oracle was consulted not only on such questions as land disputes and personal problems, but also about such calamities as plague and disease.

Typical of the gods, Apollo was insanely jealous of anyone questioning or challenging his talents. It was in situations like this that the violent side of the god emerged, a lesson to man that no matter how advanced one becomes, it is always possible to fall back into the old primitive, violent ways.

THE MYTH OF MARSYAS

One day Athena, the goddess of invention, constructed a flute. At first, she was pleased with her creation because it made such beautiful sounds. But when she realized that her cheeks puffed out when she played, distorting her otherwise perfect face, she threw the instrument aside.

A Satyr (a woodland spirit of virility) named Marsyas came across the discarded flute, picked it up, and began to play. After some time he became so proficient in his playing that he believed himself to be the finest musician ever, better even than Apollo. He was so certain of his talents that he challenged the god to a musical contest. The nine Muses, the spirits of artistic endeavors, were to be the judges. Apollo, calmly cradling his lyre, waited for Marsyas to finish his songs, which, although very good, couldn't compare to the music Apollo could make. The Muses were overcome by their lord's playing. Apollo was deemed the winner, and in retribution for having challenged him in the first place, he strung Marsyas to a tree and skinned him alive, the Satyr's screams now filling the woods with a much more sinister music.

ARTEMIS—
GODDESS
OF THE HUNT

Diana of Versailles,
Leochares,
fourth century B.C.,
Roman copy after
Greek statue. Diana
was the Roman name
for Artemis.

Artemis became aware of her new duties as a goddess mere seconds after she was born—immediately after Leto delivered her, the newborn Artemis helped deliver her brother Apollo, and from that point on, Artemis was the goddess of childbirth and the protector of children. This, however, is generally considered a secondary aspect, for Artemis is most well known as the goddess of the hunt.

Tall in stature and strong of build, Artemis would have proved a match for any of the male gods. Without peer as a hunter and Ares' equal as a warrior, Artemis nonetheless possessed enough physical beauty to make even Aphrodite jealous. Unlike the goddess of love, however, Artemis was forever chaste. In fact, Aphrodite's promiscuousness infuriated Artemis; she found it very distasteful that marriage vows could be so easily forgotten. Because of this, she avenged the victims of infidelity whenever she could. She also considered rape, especially the rape of virgins, to be an inexcusable crime. When she learned of a rape, she would immediately punish the rapist, showing him not the slightest bit of mercy.

While Apollo was the god of truth and prophecy, Artemis was the goddess of human rights. It was she

who stood up for the quiet and just, the meek and unthreatening, the defiled virgins, the underdogs. Together, these two illustrate the classical conception of justice.

THE MYTH OF ACTAEON

On occasion, Artemis' steadfastness in her beliefs caused undue pain and suffering and served as a reminder to man that any cause, if taken to extremes, can prove to be just as unjust and damaging as the evil it purports to fight against.

While hunting in the woods with his faithful pack of hunting dogs one day, the great hunter Actaeon accidentally came across the naked Artemis bathing in a woodland pond. Since she was a goddess, possessing a beauty never before dreamed of in his mortal mind, his human curiosity led him to hide in the bushes and stare in wonderment and admiration.

A gentle snap of a twig alerted Artemis to his presence. Her first reaction was to let him go since he'd come across her purely by accident. But she realized that to let him go would only lead to trouble—soon he would be back home, drinking with his friends, and would brag about having seen the "virgin goddess" naked. Artemis, who had sworn a vow of chastity and had vowed that no one would ever see her naked, could not allow this mortal to remain at large. She transformed the poor hunter into a stag of such noble and grand stature that his hunting dogs immediately fell upon him, having no idea that it was actually their master they were tearing limb from limb, his blood on their muzzles.

Diana and Actaeon, Cavalier d'Arpino, late sixteenth–mid seventeenth century.

ATHENA AND HEPHAESTUS—ARCHITECTS OF CIVILIZATION

ATHENA—GODDESS OF INVENTION

Of all the births in the Greek pantheon, Athena's is one of the oddest. She was not born of a female, but from the head of her father, Zeus. Her mother was Metis, whom Zeus swallowed when he learned she was pregnant with his child. Soon after this terrible deed, the king of the gods experienced a great deal of pain, which for a long time he thought was simply a massive headache. The pain grew and grew, and eventually, out of desperation,

---

Minerva (the Roman version of Athena),
head for Lemnian statue, Hellenistic period,
Roman copy after Phidias.

Athena Repulsing Mars, Tintoretto, 1576.

Zeus asked Hephaestus to take his hammer and bash open Zeus' head. When Hephaestus split Zeus' skull, Athena leapt out, fully grown and fully armed.

The goddess of wisdom and invention, Athena was credited with creating such tools as the bridle, the yoke, the plow, and the rake. She also created the flute and the trumpet, as well as mathematics. The clay pot and the skills of homemaking also came from Athena. She gave man not only the essentials for making a home but also the tools and ideas for creating a civilization. All this considered, it comes as no surprise that Athens, one of the most advanced cities of the ancient world, was considered her home city.

In the minds of the early Greeks, Athena was not as peace-loving as her generosity may imply. Homer described her as a rather warlike goddess, and she was in fact considered to be the goddess of war, the female counterpart of Ares. For her, however, war was not blind, unplanned battle, as it was for Ares, but strategic and ordered combat.

LEFT: As the rest of the Olympians look on, Athena leaps out of her father's head.

BELOW: In one version of the myth, Hephaestus, the god of metallurgy, was lamed after Zeus threw him off Mount Olympus angry at his defense of his mother, Hera.

BELOW LEFT: Hephaestus informs Athena of his desire for her, but the goddess of invention stands aloof. This desire eventually overcame Hephaestus and he attempted to rape the goddess.

During the Trojan War, Athena sided with the Greek army. It was while under her influence that the mortal hero Diomedes successfully attacked and wounded Ares, who then complained about his half-sister to an inattentive Zeus. This situation points out a major difference between the two deities of war—Athena was level-headed and intelligent; Ares was, both intellectually and emotionally, a child.

Like Artemis, Athena was a chaste goddess, but for different, less prudish reasons—she simply found the advances of the male gods infantile and silly. She was attracted to none of them, and therefore did not desire their affections. Unfortunately, the disinterest was not mutual; she was constantly being hounded by the other gods, and countered their flirtations with silence and their advances with swift, brutal kicks in tender areas.

HEPHAESTUS— GOD OF SMITHS AND METALLURGY

Hephaestus was the god of craftsmanship, the deity of those who worked with fire. He was the god of blacksmiths and artisans. He was married to Aphrodite, but he rarely received her affections.

There are two versions of the story of Hephaestus' birth. According to one, he was the son of Zeus and Hera; in the other, he was the son of Hera, who had conceived him alone in an attempt to spite Zeus for Athena's parthenogenetic birth. In both versions, when Hera saw what she had given birth to—Hephaestus was both ugly and deformed—she hurled the infant from the heights of Mount Olympus. He landed in the ocean and was immediately rescued by the nymphs Thetis and Eurynome, who raised the god and encouraged his interest in blacksmithing, providing him with a suitable smithy where he created not only weapons and armor but also beautiful pieces of jewelry.

Hera once visited Thetis on a social call and complimented her on a lovely jeweled pin she was wearing. She asked Thetis where she had acquired such a beautiful object, but Thetis was reluctant to answer, as she did not want to let Hera know that her deformed son was still alive for fear she might again try to murder him. Eventually, Hera dragged the truth from Thetis and took her son back to Olympus, where she provided him with the finest forge imaginable.

Hephaestus was very happy that his mother had finally accepted him, and when Zeus punished Hera by hanging her from her wrists after discovering her role in one of the

Greek statue of
Athena and
Erichthonius (nestled
at her bosom), copy
after Cephisodotus,
4th century B.C.

many attempted coups against him, Hephaestus became very angry. He approached the king of the heavens and condemned him for his actions. Disgruntled, Zeus threw the god of blacksmiths from the heights of Olympus, and this time Hephaestus landed on the island of Lemnos. The impact broke both of Hephaestus' legs and from that point on he was permanently lame, able to walk around Olympus only with the support of crutches or, in some mythological accounts, golden leg braces of his own design.

While Athena provided man with sophisticated instruments, Hephaestus supplied the basic, rudimentary tools. It was Hephaestus who created the plow blade, the sword, the spearhead, and other such implements. Together these two gods gave man the tools needed for civilization to take root; without their gifts, it would have taken man much longer to stop living nomadically and to settle down into cities and towns.

THE RAPE OF ATHENA

It was no secret that Athena considered herself "unattainable," and this attitude often prompted cruel and malicious acts on the part of her fellow Olympians.

Once, when Athena was planning to go and see her half-brother Hephaestus to ask him to make her some armor, Poseidon told the smith that she was on her way with lust on her mind and expected to be made love to. When she arrived at the smithy and requested the arms, Hephaestus would not allow her to pay him, stating instead that he would do the job for love. Thinking this to mean that the god would do the work for free, with her gratitude his only compensation, Athena agreed and watched the god work his wonders, toiling away at a magnificent set of arms. When he was finished he threw himself upon her, his mind racing with lust. Athena threw him off herself, but not before he deposited some of his semen on her thigh. Outraged at such a violation, Athena wiped the semen off her leg and flung it down to the earth, which then became pregnant with Hephaestus' child. Gaea was revolted at the thought of giving birth to a child of Hephaestus and refused to be held at all responsible for the child's welfare.

Because of her kind nature, Athena could not just let the child perish. She assumed responsibility for the infant, whom she named Erichthonius. The child was hideous, not simply deformed like his father but a new sort of creature—half-serpent, half-human. Eventually, this man-snake would become the first king of Athens, teaching his subjects to revere and worship his adopted mother. In another version of this myth, Hephaestus' semen falls onto a snow-covered mountainside, from which the first statues sprout. Metaphorically, this version is much more satisfying, since it makes sense that the union of wisdom and handicrafts, whether or not it was fully successful, should produce art.

Black-figured amphora, sixth century B.C., depicting Athena standing between two columns on which cocks are perched. This amphora was given as a prize for a footrace winner at the Panathenaic Games.

HERMES
AND DIONYSUS

HERMES—GOD OF THIEVES,
COMMERCE, AND CUNNING

S on of Zeus and the nymph Maia, daughter of the Titan Atlas, Hermes earned
his reputation as a trickster early on. Soon after his birth in a cave on Mount
Cyllene, Maia, satisfied that her newborn was healthy, turned her back on
him for a few minutes in order to freshen up and regain her composure. In
the short time that her back was turned, the young Hermes sprouted into

Mercury, Giambattista Tiepolo, eighteenth
century. Mercury was the Roman version
of Hermes.

boyhood and sneaked away from the cave to explore the surrounding countryside.

He soon came across Apollo tending a herd of cattle, which the young god immediately decided to steal as a prank. He waited until Apollo was asleep, and to make sure he covered his tracks, as well as those of the cows, he led the cattle off the field backward, making them walk in their own hoofprints so that no fresh ones would be made. Once he was out of sight he fashioned shoes for the cattle that would make no impressions on the soft earth. He then led the herd back to the cave of his birth, feeling quite successful in his first escapade.

When Apollo discovered that his cattle were missing, he enlisted the aid of the Satyrs, the forest spirits who were the personifications of unbridled nature, to find them. The wood spirits searched the forest from end to end, leaving no path or clue unchecked. Eventually, one of the scouting parties came across the cave on Mount Cyllene, hearing enchant-

ing music coming from its mouth. As they approached, Hermes' nurse emerged from the cave and told them that the music was being made by the young god. The divine child, she told them, had constructed a wonderful musical instrument from the shell of a tortoise, using fresh cowgut as strings. The Satyrs immediately returned to Apollo and told him what they had discovered. Apollo went to the cave, seized the young Hermes, and brought him to Olympus to answer to Zeus for the obvious crime.

Zeus didn't want to find his young son guilty but, after hearing the evidence, he found he had no choice. When Hermes realized that his father didn't believe his lies, he confessed to the theft and promised to return the majority of Apollo's herd. He couldn't return all the animals, he said, because he'd already killed two of the cows, used their guts for his lyre's strings, and divided the succulent meat into equal portions that he'd offered to the gods in sacrifice.

Zeus then examined the slaughtered cows and noticed that there was one sacrificial portion too many. When he asked Hermes about this miscalculation, the young god responded that he had apportioned one sacrificial lot for himself. Zeus couldn't help but smile inwardly at this boldness. In order to clear the air between himself and his half-brother, Hermes offered Apollo not only the return of his herd but the lyre as well. Intrigued by the new instrument, Apollo agreed; soon, after Apollo had practiced with it for a while, the lyre became Apollo's signature instrument.

Zeus was so impressed by the ingenuity and resourcefulness of his young son that he bestowed upon him many duties and honors, all worthy of his crafty nature. Although Zeus knew that Hermes would try to tell the truth whenever he was asked a question, he realized that his son would not always tell the entire truth if it was not in his best interests. Because of this, Hermes became the god of business and commerce.

Hermes soon found that his new duties weren't limited merely to business. Because of his cunning, he also became the god of rhetoric and the misleading sentence. His sphere of influence was soon extended to include lovers, coworkers, and government officials. Because of his stealth and quickness of foot, Hermes became the messenger of the gods; he was dispatched whenever one god needed to speak to another over great distances. He was also the guide of the dead. Only Hermes knew the path leading to the underworld, and it was he who led the recently departed souls down to Hades' dark domain.

Since he was the errand-boy of the gods, knowledgeable of all roads and pathways on heaven and earth, Hermes became the patron god of travelers. At major crossroads through-

out ancient Greece rectangular pillars topped with the bearded face of Hermes were erected. If a traveler approached a fork and found himself confused as to which way to go, he would put his faith in Hermes to guide him down the correct path.

Hermes' occupation as messenger of the gods ensured that he figured prominently in many myths, more so than almost any other god except for Zeus.

DIONYSUS— GOD OF INTOXICATION

Dionysus was the only Olympian whose mother was mortal. He is also the only Olympian to be "born" three times.

Greek vasepainting,
c. fourth century B.C.,
depicting Dionysus
and his mother,
Semele.

One of the many mortals desired by Zeus was a beautiful princess of Thebes named Semele. The king of the heavens courted her time and again, finally swearing by the river Styx that he would do whatever she asked of him. When Hera learned of her husband's newest infatuation, she immediately began to scheme against him. She planted in Semele's head the desire to see Zeus as he truly was, not in the guise of a mortal.

When Semele told Zeus of this desire, he tried very hard to change her mind, but to no avail. With a heavy heart, the king of the gods revealed his true form to her and she fell down dead. Zeus removed the unborn Dionysus from her womb and placed him in his thigh, where he continued to grow until he was born. When the child was fully grown, he emerged from Zeus' thigh.

As soon as the young Dionysus was born, Hera ordered a group of Titans to lure him away from his father's protective gaze with wondrous presents and toys. The lures proved too tempting to the young god, and as soon

as he was out of range of his father's watchful eye, the Titans grabbed him, tore him limb from limb, and roasted and ate his flesh.

Athena, however, found and saved the child's heart, and Zeus was able to salvage his limbs. They buried the remains, and Rhea, re-combining the pieces, brought the child back to life. This was the first time the god experienced the cycle of death and resurrection, a cycle he would repeat again and again, just as the grapevine dies every winter and is born again in the spring.

Zeus now placed his bastard son in the care of Athamas, king of Orchomenos, and his concubine, Semele's sister, Ino. On the advice of Hermes, the two mortals disguised the young Dionysus in girl's clothes, hoping to trick Hera, who was not in the slightest deceived. In retaliation, she caused Athamas to fly into an insane rage and kill his son Learchus. With the blood of his child not yet cold on his hands, the king turned his murderous attention to Ino. As he advanced, Dionysus blinded him so that instead of killing

his lover he slaughtered a goat. Filled with grief, Ino threw herself into the sea soon after. Zeus, remembering her kindness toward the young god of wine, decided that she would not be sent to Hades; instead, he transformed her into the sea goddess Leucothea. At the same time, Dionysus was transformed by Zeus into a young goat, and then entrusted to a group of oreads (mountain nymphs) living on Mount Nysa. It was here that Dionysus learned of the grape and, through experimentation, created wine.

Dionysus, more than any other god, personifies the extremes of human nature. As the god of intoxication, he is the god of both the insane, drunken rage and the introspective, drunken calm—he is at once man's destroyer and his benefactor. The god of wine appears in many myths, and is often a stock character in stories that involve drunkenness. He is also the personification of the cyclical pattern of nature. Like the grapevine, Dionysus was said to die every year, only to be reborn when the first new shoot appeared in the spring.

CHAPTER
XI

THE
LESSER OLYMPIANS

While it is the major Olympians who flavor classical mythology with
their strong personalities (and who are at the center or on the sidelines
of most Greek myths), there is a second tier of gods that supply the
canon with the subtle colorings that are related more to purely human
nature. These lesser gods were never called upon for help by heroes in crisis and
never figured prominently in any myths; they were the gods and goddesses of
everyday life.

The Muse Calliope, Eustache Le Sueur, c. 1650.
Though Calliope was generally portrayed holding a scroll or stylus, the artist chose
to paint her playing the harp.

HESTIA—GODDESS OF THE HEARTH

Hestia was one of Zeus' sisters. Although she was one of the original Olympians, along with Hera, Poseidon, Demeter, Hades, and Zeus, her duties in the pantheon relegated her to a role that was lacking in drama. Hestia was the goddess of hearth and home, the deity who kept watch over the homestead, making sure that no harm came to the family. She had no discernible personality and never played an essential role in any major myths. She was quite simply the "home goddess." Like the hearth itself, she was content to serve those who drew warmth and comfort from her.

The Temple of the Vestal Virgins in ancient Rome was dedicated to the goddess Vesta (the Roman name for Hestia). Inside this temple, six virgin priestesses continually tended and monitored her sacred fire. If any citizen wanted to leave the city and make a place for himself elsewhere, coals would be taken from the sacred hearth and used to ignite the first flame in the land where he settled.

HEBE—GODDESS OF YOUTH

The daughter of Zeus and Hera, Hebe was the goddess of youth, able to restore the spark of life in the aged and decrepit. Other than her eternal youth—of both form and spirit—she had no personality to speak of. In some myths, she was the cupbearer for the gods, keeping their cups filled with nectar during banquets.

IRIS—GODDESS OF THE RAINBOW

Iris, whose parentage is undefined, was the goddess of the rainbow. While Hermes was responsible for carrying messages from one god to another, Iris was the gods' messenger to mankind.

THE GRACES—GODDESSES OF SOCIAL INTERACTION

The three daughters of Zeus and Eurynome, daughter of the Titan Oceanus, or in some accounts the daughters of Aphrodite and Dionysus, the Graces were the deities who presided over all social functions. They always worked together.

Aglaia, the youngest of the three, was the most stately; it was Aglaia who gave a speaker the presence to captivate a crowd. Euphrosyne was the one who infused a party with good-natured laughter; without her, all parties and social functions would have been intolerably serious. Thalia, the third sister, served a double purpose, in that she was also one of the Muses; she was the spirit of comedy, the mother of the joke, however refined or crude.

Jean Baptiste REGNAULT 1754-1829

ΚΑΛΛΙΟΠΗ   ΚΛΕΩ   ΕΡΑΤΩ   ΜΕΛΠΟΜΕΝΗ

THE MUSES— GODDESSES OF ARTISTS

The daughters of Zeus and Mnemosyne, whose name means "memory," the Muses were nine in number. In early accounts they are all lumped together and not treated as separate personalities—they are thought of simply as the goddesses of creative invention, hence Homer's immortal lines "Sing O Muse of the wrath of Pelleus' son Achilles" and "Tell me, Muse, of the man of many ways..." (*The Iliad* and *The Odyssey*, respectively). Later, each would be given her own personality, and special artistic endeavors would be attributed to her.

Calliope, usually depicted holding a scroll or stylus, was the Muse of epic poetry. Clio, generally portrayed holding either a scroll or

ΤΕΡΨΙΧΟΡΗ
ΠΟΛΥΜΝΙΑ ΕΥΤΕΡΠΕΙ
ΘΑΛΕΙΑ ΟΥΡΑΝΙΑ

set of tablets, was the Muse of written history. Erato was the Muse of erotic poetry; Sappho, the famous female poet of Lesbos, undoubtedly owed a debt to her. Euterpe was the Muse of lyric poetry and Dionysian, rapturous music; she was most commonly pictured holding a flute, representing the musical nature of the lyric poem. Melpomene, usually depicted holding the frowning mask of tragedy and wearing the cothurnus, a high, thick-soled boot commonly worn by Greek tragic actors,

was the Muse of tragedy. Polyhymnia was the Muse of religious poetry and song; her demeanor was described as pious and thoughtful. Terpsichore was the Muse of dance; like Euterpe, she was usually shown grasping a lyre. Thalia was the Muse of comedy; the opposite of Melpomene, Thalia was generally portrayed holding the classic laughing mask of comedy. Urania, typically depicted holding a globe, which served as a symbol for all the celestial bodies, was the Muse of astronomy.

Apollo and the Muses, Giulio Romano, sixteenth century. The Muses were Apollo's mistresses.

THE
QUEST FOR
THE GOLDEN FLEECE

THE ORIGIN OF
THE GOLDEN FLEECE

There was a king of Boeotia named Athamas who, although married to Queen Nephele—with whom he had fathered two sons, Phrixus and Leucon, and a daughter, Helle—was in love with a woman named Ino. The affair between Athamas and Ino intensified until even the servants knew of their relationship. Through hearsay, Nephele learned of the tryst. When she

The Argonauts, Costa Lorenzo,
late fifteenth–early sixtenth century.

Phrixus and Helle on the back of the golden ram. In most accounts of this myth, the ram is said to have flown from Boeotia to Colchis. In this picture, however, the beast is swimming.

stricken with famine, Athamas would dispatch a messenger to the Delphic Oracle to ask for Apollo's aid and guidance.

The singed seeds didn't sprout and the fields were as barren as a desert. Desperate for guidance, Athamas sent a messenger to the Delphic Oracle. Unbeknownst to him, the messenger was in Ino's employ. On his return, the messenger told Athamas not what the Oracle had said, but the words that Ino had instructed him to say, words that would seal the doom of Prince Phrixus.

According to the messenger, the Oracle foretold that the only way to make the fields fertile again was to sacrifice the king's eldest son on top of Mount Laphystium. Even though the thought of slaying his only son sickened him, Athamas felt he had no choice. With a heavy heart, he led Phrixus to the top of the mountain. Helle followed them, pleading with her father not to kill her beloved brother.

Hera, taking notice, became enraged. For a father to kill his son because of lies from an adulterous woman was too much for her. She sent Hermes down to Boeotia with a wonderful flying ram whose fleece was made of pure gold. She told Hermes that Phrixus was to be saved and that the ram would be his ticket to safety. As the knife drew close to Phrixus' neck, Hermes appeared and placed the prince on the back of the ram. Helle, not wanting to be left behind, jumped on as well, and soon the two of them were flying away from the land that had caused them so much trouble.

Helle had great difficulty containing her excitement. She began to laugh and flail about, losing her balance over the strait that separates the landmasses that are now Asia

confronted her husband, Athamas imprisoned his queen, opening the doors of the palace and his bedchamber to Ino.

It wasn't long before Ino became obsessed with doing away with Nephele's children. She realized that if Athamas were to die, Phrixus would inherit the throne, making her position in the palace highly uncertain. She quickly devised a plan to secure her status. Ino was a princess of Thebes, a position that brought with it a great deal of respect. Knowing that the women of Boeotia held her in high regard and would do whatever she asked, Ino requested that they scorch the corn that was to be planted. Her plan was to make sure that the season's harvest never even sprouted—she knew that if the kingdom were and Europe. She fell into the water and died almost instantly. In her honor, the area was named the Hellespont.

So it was a lone boy that the golden ram brought to the kingdom of Colchis, where he was accepted by King Aeëtes as his own son. In gratitude to the gods, Phrixus sacrificed the ram to Zeus and gave the Golden Fleece to his new father, who treasured it above all things.

JASON
ASSEMBLES THE
ARGONAUTS

There was a time in the kingdom of Iolcus when King Cretheus died, leaving his son Aeson the throne. But Aeson's half-brother, Pelias, was ruthlessly ambitious; he usurped the throne from Aeson and imprisoned him. Unbeknownst to Pelias, however, Aeson had a son named Diomedes whom Aeson had placed in the care of the learned Centaur Chiron, a noble creature who was half-man and half-horse. Chiron took to calling the boy Jason.

When Jason was a young man, Chiron decided to tell him of his true heritage. Jason then became determined to reclaim his throne. Although now feeble with age, Pelias still possessed a sharp mind. Fearing that he might lose his ill-gained power, he consulted the oracles regularly. For years they reported nothing. But around the time Jason became aware of his lineage, Pelias was told that he should beware of a man wearing one sandal.

En route to Iolcus, Jason came to a river that proved to be an obstacle for an old woman stranded on its bank. As he was of a kind nature, Jason offered to carry the woman across. The old woman was none other than Hera in disguise; she didn't like Pelias and knew that Jason would lose one of his sandals in the mud of river if he carried a heavy load through its waters.

Now wearing only one sandal, Jason came to the city. Word soon reached Pelias that someone fitting the oracle's description had come to town. In a slight panic, Pelias ordered the man to be brought to him.

When the two met, Pelias demanded to know the traveler's identity. Jason said that in the past he was called Diomedes, and that he was the son of the king's half-brother, Aeson.

Greek krater, fifth century B.C., depicting a group of Argonauts.

RIGHT: Heracles (right) and his squire Hylas, who met his doom at the hands of a group of amorous water nymphs.

BELOW: Water nymphs bathe and seduce Hylas while Heracles looks on from behind a rock.

Jason then demanded that the king relinquish the throne to him, the rightful heir. Upon hearing this, Pelias knew that he had no choice, since he couldn't stand up to this athletic youth, but he was not willing to simply hand over the power.

"You will have the throne," said Pelias, "but first you must undertake a great journey. My land is haunted by the ghost of Prince Phrixus. In order to put his soul to rest, the Golden Fleece of the ram that carried him from here to the far-off land of Colchis must be found and brought back. If you bring me the Golden Fleece, I will give you the throne."

Jason accepted Pelias' proposal and soon made it known that he was looking for the bravest and noblest warriors in the land to help him in his search.

He hired the famous shipbuilder Argus to construct a vessel for the voyage; upon completion, this ship was named the *Argo*, in honor of its creator. Men from all over the world came to give Jason their aid; this assemblage of brave warriors was christened the Argonauts. Among them were such heroes as Heracles; the twins Castor and Polydeuces; the master musician and poet Orpheus; Atalanta, the huntress whose skill with a spear rivaled that of any man; and the shapeshifter Periclymenus. Echion, son of Hermes; Ascalaphus, son of Ares; Great Ancaeus, son of Poseidon; and Idmon, son of Apollo, were also members of the crew. All in all, the *Argo* had a crew of around fifty of the bravest and most gifted heroes of the ancient world.

In the course of their quest, the Argonauts had many great adventures. Some of these are accorded full-length stories, others only brief mention.

THE DEATH OF HYLAS AND THE LOSS OF HERACLES

Among the first few stops of the *Argo* was a brief visit to an unnamed island to gather supplies. Shortly after the Argonauts beached, Heracles went into a nearby forest to search for a sturdy tree from which to fashion himself a new oar, since his had recently broken. After an hour or two, he came across a suitable candidate and dragged it back to camp to begin carving.

Upon his return he realized that his young squire, Hylas, was nowhere to be found. He returned to the forest to search for him, but met with failure. He found only Hylas' water pitcher, lying next to a pond. While the lad was gathering water, a group of water nymphs had surprised him. Entranced by the young man's beauty, they had dragged him down into their watery home, unintentionally drowning him. The next morning,

when Heracles still had not returned from his search, Jason decided that the *Argo* would have to sail without him.

BOXING WITH KING AMYCUS

Coming to rest on the island of Bebrycos, the Argonauts found themselves in the company of King Amycus, a belligerent man who fancied himself the greatest boxer in the world. He held such a high opinion of his skills that he challenged any and all visitors to a fight to the death.

Polydeuces, the twin brother of Castor, agreed to represent the Argonauts in the fight. A lesser man would have amended his decision when he set eyes on Amycus. The king was built like a bear, huge and muscular; the sight of him brought to mind Heracles himself. Amycus also arranged for the fight to be unfair; he supplied Polydeuces with a pair of simple leather gloves while his own were covered with sharpened steel spikes. But Polydeuces knew that an opponent of Amycus' enormous size and build would be slow and sluggish in his punches. The quick and agile Polydeuces figured the king would prove to be no great threat.

As the fight began, Polydeuces quickly recognized the weak points in Amycus' fighting style, and with one blow crushed Amycus' temple, sending bits of bone into the man's brain and killing him instantly. When Amycus' men saw their king drop to the ground dead, they raised their arms to avenge his death. The Argonauts, however, proved to be as well trained in the art of combat as Polydeuces, and the battle was soon over.

PHINEUS AND THE HARPIES

Soon the Argonauts came to eastern Thrace, where they met a seer named Phineus. Having been given the gift of prophecy by Apollo, Phineus had used his talents all too well, and had angered Zeus for predicting the future too accurately. In retribution for Phineus' "crime," Zeus had sent a band of Harpies to torment the old man.

The Harpies were evil creatures with the heads and torsos of women but the wings and talons of vultures. They had no control over their defecation and left a terrible stink wherever they went. Whenever Phineus would sit down to a meal, the Harpies would descend, snatching up what food they could and covering the rest with their droppings, making it inedible.

Phineus pleaded for help, and the Argonauts agreed to aid him any way they could. Phineus knew that the only way his curse could be lifted was with the aid of the Argonauts Calais and Zetes, the winged sons of the North Wind. The next time Phineus sat down to a meal and the Harpies darkened the skies, Calais and Zetes flew into the air after them, killing many and making the rest flee in mortal terror, never to return.

The Lemnian Women and their queen tempt Jason and the Argonauts to stay with them on the island of Lemnos. They had earlier killed their husbands and sworn to have nothing to do with men, but the beauty and valor of the Argonauts changed their minds.

The Argo approaches the Symplegades. With the aid of Phineus, the blind seer, the Argonauts were able to manuever safely past this enchanted obstacle.

THE SYMPLEGADES

That night, while sitting down to his first meal in a long time, Phineus told Jason how to maneuver the *Argo* through the Symplegades, two enormous rocks that framed the only inlet to the Bosphorus Strait. These rocks were enchanted so as to clash together unexpectedly whenever a ship passed between them, crushing the vessel and its hapless crew.

Phineus told Jason that as the *Argo* approached this magical obstacle, a dove should be released. If the bird made it through unscathed, so would the ship; if, however, the dove was not successful, Jason must give up the quest then and there, for the *Argo* would not pass through safely.

The dove made it through with the loss of only a few of its tail feathers; likewise, the *Argo* made it through with the loss of only the smallest bit of its stern. They soon landed on the shores of Colchis, land of King Aeëtes, keeper of the Golden Fleece.

COLCHIS AND THE GOLDEN FLEECE

Upon reaching the city, the Argonauts were made very welcome. Baths were drawn and a splendid feast was prepared.

After the men had eaten and were sitting around the table leisurely picking their teeth, Aeëtes asked Jason the reason for the visit. When Jason told him he was in Colchis to obtain the Golden Fleece and bring it back with him to Iolcus, Aeëtes burned inwardly; he had absolutely no intention of parting with such a prize.

By Aeëtes' silence Jason could tell that the king wasn't going to simply hand over the Fleece. Not wanting to seem ungrateful, he offered to perform any task the king might wish. Seeing the opportunity to rid his kingdom of these adventurers, Aeëtes concocted a plan: He asked Jason to plow, sow, and reap a field. The king's oxen, fire-breathing beasts famous for their malice toward men, would have to be yoked and somehow forced to plow the field. The seeds Jason was to sow were the teeth of a dragon that, when planted, would yield not corn or any other grain, but armed men ready for battle. Jason was to "harvest" this crop by emerging victorious from a battle with the Teeth-Men.

Jason agreed to Aeëtes' wishes, knowing that the next day would probably be his last. At this very moment, Medea, the king's daughter, peeked out from behind a curtain to gaze on the strangers and immediately fell in love with Jason. Overhearing what her father had planned for the beautiful young man, she vowed to help him by any means at her disposal.

Later that night, Medea sent a messenger to the *Argo*. The messenger told Jason that the king's daughter wanted to help him in his perilous endeavor, and told him where to meet Medea that night.

When the two met at the appointed place and time, Medea gave Jason a magical ointment of her own making. Once applied, this salve would make the wearer invincible for a day—the oxen would not be able to harm him. She also told him that if the Teeth-Men became too numerous, he should throw a stone in the middle of them. This would cause them to turn and fight each other until none remained.

As Medea described the ointment and the strategy of the stone, Jason found himself staring deeply into her eyes, unable to tear away. He had become as enamored of her as she was of him.

The next day there was a great gathering around the unplowed field. Jason had already applied the ointment, which flooded him with a feeling of tremendous power. When the oxen were released, he had little trouble overpowering and yoking them; their flames didn't even redden his flesh. He then guided them up and down the field, plowing the rows and sowing the teeth as he went.

When the seeds were sown, and an army of bloodthirsty men were poised for battle, Jason threw a stone in the middle of them and soon the men were fighting each other. It took only minutes for the entire army to kill one another. When the Argonauts saw the last man fall, they let out a raucous cheer. Their captain was victorious and the Fleece would soon be theirs.

Aeëtes, however, was not as pleased with the situation as were the Argonauts. He stormed back to his palace and began plotting against Jason and his men, finally deciding that he would have his army attack them that night. But Medea, knowing the way her father thought, sped to the *Argo* and warned Jason that he must leave soon or be ready for the worst fate her father could imagine. She told him that the Fleece was kept in a cave guarded by a horrendous dragon that never slept. She

told Jason that she would magically coax the beast to sleep, after which the Fleece could easily be taken.

While Jason went to the cave and retrieved the magnificent Fleece, Medea stole back to the palace and convinced her little brother Apsyrtus to come along with her, telling him that they were going to sail off with the Argonauts for a great adventure. The unwitting boy readily came along, and Medea and her brother were waiting on the *Argo* when Jason came running back to the ship, Fleece in hand.

Jason clambered back on board and gave the order to start rowing. Soon the *Argo* was at sea, with King Aeëtes and his best warriors in pursuit. Medea knew there was no way the *Argo* could outrun her father's ships; this was the reason she had brought her brother along. In an act of sheer brutality, she slew her young brother and dismembered him, flinging the pieces off the side of the ship one by one. Aeëtes, realizing what had happened, was forced to call off the pursuit in order to retrieve each piece of his young son so that he might have a proper burial.

Soon, the *Argo* was back at port in Iolcus. Jason gave the Golden Fleece to King Pelias and as promised, the old man stepped down, relinquishing the throne to Jason.

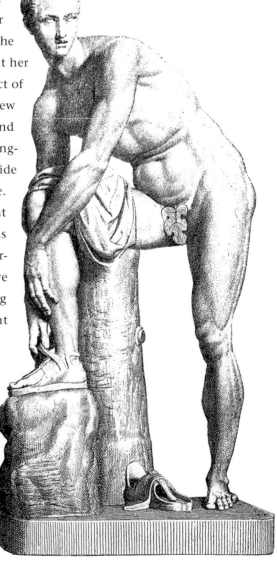

Jason's quest for the Golden Fleece begins with a prophecy telling his Uncle Pelias to beware a man wearing only one sandal—Jason. In most accounts, Jason loses his sandal in the muddy banks of a river while carrying a disguised Hera across. In one alternate version, however, Jason removes the sandal himself after the strap breaks en route to Iolcus.

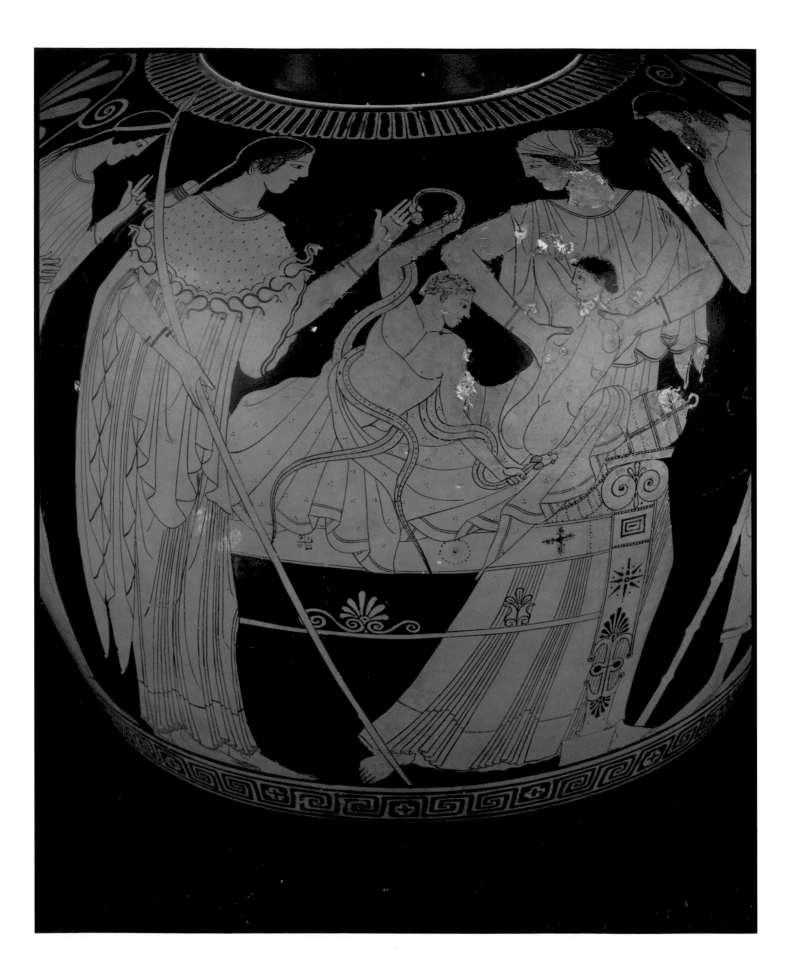

THE TWELVE LABORS OF HERACLES

THE ORIGIN OF HERACLES

There once was a great Theban general named Amphitryon. This general's wife was Alcmene, and it was this woman whom Zeus decided would be his last mortal "diversion."

While Amphitryon was leading his army into battle with the Teleboans and Taphians, Zeus—disguising himself as Amphitryon because he knew that Alcmene was very much in love with her husband—came to

Red-figured stamnos, fourth century B.C., depicting the infant Heracles "playing" with and inadvertently killing the two serpents sent by Hera.

Alcmene's bedchamber. Before coming to Earth, Zeus had arranged for the sun not to cross the sky for three days; he had also convinced the moon to take three days to cross the sky that night. By doing this, he was sure to have enough time to lie with Alcmene as many times as he might desire.

Nine months later Zeus was strutting around Olympus, boasting that soon a son of his would be born who would rule the land of Thebes as no other king had ruled before. When Hera learned of this, she went to Zeus and made a deal with him that any prince born to the House of Perseus (the ruling family of Thebes) that night would be the next king. Zeus agreed, certain that his new son, Heracles, which means "Hera's Pride," would be brought into the world that evening.

Hera then went down to the palace of Sthenelus, whose wife, Nicippe, was seven months pregnant. Using her godly talents, Hera sped up Nicippe's labor so that the first prince born that night was not Heracles but Eurystheus, a weak, timid little soul who was as unlike Heracles as water is to fire. From the moment of his birth Heracles was destined to never be a king.

Soon after he was born, Heracles demonstrated his enormous strength. One night Hera sent two serpents into his crib to kill him. Instead of crying at the sight of the snakes, as his half-brother Iphicles did, the infant Heracles saw them as toys and began playing with them. It wasn't long before he'd accidentally killed both of the serpents. Alcmene soon discovered him looking dejectedly at the two limp things that, until a moment ago, had been so quick and playful.

During Heracles' adolescence he often had trouble containing his godlike strength. He was able to quickly master the more athletic arts, such as archery and swordplay, but when it came to academia he was rather thick. Once, during a very discouraging lyre lesson,

he grew irritated with his lack of skill and the beatings he was receiving from his teacher and, unaware of his own strength, hit the man over the head with the instrument, mistakenly crushing the teacher's skull. Amphitryon then sent him to a cattle farm where he stayed until he was eighteen, further developing his strength and skills and learning the benefits of an outdoor life.

When he was eighteen, Heracles decided to leave the farm and kill the Cithaerian Lion, because the herds he tended, as well as some neighbor's cattle, had been falling prey to this beast. He tracked the Lion to its lair on Mount Helicon and killed it in a matter of seconds. It was from this creature that Heracles got his characteristic cloak, which consisted of a lion's pelt for a cape and the head and jaws of the beast serving as an elaborate headpiece.

THE
TWELVE LABORS

During his adulthood, Heracles found himself pitted against the Minyans, who were enemies of his countrymen, the Thebans. In defense of his land, he led the attacks against the invaders and was victorious. In gratitude, King Creon of Thebes offered him the hand of his eldest daughter, Megara, which he accepted.

Hera decided that now was the time to take her vengeance. One day she sent a streak of insanity into Heracles' brain. The hero was thrown into a mad rage and slew his wife and children. When he came to his senses and realized what he had done, he secluded himself in a dark room of the palace, his mind full of the realization that the hands that cradled his crying face had also slain his family. He wanted nothing more than to kill himself. Fortunately, his longtime friend Theseus convinced him that he wasn't responsible for the

In an alternate version of the snake story, Hera sends only one serpent to kill the infant Heracles.

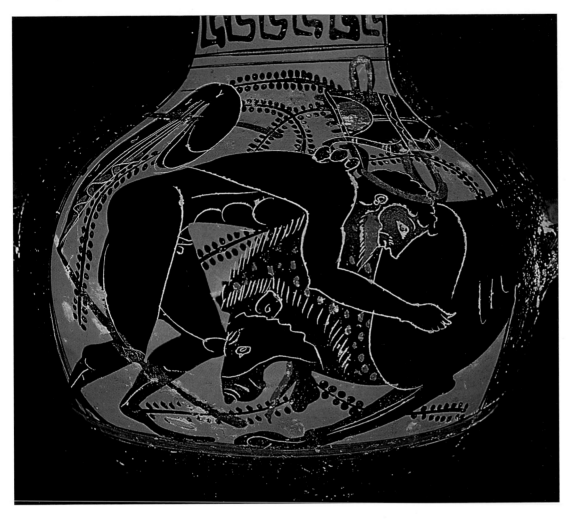

deaths because he had been insane at the time. He advised Heracles to journey to Delphi and ask the advice of Apollo's Oracle.

The Oracle told Heracles that in order to cleanse his soul, he must offer his services to King Eurystheus for twelve years. This was a repellent idea to Heracles, who considered Eurystheus to be nothing more than a weakling, undeserving of any respect. But the voice of Apollo could not be denied.

Although Eurystheus was physically weak, his mind was quite sharp, and he devised a series of twelve tasks that he felt would tax his cousin to the limits.

THE FIRST LABOR— THE NEMEAN LION

The first task was to bring back the hide of the Lion of Nemea, which was impervious to any weapon ever made.

Heracles tracked the beast to its lair on Mount Tretus. It had just returned from a kill and was sluggish with sleep and a full belly. Heracles attacked, but his weapons were of no use. The Lion, too sleepy to retaliate, sauntered into its cave and fell into a deep sleep. Heracles then blocked off the cave's exit and throttled the Lion with his bare hands. The creature awoke in a fury but soon perished under Heracles' grip. Using the Lion's own claws, Heracles flayed the beast and brought its magnificent pelt back to King Eurystheus.

THE SECOND LABOR— THE LERNAEAN HYDRA

Heracles' second task was to kill the Hydra of Lernaea, a fire-breathing, hideous-smelling reptilian monster with nine serpentine heads, one of which was immortal. Heracles' cousin Iolaus accompanied him on this journey.

Hercules and the Hydra, Antonio Pollaiuolo, fifteenth century.

Seeing the trouble his cousin was in, Iolaus happened upon a brilliant idea. He quickly made a fire and soon had a makeshift branding iron glowing red hot. Firebrand in hand, Iolaus approached the battle and seared the Hydra's necks as soon as Heracles had dispatched their heads, making it impossible for new heads to sprout. Soon the Hydra was down to its last, immortal head.

Heracles cut off the immortal head with a sword and buried it, still hissing and spitting, under a gigantic boulder. Packing up to leave, Heracles noticed that the blood from the Hydra's corpse was killing everything it came into contact with. Thinking quickly, he dipped his arrows into the poisonous blood, making them the most lethal weapons in the mortal world.

Eurystheus decided that since Iolaus had helped Heracles, this task was completed unfairly. Heracles nodded his apologies, not really caring what the spindly little king thought. As far as he was concerned, the labor was finished.

THE THIRD LABOR— THE ERYMANTHIAN BOAR

Heracles' third task was to capture the invincible Boar of Erymanthia. When Heracles first saw the monster, he realized that a direct attack would result in defeat. Again, a special plan would be necessary.

Some months later, after the first snowfall, an idea came to him. After a thick blanket of white covered the land, Heracles lured the Boar into a clearing in which a huge snowbank had built up. He waited until the Boar was facing into the snowbank, then leapt out of hiding, frightening the Boar directly into the drift, where it became stuck.

Heracles bound its legs together and carried it back to Eurystheus. When the hero reached the city, the scrawny king took one look at the terrible creature on Heracles' back

Athena assisted Heracles by showing him the way to the creature's lair. She also told him that fighting the Hydra in its cave would mean his certain death; only by forcing it out into the open would he stand a chance of achieving victory.

Taking Athena's advice, Heracles sent a volley of flaming arrows into the Hydra's lair. The monster emerged screaming from the dank swamp, lunging for its tiny attacker. At first, Heracles thought he could simply bash each of the heads into oblivion, but he discovered that as soon as one was pulverized, a replacement immediately grew in its place.

and ordered his artisans to quickly fashion for him a bronze jar that would be buried in the ground, in which he could safely sit while Heracles came to town with his terrifying trophies. He also told Heracles that from now on he would have to leave all proof of his completed tasks outside the walls of Mycenae.

Passing through Iolcus en route to his fourth task, Heracles learned that Jason was amassing a small army to go off and retrieve the fabled Golden Fleece. Abandoning his labors, Heracles joined the Argonauts and returned to his labors afterward.

THE FOURTH LABOR— THE CERYNEIAN HIND

Artemis' chariot was drawn by a team of the most beautiful hinds (female deer) ever seen, which the goddess had captured as a child. There had been one deer, however, that had eluded her; it had spied her approaching the flock and bolted, quicker than the wind, into the Ceryneian Hills. Heracles' fourth task was to capture, but not kill, this last deer. He would have to succeed where Artemis, the goddess of the hunt, had failed.

It took Heracles an entire year to locate the timid, lightning-fast animal. During that time he honed his archery skills—he'd devised a plan to take the deer alive but knew that if the plan was to meet with success, his skill with an arrow would have to rival that of Artemis herself.

After tracking the Hind to Mount Artemisium, he crouched under a bush on the grazing path that the deer walked every day. When the animal came near, Heracles shot an arrow between the tendon and bone of its front legs. The arrow passed through skin, shedding no blood. Hobbled, the deer was easy to capture. The fourth labor was finished.

THE FIFTH LABOR— THE STYMPHALIAN BIRDS

Very few animals were sacred to Ares. It is only fitting that his sacred beasts—the Stymphalian Birds—were as foul as the Greeks found unbridled battle-lust to be. The Stymphalian Birds, so called because of their residence in the Stymphalian Swamp, were ugly creatures with beaks, talons, and wings of bronze. They had a habit of eating anyone who came near their rookery. Because there was no animal in the swamp brave enough to consider the birds as possible food, within a short time the swamp was overflowing with the foul beasts. Occasionally, groups of them would fly off in hopes of finding a new home. As they flew, they passed over countless nearby fields, befouling them with their noxious defecations, making them unfit for farming.

Clearing the Stymphalian Birds out of the marsh was Heracles' fifth labor. A single bird by itself was not terribly daunting, but Heracles was faced with countless hordes of the horrible creatures. He first went to the edge of the swamp with a great number of arrows, planning to shoot any bird that flew above the trees, thus diminishing their number to a point where the remainder could be easily dealt with.

As it turned out, the Birds were too numerous for this plan to work. Heracles could have shot a thousand in a day and it would have done no good. He prayed to Athena for guidance. Hearing his pleas, the goddess had Hephaestus create a magnificent bronze rattle

In an alternate version of the story of Artemis' capture of the deer of Ceryneia, the deer are not hinds but stags.

that, when shaken, would fool the birds into thinking they were in the middle of an earthquake.

Positioning himself on a mountainous shelf overlooking the infested swamp, Heracles shook the rattle for all it was worth. The noise traveled down into the swamp and into the ears of the Birds, and soon the sky was black with the fleeing flocks. With nearly the entire sky full of targets, Heracles had no trouble shooting down the majority of the birds. The survivors, of which there were few indeed, worked their way east to a remote island in the Black Sea where they never caused anyone trouble again.

THE SIXTH LABOR— THE AUGEIAN STABLES

King Augeias of Elis had the largest herd of cattle the ancient world had ever known. Augeias had a bit of a tidiness problem though—no one could remember the last time the stables had been cleaned, and the manure was piled so high that it was almost impossible for a man to walk through the stables without suffocating. And the stench was so strong that it carried throughout all of the Peloponnese.

Heracles' sixth labor was to clean Augeias' stables in one day. He went to the king, told him of his task, and was met with resounding howls of laughter. Augeias, laughing so hard there were tears in his eyes, gave Heracles permission to take whatever steps necessary to get the job done. Heracles climbed to

the top of a nearby hill and noticed that two rivers, the Alpheus and the Peneius, ran nearby. He went down to the stable yard and punched two great breaches in the wall. He then went to the banks of both rivers and dug huge troughs running from their flooded banks to the stable. By diverting these rivers, Heracles cleaned out the stables in minutes.

THE SEVENTH LABOR— THE CRETAN BULL

Heracles' seventh labor was to capture the dreaded fire-breathing white bull of Crete, which had lately been rampaging through the

ABOVE: Heracles slays the Stymphalian Birds, whose beaks, talons, and feathers were made of bronze. The Birds would have torn Heracles to shreds were it not for his protective armor, the skin of the Nemean Lion.

RIGHT: Black-figured amphora, c. fourth century B.C., showing Heracles capturing the Cretan Bull.

country, burning fields, uprooting crops, and slaying the occasional passerby. When the hero arrived in Crete, King Minos offered him all the aid he might need. Heracles refused the king's kind offer, preferring to confront the animal one on one. It was a long struggle, possibly the longest single battle of his twelve labors, but Heracles was eventually successful. He muzzled the animal so that its flames were temporarily snuffed, and loaded it on a boat for the return to Eurystheus.

THE EIGHTH LABOR—
THE MARES OF DIOMEDES

There once was a king of Thrace named Diomedes who had a particularly nasty habit—whenever guests would land on his shores he would offer them all the kindness and hospitality in the world, only to later feed them to his four flesh-eating horses. Heracles' eighth labor was to capture these savage animals.

Upon arriving at Diomedes' palace, Heracles was made most comfortable. Diomedes' attendants, however, soon tried to throw Heracles into the horses' pen. Heracles quickly overpowered the men, then approached Diomedes himself and, taking hold of the savage king, threw him into the pit. The eyes that had seen so many perish in that pit were now, along with the rest of him, just another meal for his treasured horses.

After that last gruesome meal, the horses' appetites became permanently sated and the beasts gave Heracles no trouble as he yoked them and brought them back to Mycenae.

THE NINTH LABOR—
THE GIRDLE OF HIPPOLYTE

The Amazons were a fierce race of female warriors who held men in low regard, believing the female to be the true warrior. Their men were relegated to the common household tasks that women performed elsewhere in the ancient world. To the women went the thrill of battle and the spoils of war. It is not surprising that the Amazons had a great affinity for Ares; likewise, he had an affinity for them, so much that he gave Queen Hippolyte his sacred girdle.

Eurystheus had a daughter named Admete who desired Hippolyte's girdle. She pleaded with her father, who in turn decreed that Heracle's ninth labor would be to retrieve Hippolyte's girdle for his daughter.

Upon landing on the shores of Themiscyra, Heracles was met by Hippolyte, who found herself greatly attracted to him. Never before had she met a man who so exemplified everything she respected. He had the physical strength of a god, was steadfast in his beliefs, and was a little on the dim side. She quickly agreed to give him Ares' girdle.

Hera, observing the ease with which the charming Heracles was about to obtain the girdle, decided to complicate matters. In the guise of an Amazon, she infiltrated the city and began spreading rumors that the male stranger was planning to kidnap Hippolyte.

The Amazons were quick to come to arms. Heracles, seeing the great rush of warriors, figured he had been set up. He killed Hippolyte without a second thought, removed the girdle from her cooling corpse, and with the small army that had accompanied him, fought off the Amazons.

THE TENTH LABOR—
THE OXEN OF GERYON

Geryon, the king of Tartessus, an area in what is now Spain, was reputed to be a man composed of three individual bodies, all joined at the waist. He was also known for his fabulous oxen, the finest in the world. Heracles' tenth labor was to travel to the kingdom of Geryon and return with his oxen. There was one stipulation, however: Heracles was not able to

Amazon warriors were reputed to have cut off their right breasts so that they wouldn't get in the way of their bowstrings.

THE
TROJAN WAR

THE ROAD TO WAR—
THE JUDGMENT OF PARIS

Weddings were cause for great celebration in classical times, both for mortals and for gods. Not to be invited to a wedding meant that a person wasn't considered important. When the wedding of King Peleus and Thetis, a Nereid, or water nymph, was being planned, the last person the Olympians wanted to see at the festivities was Eris, the goddess

Story of the Destruction of Troy,
studio of Colombe, c. 1500.

RIGHT: At the wedding of Peleus and Thetis, Eris, the goddess of discord, threw her infamous golden apple into the middle of the revelry, generating the famous dispute between the goddesses that led to the Judgment of Paris and eventually the Trojan War.

BELOW RIGHT: Greek amphora, sixth–fifth century B.C., depicting Helen confronting Menelaus.

of discord and the sister of Ares. When Eris found out she was not going to be invited, she concocted a plan sure to throw a major upset into the goings-on.

She waited until the wedding was well under way and then threw a golden apple with the words "for the fairest" inscribed on it into the assemblage. At a mortal wedding, most people would be polite and would assume that such an offering was meant for the bride. Hera, Athena, and Aphrodite, however, all jumped for the gift at once, none of them willing to relinquish it and admit mediocrity. After much argument, they turned to Zeus to resolve the matter. Wisely, the king of the gods decided that it would be in his best interest to remain an impartial observer, for he knew that if he chose one as the fairest, the others would have no qualms about getting even with him later.

Zeus gave the job of judging to Paris, a young prince of Troy who as an infant had been exposed to die on the slopes of Mount Ida because of a prophecy that the next royal child born would be the cause of the fall of Troy. Paris had not died, however—unbeknownst to his true father, King Priam of Troy, Paris had been rescued by a shepherd who had raised the boy as his own son.

Each of the goddesses offered Paris a bribe of incredible magnitude in return for choosing her as the most beautiful. They handed

him the golden apple and told him to give the apple to the one whose proposal he liked the most. Hera offered Paris worldly rule over all of Europe and Asia; if he had taken her offer, it would have resulted in the largest empire ever conceived. Athena promised the young lad victory over the Greek army, total conquest of the Trojans' enemies. But Aphrodite, realizing that Paris was a young boy with the majority of his thoughts not on world domination but on softer, more personal victories, offered him the most beautiful woman in all the world: Helen, the wife of Menelaus, king of Sparta.

Even though Paris was involved with a beautiful nymph at the time, he had heard stories of Helen's beauty and found himself intoxicated at the idea of having her. He quickly handed over the golden apple to

Aphrodite, who now, even though the judgment was not based solely on merit, could call herself the fairest of the Olympians.

Following the Judgment, Paris returned to Troy to compete in the annual games held in honor of Priam's "dead" son (who was, in fact, Paris himself). During the course of these games, Paris' true identity was revealed to his father and brothers, and the young prince was accepted back into the fold. Soon after this, Paris went to Sparta, home of Menelaus and Helen, where his bribe was paid: Helen fell in love with him, and the two returned to Troy. (It is sometimes said that she was abducted, but there is much evidence to the contrary.)

Paris and Helen's relationship led to the Trojan War, the longest, most brutal, and most romanticized war in the classical canon. And at the true moment of birth of this war, we find a vain and stubborn goddess.

The Love of Paris and Helen, Jacques Louis David, 1788.

THE
TROJAN WAR

After Paris was transported by Aphrodite to Sparta, he was made most welcome by King Menelaus and Queen Helen. Menelaus soon announced that he must leave to tend to

White-figured
skyphos, c. 490 B.C.,
showing Greek heroes
discussing the siege
of Troy.

some unfinished business on Crete. During his absence he entrusted his home to his new Trojan friend. The night after Menelaus left, Paris seduced Helen on the island of Krani, en route back to Troy, where Paris promised her she would soon be his wife.

Upon his return, Menelaus sent out a call to all the kings and allies of Greece. He knew they would reply because they had all courted Helen and sworn an oath, forced upon them by Tyndareus, Helen's stepfather (her true fa-

ther was Zeus). Tyndareus had been worried that as soon as one man had won Helen's hand, her slighted suitors would retaliate violently. To put his fears to rest, he had made each suitor swear to defend the house of Helen's eventual husband, whoever he might be, if wrong was ever done to him because of the marriage. When word of Menelaus' situation reached the royalty of Greece, they called their armies together to travel to Troy and reclaim Helen.

The fleet assembled at Aulis, on the northern coast of Greece. Agamemnon, king of Mycenae, was chosen as leader. Under him was a cast of heroes: his brother Menelaus; Odysseus, king of Ithaca; Achilles, king of the Myrmidons; Achilles' friend and companion, Patroclus; Greater Ajax; Lesser Ajax; Diomedes, king of Argos; Teucer the archer, half-brother of Greater Ajax; and Nestor, who was considered the wisest of the assembled men. In all, there were 100,000 men in the Greek army; the fleet consisted of 1,186 ships. It was an army the like of which had never been seen.

When all was ready, the men sat down for a final feast before setting sail. During the meal a snake climbed a nearby tree and devoured eight baby sparrows and the mother bird. The snake then turned to stone. Calchis, the army's prophet, interpreted this to mean that the war against Troy would rage for ten years, the total number of living things that died on the tree. The first nine years would be futile, with nothing gained for either side, but the tenth year would end with the fall of Troy.

The fleet soon reached Troy, which was located on the northeastern coast of what is now Turkey. And as Calchis had foretold, nothing significant happened for nine years. The sheer vastness of the Greek army mattered little against the indomitable walls of Troy. Inside the city, King Priam, Queen Hecuba, Paris, and Helen all wondered how long the siege would last.

Hector, son of Priam and brother of Paris, was the mightiest of the Trojan warriors. Only Achilles was a fair match for him. The most tragic event of the Trojan War centered around these two warriors. It was this story of the frailty and stubbornness of human pride that Homer told in *The Iliad*, an epic tale that depicts fifty-one days of the Trojan War and the consequences of one man's selfish dignity.

Homer's epic begins at the start of the war's tenth year. Both sides are weary of fighting. The whole war seems to be an exercise in futility. The touchstone for the tragedy is, as the first line of the poem says, "the wrath of Peleus' son Achilles." During a meeting of the Greek leaders, Agamemnon is approached by an old man named Chryses, a priest of Apollo. During a raiding party on the nearby island of Tenedos, Chryseis, the old man's daughter, had been taken away to become Agamemnon's concubine. Out of love for his child, Chryses had come to plead with the king, but Agamemnon sent him away without a second thought. Chryses, calling on Apollo, demanded that justice be served. Apollo, who was quite willing to help so loyal a priest, sent a deadly plague upon the Greek forces.

Agamemnon asked Calchis for aid. The seer said that the plague would be lifted when the daughter of Apollo's priest was returned to her father. Agamemnon immediately sent Chryseis back to Tenedos, and the plague soon ended.

A meeting was then called in which Agamemnon informed his colleagues that since his bedmate had been taken from him, he required another. As a replacement, he chose Briseis, Achilles' concubine. Enraged

that Agamemnon could care so little about the happiness of his generals, Achilles decided, from that point on, to abstain from the war. He had been slighted by his leader and therefore felt that he no longer owed him allegiance. He retreated to his tent, where he was consoled by his longtime friend and companion, Patroclus.

That night Thetis, Achilles' mother, visited her angry son. She learned of the wrong her son had suffered and became infuriated. She flew to Olympus to demand Zeus' aid. She implored the king of the Gods to give quick and decisive victory to the Trojans.

At this time all of Olympus was buzzing about the war. It had become such an item of conversation that the gods had chosen sides. Zeus favored the Trojans, but kept it a secret from Hera, who favored the Greeks. Athena wanted to see the downfall of the Trojans. Aphrodite sided with the Trojans, and Ares, who was for the most part incapable of original thought, wanted whatever Aphrodite wanted. Poseidon sided with the Greeks. Apollo and Artemis favored the Trojans. Zeus answered Thetis' request. He sent a dream to Agamemnon, promising him victory if he attacked the next day. Zeus knew that without Achilles, the Greeks had no hope of winning.

The next day, in the middle of the battle, the armies ceased fighting and spread apart. A decision had been reached to let the two warriors whose hearts were closest to the actual cause of the war fight it out between them. Menelaus and Paris soon advanced on each other. Paris threw a spear that was easily deflected by Menelaus. The king of Sparta then threw his own spear, which nicked the prince of Troy. Menelaus charged, grabbed hold of Paris' helmet, and flung the man around by the head. A dizzy Paris soon found himself being dragged toward the Greek camp. Victory was within reach, but Aphrodite caused Paris' helmet strap to break, freeing him. She then swept him up in a cloud and returned him inside the walls of Troy.

Seeing what had happened, Agamemnon declared the battle over. The Greeks had won. He promised no more blood would be spilled if the Trojans surrendered and returned Helen to Menelaus. It seemed certain that the Trojans were going to surrender.

Hera, who was determined that the war shouldn't end until the walls of Troy lay in ruin, dispatched Athena to start things up again. Athena flew to the battlefield and convinced a young Trojan named Pandalaus to take aim at Menelaus with his bow. He wounded the king, incurring the wrath of the Greeks, who now would be satisfied only with the total obliteration of Troy.

The next significant battle was between Diomedes and Hector. The two were going at it tooth and nail when Diomedes realized that Ares was fighting alongside Hector, guiding his blows. His first reaction was unabashed fear, but Hera soon came to him and convinced him that he was a better fighter than Ares. Taking strength from her words and from Athena's guiding hand, Diomedes launched a spear that pierced the god of war. Ares let out a bellow of such fury that, for a moment, all fighting on the battlefield stopped.

Ares flew up to Zeus and complained about the treatment he had just received. Zeus had no pity for the cowardly god and ordered him to remove himself from the fighting. With Ares gone, the Trojans felt much less enthusiastic about the battle and retreated back inside the protective walls of their city. Zeus then remembered his promise to Thetis and went to Earth to hasten the Trojan victory.

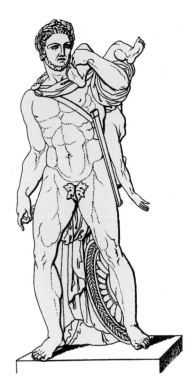

OPPOSITE: *Jupiter and Thetis*, Ingres, 1811.

ABOVE: Hector returns from battle carrying the dead body of a Greek warrior over his shoulder.

LEFT: King Menelaus and Paris engage in battle. Menelaus would have dragged Paris into the Greek camp if Aphrodite had not transported the young prince back inside the walls of Troy.

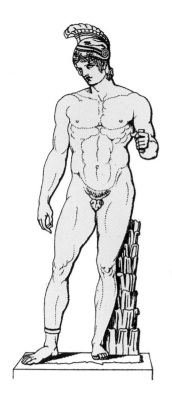

ABOVE: The warrior Achilles, whose wrath and stubbornness caused the death of many Greek soldiers.

RIGHT: Greater Ajax wounds Hector before the walls of Troy. Apollo healed Hector's wound quickly so that the Trojans would not become disheartened.

The next battle was a near-disaster for the Greeks. With Achilles still refusing to fight, and with Zeus supporting the enemy, the Greeks soon found themselves pushed back to their ships. Luckily for the Greeks, night fell and the battle ended. Their position, however, was less than desirable.

While the wine flowed in abundance in Troy that night, in the Greek camp remorse was the intoxicant. Agamemnon was near the point of giving up and sailing home. Nestor persuaded him that if he would simply apologize to Achilles and return Briseis to him, things would change. With Achilles fighting once again for the Greeks, the Trojans would not be able to duplicate the ferocious attack they had managed that day. After some reflection, Agamemnon realized he had been foolish. He asked Odysseus to go to the noble warrior and relay his apology.

Achilles received Odysseus graciously. Food was served and the conversation was friendly and most enjoyable. But when Odysseus told Achilles of Agamemnon's apology, the conversation turned cold. Achilles told Odysseus that Agamemnon could offer a thousand apologies and it still wouldn't be enough. He continued to refuse to fight.

The next day the fighting picked up exactly where it had left off. Soon it became evident that the Trojans were going to win. When Hera realized this, she devised a plan. She came across her husband on top of Mount Ida, watching the carnage below. With her soothing words and caresses, Hera seduced Zeus into lying with her. For a while Zeus forgot about the battle, giving the weary Greeks the advantage they needed.

Soon the tide of the battle turned. Greater Ajax had wounded Hector, greatly disheartening the Trojans. The Greeks were fighting with renewed fury, urged on by a supportive Poseidon.

When he awoke on Mount Ida, Zeus realized what had been done and became enraged. Seeing the wounded Hector lying gasping on the field, he ordered Apollo to amend the situation quickly. The god of healing quickly revived the fallen Trojan. With Apollo by his side, a renewed Hector once again leapt into the fray, turning the tide once again for the Trojans. They fought furiously, pushing the Greeks farther and farther back until it became evident that the Greek ships would be set aflame.

Meanwhile, in Achilles' tent, Patroclus could no longer remain idle. He convinced Achilles to trade armor with him. By dressing as the Greeks' greatest warrior, Patroclus was sure he culd fool the Trojans into believing that Achilles had reentered the battle, which would greatly discourage them, possibly even turning the advantage back to the Greeks. Achilles, still refusing to fight, agreed to Patroclus' urgings. The ruse was immediately successful; Patroclus entered the fray, and soon the tide was turned. The Trojans shrank in fear from the sight of an enraged Achilles, and soon no warrior would even approach the disguised Patroclus except Hector.

Even though Patroclus fought valiantly and with a skill he had not known he had, he was still no match for Hector. The prince of Troy quickly dispatched Patroclus to the underworld by letting loose with a well-aimed spear. In mockery of his fallen enemy, Hector stripped Patroclus of Achilles' armor, which he then donned himself.

It was Antilochus, the son of Nestor, who brought the bad news to Achilles. While the death of hundreds of his countrymen had not been enough to bring Achilles out of his tent, the death of his friend was. Embittered and enraged, he vowed to avenge the death of Patroclus. Thetis, hearing this, asked Hephaestus to fashion for Achilles a new set

of armor. This armor was so glorious that when Achilles took to the field the next day, the Trojans were filled with dread.

Never before had Achilles raged so furiously. He cut down men before they even knew he was upon them. Even the waters of the fierce river Scamander were not able to stop Achilles' advance. He was filled with an impossible fury. He wouldn't rest until Patroclus was avenged. The Trojans were soon filling the walls of their city, for their advances had turned into retreats under the mighty arm of Achilles. Soon there was only one Trojan not within the safety of the walls—Hector stood in Achilles' old armor beneath the walls of Troy, spear and sword at the ready.

Athena, who was fighting alongside Achilles, made herself visible to Hector. Seeing that Athena herself was against him, Hector's strong resolve faded. Achilles chased Hector around the walls of Troy three times. Eventually, Athena, growing bored of such childishness, appeared before Hector in the form of his brother Deiphobus. Thinking he now had an ally, Hector stopped running and turned to face Achilles. He tried to strike a deal with Achilles, suggesting that the victor should return the loser's body to the appropriate camp.

Achilles spat at Hector's offer, his rage and grief over the loss of Patroclus not forgotten. Spears were thrown by both men, but only Achilles' aim was true. He stripped Hector's cooling corpse of its armor, pierced Hector's feet, threaded them with a rope that he tied to the back of his chariot, and dragged the

Achilles Contemplating the Body of Patroclus, G.A. Pellegrini, eighteenth century.

than Priam's loss of Hector. This knowledge moved the warrior to tears and he agreed that Priam should have his son's body. He also asked the old king how many days he needed for the funeral, and said that he would hold off the Greek forces for that many days.

For nine days Troy grieved over Hector, and for those same nine days the Greeks grieved the loss of Patroclus. Both were buried. It was a wiser and kinder Achilles that knew both his days and those of Troy were now short in number. At this point *The Iliad* comes to a close. The Trojan War, however, does not.

Achilles was soon killed by none other than Paris. After Achilles' birth, Thetis had taken her infant son to the river Styx and dipped the newborn in its waters, thereby

ABOVE: **Achilles drags Hector's body around the walls of Troy while Hermes gathers Hector's soul for its trip to Hades.**

RIGHT: **White-figured skyphos, fifth century B.C., depicting Priam begging Achilles for Hector's body.**

body around the walls of Troy, an added indignity. After Achilles' wrath had died and Hector's body lay in the Greek camp, Priam went to the Greek hero and pleaded for the return of his son's body.

Achilles was deeply moved by the old man's words. In Priam's grieving he recognized the universality of death, realizing that all men would lose those close to them, that his loss of Patroclus was no more painful

making him invulnerable except for his ankle, which was the spot where she had held him when she dipped him in the river. It was at this vulnerable spot where Paris' arrow, guided by the hand of Apollo, had pierced the hero's flesh; Achilles died from an infection soon after.

The glorious arms of Achilles, fashioned by Hephaestus himself, were now a matter of contention among the Greeks. Who should rightly receive the armor? Much discussion was held, and the choice was narrowed down to either Odysseus or Greater Ajax. After a vote, the arms went to Odysseus.

Feeling that he had been disgraced, Ajax became determined that both Agamemnon and Menelaus should die. That night, as he approached their tents, he went slightly mad. He wandered until he came to the area where the Greeks kept their flocks of sheep. In his deranged state, he thought the sheep to be a collection of Greek soldiers. He ran pell-mell into the flock and began slaughtering them at random. He then singled out the sheep he

thought to be Odysseus and brought it back to his tent, where he beat the poor creature with his fists until only a bloody bag of broken and crushed bones remained. His senses were then returned to him. Realizing what he had just done, he threw himself upon his sword, unable to face the disgrace he had brought upon himself.

The Greeks were now very distraught. Two of their finest warriors had perished in a short time. They wondered if victory would ever be attained.

The Greeks then learned through a prophet that Troy would survive until a fabulous statue of Athena was taken from within its walls. Odysseus and Diomedes decided that they must steal the statue. In the dark of night, Odysseus helped Diomedes scale the walls. Diomedes quickly located the statue and brought it back to the Greek camp.

Their spirits now lifted, the Greeks decided the time had come for action. It was Odysseus who realized that the only way to be certain of a victory would be to get the violent sea. Many ships and many men were lost. A few survived, however, and did return home, despite Athena's wishes.

Such was not the case for Odysseus, the king of Ithaca. His ships were tossed by the storm to the island of Ismarus, where he led a raid on the inhabitants, the Cicones. Odysseus underestimated the strength of his opponents and suffered a sizable loss of seventy-two men. Leaving Ismarus, Odysseus set course to sail around the southeastern tip of the Pelopennese. This was the most direct route back to Ithaca. But again Poseidon threw the ships off-course, this time blowing them around for nine days until they came to the northern coast of Africa. Here Odysseus discovered a race of men who ate the fragrant blossoms of the lotus plant, which caused them to fall into an opiated state. Some of Odysseus' men fell under the flower's spell and had to be forcibly removed lest they forever forget their homeland, still so far away.

They soon beached beneath the mouth of an enormous cave. Around the cave was a fence that served as a containing wall for a sizable number of sheep, all very fat and obviously well tended. Realizing that whoever tended the sheep might possibly give food, rest, and aid to the weary sailors, Odysseus set off with twelve of his men and a full wineskin—an offering of friendship to the unknown shepherd.

The cave contained a wealth of food. Milk pails were everywhere, filled to the brim. Meat, dried and fresh, hung from the walls. Everywhere was something that made the mouths of the tired sailors water. And since no one was home, they were soon feasting to their heart's content. Bloated and slothful from the meal, they hardly noticed the huge shape that soon blocked the entranceway. It was the Cyclops Polyphemus, a son of Poseidon, and he was in no way pleased to see his home pillaged by humans.

Before Odysseus could do anything, Polyphemus had snatched up a few of the slowest sailors and bashed in their skulls on the floor of the cave. The monster then rolled a large rock in front of the entrance, blocking the only escape route. He then took his time feasting on the still-warm bodies.

When Polyphemus left the next morning to tend his flock, Odysseus had time to come up with a plan. When the Cyclops returned that evening he once again slew and ate some sailors. Odysseus approached the monster while he was heavy with food and offered him a cup of the wine he had brought. Poly-

phemus, who had never before tasted wine, downed it instantly and demanded another cup, then another and another. Soon, the monster had passed out drunk.

Odysseus' men took up the large pointed stick they had fashioned earlier and rammed it deep into Polyphemus' only eye. The monster woke up howling and frantically groped around the floor of the cave, searching for his attackers. He met with no luck, though, since Odysseus had ordered his men to hide under Polyphemus' sheep. The Cyclops rolled the enormous rock aside, figuring the humans would be easy to find as they ran out through the opening.

All he felt, however, were the backs of his sheep; he never thought to search underneath them. As soon as the men were out of Polyphemus' reach, they emerged from their hiding places, ran back to the ships, and set sail, leaving a raging Polyphemus behind.

Poseidon's hatred of Odysseus grew a thousandfold. He now had a personal vendetta against Odysseus and no longer needed to be asked by Athena to cause him trouble. But by this time Athena had forgotten her anger toward the Ithacan king. Quite the opposite—she had remembered her fondness for his cunning and intelligence and found herself liking him more with each passing day.

The next area Odysseus came to was the floating island of Aeolia, home of Aeolus, the keeper of the winds. Aeolus received the travelers with open arms and a full table, and

Black-figured vasepainting, sixth century B.C., showing Odysseus and three companions blinding Polyphemus.

his mother, Antikleia, and his friend Agamemnon. But heeding the words of Circe, he held them all off until he spied the visage of Tiresias. He then directed the spirit to the pit and let it drink its fill of the pungent froth. After Tiresias' thirst was quenched, Odysseus asked him how he might return to Ithaca.

The ghost told him that all would be well as long as none of his crewmen harmed the oxen of Helios, the god of the sun, at whose island they would soon arrive. He then told Odysseus to take heart, for even though many troubles might lie before him, he would eventually reach his beloved home and family. Odysseus returned to the surface world, letting the countless ghosts gorge themselves on the pool of blood.

Odysseus again set sail, stopping on the way at Circe's island to tell her what had happened. She informed him that soon he would come upon the island of the Sirens. The Sirens were fearful creatures, she told him, but not in the usual ways. They were quite beautiful and had voices radiant with life when they sang. It was their singing that Odysseus should beware. Once again, Circe told Odysseus how to overcome the next obstacle he was certain to encounter.

Taking her advice, Odysseus lashed himself to the mast of his ship as soon as it neared the fateful island. In order to prevent the rest of the crew from falling under the spell of the Sirens' song, he made each man plug his ears with cotton. The nearer they came to the Sirens' island the more Odysseus realized why these women should be feared. He saw, scattered all around their tiny islet, the wreckage of countless ships and the skeletons of their crews. The men, so intoxicated by the beauty of the Sirens' singing, had run their ships full force into the jagged reef that surrounded the island, smashing their boats to pieces. Odysseus himself was not immune to their song, and he found himself struggling to get free of the binding ropes. As the songs faded away into the distance, he found his senses returning, and was amazed at the power of the wondrous music.

The ship's next peril was the dual danger of Scylla and Charybdis, two terrible sister monsters. According to legend, whoever passed safely by one would undoubtedly fall prey to the other. Scylla had twelve legs and six heads, with each mouth containing three sets of terrible teeth. Charybdis, whose body is never described, lived beneath the water and three times a day sucked a great amount of water into her mouth, only to spit it back out again. By doing this she created whirlpools so fierce that even Poseidon couldn't stop their formation. With the aid of the now helpful Athena, Odysseus was able to maneuver past both monsters, but only after losing six of his crewmen.

The tired men next came to Island of the Sun, home of Helios. When the men saw Helios' magnificent oxen they forgot Tiresias' warning and, tired of eating only fish, killed some of the sacred oxen and feasted on the flesh. Odysseus ate none of the meat, knowing full well that to do so spelled death. When the ship left the island, Helios was quick to avenge the trespass. With a bolt of thunder he tore the ship apart, killing the sailors. Odysseus was the sole survivor, and was carried by the waves to an island ruled by the Nymph Calypso. Here he stayed for many years, unable to leave because Calypso had no ships at her disposal.

On Olympus, Athena pleaded with Zeus to give Odysseus aid since he had proven himself a worthy mortal on his many adventures. Zeus agreed and sent Hermes to Calypso with the message that she was to help Odysseus in any way possible. With a heavy heart, Calypso, who had fallen in love with Odysseus, gave him the timber needed to construct a raft and provided him with provisions for his

Ulysses and the Siren,
Friedrich Preller,
1832–1834.

journey home. His heart filled with joy, he set sail on his flimsy raft for Ithaca, nine years after the fall of Troy.

Seeing Odysseus on the ocean's surface, Poseidon immediately whipped up another fierce storm. The raft was destroyed, throwing Odysseus into the turbulent sea. He would have died if the sea goddess Leucothea hadn't come to his aid, telling him to swim until he reached land. She also gave him her veil, which would protect him from both drowning and sharks.

Two days later Odysseus awoke to find himself on the shores of Phaeacia. He was discovered by Nausicaa, the daughter of King Alcinous, who told him to go to the palace and ask Queen Arete for help, since her father never refused anything her mother asked. Odysseus did as he was told and soon found himself well taken care of. To repay the royal family's kindness and generosity, he told them of his many adventures.

Because Odysseus' journeys had kept him away from Ithaca for nineteen years, most people thought him dead. Only Penelope and Telemachus, Odysseus' son, believed he was alive. Unfortunately, many young men had come to vie for Penelope's hand. Convinced the king would never return, these men had no qualms about raiding the royal larder and using the palace to their own ends.

To keep the many suitors at bay, Penelope told them she was busy weaving a burial shroud for her father, who had recently died, and could not see anyone. Since this was a noble cause, none of the suitors challenged its validity. But it was, of course, a ruse. Every night, Penelope unraveled what she had woven that day, so that she never made any progress. This trick worked for a while, but eventually one of the suitors caught her in the act of undoing her work and demanded that she choose her new husband soon.

Having received aid from King Alcinous, Odysseus soon reached Ithaca. Upon his arrival he was met by Athena, who had disguised herself as a shepherd. She told him of the many suitors vying for Penelope's hand, of their intentions to kill Telemachus, and of Penelope's still undying love for her long-lost king. The goddess advised Odysseus to stay with the swineherd Eumaeus in order to observe the goings-on at the palace without making his presence known. To further disguise himself, Odysseus took on the appearance of a beggar.

On Athena's prompting, Telemachus abandoned the search for his father and returned home to Ithaca. He went to Eumaeus' hut first thing, since he trusted the faithful swineherd to tell him all that had happened while he was away. After Telemachus had heard all Eumaeus had to tell, he sent the swineherd to his mother to let her know of his return quietly so as not to arouse the wrath of the many suitors. Once father and son were alone in the hut, Odysseus threw off his disguise and revealed his identity. Their joy at the reunion was great, but since there was still much to do, they kept their merriment short.

The next day Odysseus, again disguised as a beggar, went to the palace, where he suffered many insults from the suitors. Upon hearing that a stranger had been treated so poorly in her home, Penelope ordered that the beggar be brought to her so she could apologize personally. Even though he yearned to reveal himself to his beloved wife, Odysseus held his tongue and instead told her of the many stories he had heard of the great Odysseus.

Penelope then told the beggar of the many suitors and how she had finally come up with a plan to rid herself of them. Before he had left for Troy, Odysseus had been renowned for his skill with the bow. He had once shot a single arrow through twelve golden rings placed in a row. Penelope told the old beggar that she would only marry the man able to string Odysseus' mighty bow (an impossible feat in itself) and duplicate her husband's feat with the golden rings.

The next day Penelope, carrying the bow, descended to the main hall of the palace, where the suitors were gathered, and told them of the decision she had come to. They all agreed to compete, and soon all were attempting to string the bow. Not one of the suitors was successful. When all had failed, the old beggar stepped forward and asked whether he might have a try. He strung the bow with no trouble at all and the suitors—and Penelope—immediately realized who was in their presence. Odysseus then shot a single arrow through the twelve rings that had been set up, thus confirming everyone's conclusions as to his identity. He then shot every one of the suitors on the spot. After twenty long years, the king of Ithaca, the mighty Odysseus, had finally come home.

Attic skyphos, fifth century B.C., showing Penelope with Odysseus in his disguise as a beggar.

OPPOSITE: Iceland's forbidding landscape contributed to the development of a people who were hardy and courageous—if somewhat reckless.

BELOW: Odin, the king of the Aesir, sits upon Hlidskialf, surveying the nine worlds. Note the ravens Hugin (thought) and Munin (memory) whispering into his ears.

in Iceland in 1643, the *Arnamagnaean Codex* was found, also in Iceland. It contained five poems very similar in nature to those of the *Regius*, but contained one new poem, "Baldrs Draumar," that dealt with the death of Balder, the god of light. Because of the similar natures of these documents, all thirty-four poems were given the collective title of the *Elder Edda* or *Poetic Edda*. Since this work is an amalgamation of many poets, who were likely separated by hundreds of years, many inconsistencies are present in these myths. Even though the poems in the *Elder Edda* were written by people who believed in the gods and heroes they were writing about, characters in

these works who have already died spring up again out of the blue. Events that have taken place in one poem have yet to take place in another. The origins of the gods and their weaponry vary from poem to poem.

Another, more important source is a text by a man named Snorri Sturluson (1179–1241), the *Prose Edda*. By the time Sturluson began writing, Christianity had taken hold in Iceland. The onset of this new religion was causing the poetic forms of the ancient Scalds, the religious bards of Iceland, to disappear.

Along with the Scaldic style, the stories of the ancient gods were also disappearing. Sturluson took it upon himself to commit to paper not only the poetic techniques of the Scalds but a good number of the most famous ancient myths as well. This stylebook became the *Prose Edda*. (Confusingly, the *Elder Edda* is the more recent work.)

Although Sturluson's work documents a number of myths not told in the *Elder Edda*, it must be kept in mind that he was writing down the myths many centuries after those who originally circulated them had died. Through the course of time many of the myths as they reached Sturluson's ears had undergone structural and narrative changes. Thus, when both the *Elder Edda* and the *Prose Edda* are combined, we are presented with a canon of myths that is rife with inconsistencies and incongruities.

THE FATALISM OF NORSE MYTHOLOGY

Another characteristic of the Norse canon that differentiates it from practically any other ancient canon is its inherent bleakness. The harshness of the barren Icelandic landscape is reflected in the stories and myths of its ancient people.

The Norse gods were a race of half-giant, half-god deities who were not immortal. These deities understood that a time would come when they would meet their own deaths. The mortal nature of these gods reflected the fatalistic mindset in the northern races. If the lives of the ancient Norse seemed surpassingly transient, it makes sense that their pantheon reflected a certain "mortality." The most a Norseman could aspire to was to

This map of Iceland is from a seventeenth-century atlas made by the famous Dutch cartographer and publisher Willem Janszoon Blaeu, who is credited with the invention of a printing press that was the first to feature significant improvements since Gutenberg built the first press in the fifteenth century. With its many fjords, Iceland has always been appealing to map makers.

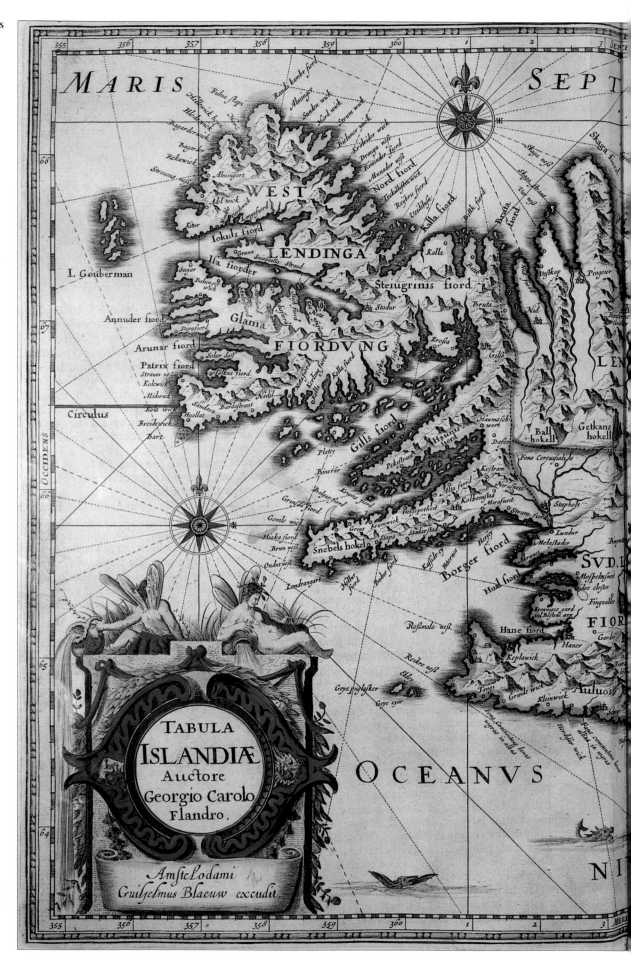

RIGHT: This ninth-century Icelandic artwork depicts the funeral ship of a dead Norse warrior; his comrades are manning the sails.

OPPOSITE: The summers are brief in Iceland, and are therefore most welcome. Not surprisingly, the most benevolent gods in the Norse pantheon were associated with the season or with the sun itself.

die fighting against the world's evils, be those evils in the form of a rival clan, inclement weather, or a pack of wolves.

For the ancient Norsemen, the noblest way to die was in battle, at an early age. By doing this they would be granted a seat in Valhala, the hall of the chosen slain, where they would fight and feast continually until the time of Ragnarok, the apocalypse, when everything in the universe would be destroyed, including the gods themselves. To die of old age or illness was considered cowardly. Since their religion told them nothing was permanent, not even the gods, the ancient Norse thought it only right to fight, violently and until the death, against the evils of the world. And the world of the ancient Norse must have seemed full of evil, where almost everything was against man. The Icelandic landscape was cold and inhospitable, the long months of winter broken by the warming rays of the sun for only a short time every year.

Iceland is situated in such a northerly position that the seasons of winter and summer are delineated by the amount of ambient light in the sky. During the summer the sun never fully sets, making nighttime a perpetual dusk. But during the long winter the darkness is nearly complete. This unrelenting darkness adds to the already harsh wintry climate, making the northern winters times of great hardship. (It is hardly surprising that the malignant characters in the Norse canon were associated with the extreme cold.)

For the ancient Norse the world was characterized by clear delineations of good and evil, light and dark. These delineations made for a mythological canon that represented good and evil as equally balanced forces that were constantly at odds, always trying to tip the scales. It was all an ancient Norseman could do to keep the balance equal by standing firm against the forces of evil, as his gods did, whenever evil arose.

The glacial rivers of Iceland no doubt inspired tales of the Elivagar.

Directly to the north of Ginnungagap was the realm of Niflheim, a dark world shrouded in continual mist. The spring Hvergelmir was in this twilight place, and from it flowed the eleven rivers of Niflheim, known collectively as the Elivagar. Individually, the Elivagar were named Fimbulthul, Fjorm, Gjoll, Gunnthra, Hrid, Leipt, Slid, Svol, Sylg, Vid, and Ylg. These rivers, having nowhere else to go, all eventually flowed into Ginnungagap. As soon as their waters hit the icy air, they froze into gigantic blocks of ice that slowly filled the massive chasm.

To the south of Ginnungagap was Muspellsheim, the world of fire and perpetual light—the opposite of Niflheim in every respect. Here lived Surtr the flame giant, the first living entity, who played a large role not only in the creation of the universe but also in its eventual destruction. It was Surtr's job to protect Muspellsheim from trespassers. But since he was the only living being, he found himself bored most of the time. In his boredom he practiced with his flaming sword, honing his skills, sending great waves of sparks and flame out into the chasm of Ginnungagap. There the fire met the blocks of ice on the abyss floor, sending great torrents of steam upward into the frigid air, where the moisture was frozen again, returning to the chasm floor as frost. From this frost were formed two creatures: Ymir, the primogenitor of the giants, and Audhumbla, an enormous cow.

Naturally, after a while both of these new beings became ravenously hungry. And while Ymir kneaded Audhumbla's udders, supplying himself with rivers of milk, Audhumbla herself had nothing to eat but the frost from the ice. She licked the ice blocks until she uncovered the god Buri, whose name means "producer." This was an apt moniker for the being who would become the grandfather of the Aesir, the ruling gods of Norse mythology.

After gorging himself on Audhumbla's rich milk, Ymir lay down on the chasm's floor to sleep off the slothfulness brought on by overeating. As he dozed unaware of the goings-on around him a sheet of fire from Surtr's sword fell very close to his sleeping body. The warmth both deepened his sleep and made him perspire. From this perspiration was born Thrudgelmir, an ugly six-headed giant who was the grandfather of the frost giants, the sworn enemies of the Aesir. From the sweat of Ymir's armpits came two other children, also giants, though not as malformed as Thrudgelmir. This brother and sister had only one head each, but they were still hideously ugly. Their names were never recorded.

Soon after his birth, Buri produced a son, the god Bor. Bor soon married the giantess Bestla, and with her produced three sons. The first was named Odin, the second Vili, and the third Ve. These children were the first of the race of Aesir, destined to become the ruling forces of good in the Norse universe.

When Thrudgelmir and his young son Bergelmir (who had sprung from his father much in the same way Bor had sprung from Buri) discovered the existence of Bor's children, they quickly enlisted the aid of their brother and sister giants to help them destroy these forces of good.

The war between the children of Thrudgelmir and the children of Bor raged for countless ages in the depths of Ginnungagap with no advantage ever going to either side. The children of Bor, though few in number, were incredibly strong. The wounds they sustained quickly healed; it was impossible to kill them. The giants, while more vulnerable than the children of Bor, kept producing new children to replenish their ranks. For thousands of years the battle between good and evil continued with neither side showing any sign of weakening or losing ground.

Eventually Odin, Vili, and Ve ambushed and defeated their most hated enemy, the original frost giant Ymir himself, who collapsed to the floor of Ginnungagap, blood flowing furiously from his wounds. It was this flood of Ymir's blood that killed the rest of the giant army, all of whom, save for two, drowned in the blood of their original father.

The giants who survived the flood were Bergelmir and his wife, whose name is unknown. They escaped the flood by piloting a

These three Viking coins, which have images of sailing vessels embossed on their surfaces, were found at an ancient Viking marketplace at Birka, located in Sweden.

ship on the ocean of blood, finally settling in a land far to the south, thereafter dubbed Jotunheim, the land of the giants. Here the two created a new race of frost giants, all of whom were taught to hate their vanquishers, the Aesir.

CREATION OF THE WORLD

Now that the war was over, Odin, Vili, and Ve decided it was time to make the universe a more pleasant place. They decided to create a world out of Ymir's corpse (it was all they had from which to fashion a world). Ymir's blood had already formed the oceans. From the corpse's flesh they created Midgard, the earth, which would soon become the home of mankind. This they positioned between themselves and Jotunheim, wanting to put as

much distance as possible between themselves and the giants. They used Ymir's bones to prop up loose pockets of flesh, creating hills and valleys. His teeth, jagged and broken, became the world's many cliffs. His hair became the earth's vegetation. His skull became the heavens above. And whatever brains were left in his skull after the massacre became the billowing, primordial clouds.

With the earth and sky now in place the gods decided that a light was needed. They traveled to Muspellsheim to collect some of the sparks that flew from Surtr's blade. They threw these pieces of undying fire into the sky, where they became the stars. Out of all the sparks there were two that outshone the rest; these became the sun and moon.

The gods fashioned two chariots, built specifically for hauling these two magnificent orbs across the sky. The sun chariot was equipped with the safety and comfort of both the steeds and driver in mind. Pouches of ice

OPPOSITE: This Viking burial plot is in Blomsholm, Sweden. The stones are laid out in the rough form of a ship.

BELOW: This bronze artifact, which dates from around 1000 B.C., is cast in the image of one of the two sacred horses that pull the chariot of the sun across the sky.

were secured behind the horses, protecting their hindquarters from the awesome heat of the sun. They also created the shield Svalin to protect both driver and steeds from the undying rays. The moon chariot did not have to be outfitted with the same safety precautions since the moon's rays were not as fierce as the sun's. The horses Arvakr, "the early riser," and Alsvin, "the quick-footed," were chosen to pull the sun chariot across the sky. Arvakr ensured that the sun rose early in the day and Alsvin made certain it wouldn't linger too long over Midgard and scorch it. The moon chariot's steed was named Alsvider, which means "always quick."

During the great war between the giants and the Aesir, numerous relationships between the two races had developed, despite their ongoing feud. Aesir became intimate with giants and giants became intimate with Aesir. Numerous children were conceived, many of whom would later become important characters in the canon. Two such children were Mani and Sol, whose names mean, respectively, "moon" and "sun." They had been so named because their father thought they were as beautiful as the orbs fetched from Muspellsheim. When searching for drivers for the chariots, Odin took notice of the pair and knew he had found the appropriate charioteers. Every day Mani and Sol drove the moon and sun across the sky, creating not only day and night, but time as well. As with everything in the Norse canon, however, such beneficence could not go unchallenged.

Quick on the heels of both Mani and Sol during their daily rides across the sky were the wolves Skoll and Hati. These ravenous beasts were possessed by a singular desire: to overtake and swallow the magnificent glowing orbs in the sky. Only at the time of Ragnarok, when all would be destroyed, would these voracious wolves overtake and devour the two celestial chariots.

Shown here is the end of a buckle cast in gold repoussé. Dating from around the ninth century, the Viking artifact displays incredible detail.

THE CREATION OF MAN

One day, while walking along the edge of the sea checking their handiwork, Odin, Vili, and Ve came across two fallen trees. One was an elm tree, the other an ash. Odin imbued each tree with the spark of life. Vili endowed them with spirit and a thirst for knowledge. Ve granted them the gift of the five senses. When all was finished the two trees no longer resembled trees at all, but appeared to be smaller versions of the gods themselves. They were the first man and woman. The man had come from the ash and was named Ask. The woman had come from the elm and was named Embla. The sons of Bor granted these new beings the realm of Midgard.

THE CREATION OF THE DWARVES AND ELVES

The sons of Bor discovered that while they had been busy, Ymir's rotting flesh had produced a slew of creatures. These creatures were dark, smelly beasts. And, although repulsive, they did have life and therefore the Aesir felt an obligation to help them.

The gods assessed the foul, wriggling creatures and quickly changed them into forms fitting their natures. The creatures who were of an evil, greedy nature took on a hunched-over, gnarled shape. They were hearty, though, and could easily survive where others could not. These beings were called dwarves and were banished to a place called Svartalfheim, a subterranean world, far below the surface of Midgard. Here they would be able

to dig through the rich earth, uncovering the precious metals and gems they so treasured. They had to be careful never to venture to the surface during the day, for the slightest touch of a sunbeam on their bare skin would instantly turn them to stone.

The creatures who possessed a gentle, kind spirit, with no ill will or greed to taint their souls, were changed into beautiful beings, light as the air itself; these were the elves. They were told they could live in the land of Alfheim, "world of the white elves," which could be found between Asgard and Midgard. In Alfheim the elves had safe haven; and whenever they chose they were permitted to fly down to Midgard for whatever reason took

their fancy, be it to play with a flock of birds soaring through the air or to tend to some flowers that needed special care.

ASGARD AND
THE AESIR

Seeing that everything was now fairly well taken care of, Odin, the ruler of the gods, ordered that a great meeting take place in the center of Asgard, the area the gods had set aside for themselves before they undertook the rest of creation. At this grand meeting the gods decided that within the realm of Asgard

warfare was not welcome. Peace would reign as long as the Aesir ruled. They then set up a magnificent metalworking shop, from which they fashioned their weapons and from which came the enormous and beautiful palaces and halls that would eventually fill Asgard.

Running through the center of it all was the great ash tree Yggdrasil, the mightiest tree ever. Its three roots, one in Jotunheim, one in Niflheim, and one in Asgard, gave the uni-

verse its stability. Near each of these roots flowed a spring. The root in Niflheim was near the mighty Hvergelmir. Here lived the evil serpent Nidhogg, who continually gnawed on the root of the mighty tree, hoping one day to bite clean through and thereby cause the universe to fall into chaos.

Near the root in Asgard flowed the well of Urd. Here was located Gladsheim, the meeting hall of the gods. The three Norns, the goddesses of destiny, whose names were Urd (past), Verdandi (present), and Skuld (future), lived near this spring, from where they controlled not only the destiny of man but of the universe as well.

The root in Jotunheim was near the spring of wisdom, which was guarded by Mimir. It was here that Heimdall, the watchman of the gods, kept the horn that would be blown at the beginning of Ragnarok. For countless eons the Aesir, giants, dwarves, elves, and man lived in harmony. Everyone kept out of everyone else's way and no trouble was caused. It was a golden age. But, like all good things, it was to come to an end.

THE WAR BETWEEN THE AESIR AND THE VANIR

There were some creatures that even the tolerant Aesir could not stand. One of them was a witch named Gullveig. Whenever she visited Asgard all she could talk about was her desire for gold and how much she loved the precious metal. Such greed was repulsive to the Aesir. On one of her visits her obnoxious rantings and unseemly gold-lust became too much for them to bear and they all rose up and killed her, throwing her body onto a large fire they'd built in the middle of Gladsheim.

But Gullveig's powers were mighty and she rose from the flames reborn. Three times the Aesir slew her and three times they set her body on the pyre but each time she rose from the flames as fresh as a newborn. After this the Aesir began calling her Heid, which means "shining one." Heid soon became the goddess of evil magic, letting loose her foul powers throughout the universe, tainting everything.

When the Vanir, the gods of the natural world, who lived in the realm of Vanaheim, not far from Asgard, learned of how the Aesir had played a part in the creation of this new black goddess, they became incensed. They declared war on the Aesir.

The battle raged furiously for eons, with neither side ever gaining much of an advantage. As soon as the Aesir delivered a crushing blow to the walls of Vanaheim, the Vanir would amass their magic and lay waste to the walls of Asgard. It eventually became obvious to both sides that there could be no winner in this war, and so a truce was called.

It was decided that the Aesir and the Vanir should live in peace. To cement this agreement the two sides agreed to exchange key leaders. The Aesir sent Vili and Mimir. Vili was widely thought of as a born leader, strong in both thought and action. Mimir, the guardian of the well of wisdom, was considered the embodiment of the well he protected. The Vanir sent Njord, the god of summer, and his son Frey, the god of sunshine and spring. Along with them came Kvasir, who was born from the combined saliva of Vanir and Aesir, and Freya, Frey's sister, who would become the goddess of beauty and love, as well as the queen of Odin's warrior maidens, the Valkyrs.

These gold brooches, which were found in Denmark, date from the tenth century. They were part of a Viking funeral cache.

THE
REBUILDING OF
ASGARD'S WALL

Many years after the war with the Vanir the
Aesir had yet to rebuild the protective wall
around Asgard. Even for the gods it seemed
too daunting a task. Yet they were all worried
that by leaving their defenses down they were
inviting an invasion by the frost giants.

One day Heimdall, the watchman of
Asgard, came to Odin telling him of a stranger
who had come demanding an audience with
the Aesir. Odin called a meeting and soon all
the Aesir were assembled in Gladsheim. The
stranger entered the hall and offered to rebuild Asgard's wall. The gods were both ex-
cited and wary, since they knew there must be
a considerable price for such a service. The
stonemason said that he would rebuild the
wall in a mere eighteen months, and that for
payment he desired the hand of Freya, the
goddess of love, as well as possession of the
sun and the moon.

The gods were ready to run the craftsman
out of Asgard right then, but Loki, the god of
evil and trickery, spoke up, asking his fellow
gods to at least consider the mason's offer. The
stranger was led outside of Gladsheim so that
the Aesir could discuss the situation.

Loki's plan was to agree to the mason's
price, but to only allow the stranger six
months, an impossibly short time, to finish
the task. Loki figured that in six months the
wall would be half-built and they wouldn't
owe anything. The Aesir were hesitant to go
along with Loki but couldn't find any fault
with his plan, so they agreed.

When the Aesir's conditions were related
to the mason, he agreed, but asked to be allowed the use of his horse, Svadilfari. At first
Odin refused, but Loki convinced the king of
the Aesir to agree to the stranger's demand.

The mason began work the next morning. Svadilfari proved to be more powerful
than the gods had thought possible. The stallion was able to haul massive amounts of rock
up to his master, who was then able to chisel
them into shape and fit them into the wall almost as fast as Svadilfari could bring them.

As the end of the six-month period neared, the gods saw that all that was left to be built was the gateway, which would take no time at all to build. Anxiety filled the gods, most of all Freya, who hated even the thought of being married to the stonemason.

Odin called a meeting in Gladsheim where it was soon decided that since Loki had gotten them into the mess, Loki would have to get them out if he wanted to continue living in Asgard. With his quick words and quick mind, Loki devised a plan that he was sure would put the minds of the Aesir at ease.

That night Loki transformed himself into a beautiful mare and seduced Svadilfari. The shape changer led the fierce stallion far away from his master so that the next day the mason would have to haul the stones himself. With this added burden on his shoulders there was no way the mason could complete the job in time.

When the stranger found Svadilfari missing he knew he had somehow been tricked. In his anger he rushed into Gladsheim and voiced his complaint. His anger was so great that it became impossible for him to maintain his disguise and soon a lumbering, bellowing rock giant stood before the gods. Odin quickly called for Thor, the god of thunder, who killed the giant with one blow from his mighty hammer, Mjolnir.

Months passed and the Aesir soon completed the wall, but still no one knew what had become of Loki. Eventually Loki returned, crossing Bifrost (the rainbow bridge that led to Asgard) with an eight-legged colt in tow. Loki went to Odin and told him how he'd tricked Svadilfari into running away, and how he'd had to mate with the stallion in order to keep the beast from returning to the mason. The eight-legged colt was the offspring of that union. Loki gave the colt to Odin, telling him that it was, without question, the fastest horse in all the universe. The young horse was named Sleipnir and grew to become Odin's faithful steed. Asgard was now complete and secure once again. The Aesir, with Odin in command, began their rule.

This detail is from a ninth-century picture stone found on Gotland that probably served as part of a funerary tribute. Made of limestone, the picture stone highlights several figures from the Norse canon; this detail shows Odin astride Sleipnir. He is being welcomed to Valhala by a Valkyr (the figure to the left of Sleipnir).

ODIN—KING OF THE AESIR

O f all the Norse gods, Odin was one of the most tragic and noble. He possessed a wisdom so vast and all-encompassing that he was unable to be of good cheer, since he was able to see forward into the future to the time of Ragnarok, when the gods and the universe would be destroyed. He is sometimes known as Wotan or Woden, and the day Wednesday is named after him. He was typically characterized as the spirit of the universe itself, the god of the wisdom that comes with age, and the protector of warriors whose hearts are

Odin, the one-eyed god, sits upon Hlidskialf (the foot of which depicts Yggdrasil and the Norns) observing the nine worlds. Clutching Gungnir, Odin is flanked by Hugin and Munin.

true and courageous. He was also thought to be somewhat connected with the few summer months of the north. During these short periods every year Odin was thought to rule. During the longer periods of winter Odin relinquished his rule to Uller, the god of winter.

Odin was one of the original gods, the sons of Bor, and therefore nearly all the other gods of Asgard are in some way descended from him; hence his other name, Allfather. Odin was the son of Bor and the giantess Bestla and is usually depicted as a distinguished old man with a wide-brimmed, floppy hat concealing his face in shadows. From Hlidskialf, his throne, he was able to view the entirety of the nine worlds and witness the goings-on of man and god alike. His second but most beloved wife, Frigga, was the only other being who was allowed to sit upon Hlidskialf.

Odin had two other wives besides Frigga. His first wife was named Jord, or Erda. She was the offspring of the Primordial Chaos surrounding Ginnungagap and an unknown giantess. With her Odin produced Thor, his mightiest child. His third wife was named Rinda. She represented the barren, cold earth of winter and only begrudgingly allowed Odin to be with her for a short time every year. During this time the land warmed and the brief northern summer occurred. With Rinda, Odin produced a son, Vali. Vali was one of the few gods to survive Ragnarok, and figured prominently in the story of the death of Balder, the god of light and truth.

Odin is usually shown holding his magnificent spear, Gungnir, and wearing the armband Draupnir, which self-replicated every seven days. Respectively, these objects symbolize Odin's strength and fer-

tility. Perched atop Odin's shoulder could be found the two ravens Hugin and Munin, their names meaning "thought" and "memory," respectively. They were Odin's far-reaching eyes and ears. Every day they left their lord, scouring the world for any news that the king of the Aesir might have overlooked.

Odin also had two wolves familiar to him, Geri and Freki. Symbolizing the innate hunting instinct of their master, these two wolves received every scrap of meat that was set before Odin. Odin himself refrained from eating, his only sustenance being the wonderful mead, or honey wine, that was served in Valhala, the hall of the chosen slain. When Odin found it essential to leave Asgard he rode his eight-legged horse Sleipnir, the offspring of Loki and Svadilfari. Sleipnir was the fastest horse in the nine worlds.

On Midgard Odin's furious spirit of battle was said to possess a certain type of warrior called a berserk. The name comes from the fact that these warriors wore bearskin shirts into battle instead of armor, believing that

mighty Odin would shield them from all harm. They fought in insane rages, slashing at anything that might come their way, including members of their own clan, or boulders and trees if nothing else was around. Their fearlessness and sheer brutality made them formidable enemies, and their undying ferocity endeared them to Odin.

MIMIR'S WELL — THE SOURCE OF ODIN'S WISDOM

Soon after Ymir had been vanquished and Odin and his brothers had constructed the world from the giant's corpse, Odin visited Mimir, the guardian of the well of wisdom. In the waters of the well one could supposedly see the future being played out.

Odin approached Mimir, pleading for a draught of the wondrous water, knowing full well that in order to fulfill his position as king of the gods he would need the magical wisdom the well could endow. Mimir agreed to Odin's wishes but on one condition: Odin must pluck out one of his eyes and leave it in the well. Odin readily complied, plucking out an eye and letting it sink to the bottom where it was still visible, a pale yet lustrous orb that became a symbol for the moon. His remaining eye therefore became symbolic of the sun.

With the water of the well flowing through his body Odin gained the wisdom he longed for. Returning from the well he tore a branch from Yggdrasil and from it fashioned his spear, Gungnir. It was not long before Odin realized the price that such wisdom exacts from its holders. He was able to see clearly the transitory nature of the universe and even the eventual fate of the gods at Ragnarok. He realized, in a fatalistic flash, that nothing was permanent, that everything would eventually

perish. The weight of this wisdom caused his normally cheerful face to sour; from that point on his countenance was that of a being who had seen his own doom. It is for this reason that Odin drank only mead and never ate. With the fate of the universe already clear to him, Odin required a great deal of solace (hence his strict diet of alcoholic beverages).

Geri and Freki, Odin's two wolf familiars, symbolized not only their master's innate cunning but his savagery as well.

THE FEAST OF THE EINHERIAR

Odin had three main palaces in Asgard: Gladsheim, the meeting hall of the gods; Valaskialf, where Hlidskialf stood; and Valhala, the palace of the chosen slain, which was situated in the middle of Glasir, a magnificent wood with trees that had leaves of red gold.

Valhala was the final resting place of those who had died with honor, in the fury of battle. To die in battle was the noblest death a Norseman could hope for. To die of old age or disease was considered a "straw" death, referring to the straw beds the infirm were placed on. Such a death was considered highly ignoble. In fact, most Norsemen preferred to fall on their own swords than face the indignity of a straw death.

When a battle raged in Midgard, Odin would dispatch his warrior maidens, the Valkyrs. These virgin demigoddesses would fly to earth on their steeds and select from the fray those warriors who had fallen with battle-lust in their eyes and blood on their hands. These chosen dead, or Einheriar, were then transported over Bifrost to Valhala.

Valhala was a palace of magnificent proportions. It was reported to have five hundred and forty doors, each one wide enough to allow eight hundred men passage at the same time. Highly polished spears lined the walls of the great hall, reflecting light from their tips, reminding the dead of the glory of battle. Long tables filled the room where the Einheriar would sit and feast with the king of the gods himself.

During the feasts the Valkyrs took on gentler roles. They served the warriors, making sure their plates were full of meat and their drinking horns full of mead. The meat was supplied by a divine boar, named Saehrimnir, who was slain every day by Andhrimnir, the cook. Miraculously, after every feast Saehrimnir would recombine, ready for the next feast. There was never a lack of food in Valhala.

After the warriors had gorged themselves they would call for their arms, proceed into Valhala's courtyard, and spend the rest of the day hacking each other to bits until the dinner horn sounded once again. The wounds they had received immediately healed and the combatants, like the best of friends, would slap each other on the back, laugh heartily, and sit down again for another mighty feast. From his seat at the head of the hall Odin watched over every feast, pleased that such noble warriors were able to enjoy each other's company both on the battlefield and at table.

One of the Valkyrs (Odin's select band of warrior maidens) summons a fallen warrior to the halls of Valhala.

CREATION OF RUNES

Of the many things Odin was credited with, the invention of runes is one of the most noteworthy. Realizing that only through pain and hardship is knowledge ever attained, Odin hanged himself from a branch of Yggdrasil for nine days and nights, staring into the inky blackness of Niflheim, contemplating his vast wisdom and the best manner to make that wisdom accessible to man and god alike. When he undertook this torturous labor, his body failed him and he died. Through sheer force of will he forced himself to be reborn with the knowledge known only to the dead intact inside his skull. From this knowledge he fashioned the runic symbols.

Their primary use was as objects of divination and fortune-telling. Later on people realized the value of the runes as symbols for record-keeping and decoration, especially on weapons. These runes became the characters in the earliest northern alphabets.

(TRANSLITERATION OF THE LEADEN TABLET.)

✝ (AT) Þ(E)R KUEN(E) SINE PRINSINED (B)AD (M)OTO LAN-
ANA KRISTI DONAVISTI GARDIAR IARDIAR
IBODIAR KRISTUS UINKIT KRISTUS REG-
NAT KRISTUS IMPERAT KRISTUS AB OMNI
MALO ME ASAM LIPERET KRUX KRISTI
SIT SUPER ME ASAM HIK ET UBIQUE
✝ KHORDA ✝ IN KHORDA ✝ KHORDAE
(t) (M)AGLA ✝ SANGUIS KRISTI SIGNET ME

RUNES, A. D. 1000.*

ABOVE: This ninth-century limestone tablet depicts some of the rather visceral pleasures to be enjoyed by the Einheriar in Valhala, where the feasting and fighting was endless.

LEFT: This tablet, which dates from around A.D. 1000, was discovered in Denmark in 1883. The first two lines of runes are in early Danish, and the remaining lines are in Latin.

side of the table, had left nothing. He had eaten both meat and bone and therefore was declared the winner.

Next to meet the challenge was Thialfi. He boasted that he could outrun anyone Utgard-Loki cared to match against him. The giant Hugi was chosen to compete against the young boy in a series of three races. Everyone adjourned outside the palace to a strip of open ground. There the two runners positioned themselves for the first race. At Utgard-Loki's word the runners sprinted from their points. Even though he ran akin to the wind, Thialfi was not fast enough to beat Hugi, who proved to be so quick that he was able to turn around and greet the young boy when the youth passed the finish line.

The second race ended no better than the first. Hugi beat Thialfi by almost three times the distance he had in the first race. The third race was even more of a failure. Hugi reached the finish line before Thialfi was even half-way done.

Utgard-Loki then turned to Thor and asked him what type of competition he would like to enter. Without hesitation the god of thunder challenged anyone in the palace to a drinking contest.

Utgard-Loki had a massive mead-filled horn brought out. He told Thor that among the giants most could drain the horn in one draught. Some of the weaker giants needed two drinks to do the job, but none was so weak as to need three sips.

Thor lifted the horn to his lips and took a massive draught. He thought he'd certainly drained the entire horn. But when he put it down he saw that the level of the mead had only gone down a little. On his second attempt the level was again slightly lower than before, but the horn was no where near empty. Thor's third attempt drained an enormous amount of liquid from the horn but still it was not drained when he put it down. Utgard-Loki chuckled to himself and asked the god of thunder if there was any other contest he would like to undertake. Thor boasted that he could meet any challenge the giant King set before him.

Utgard-Loki told him that many giants considered it a great challenge to lift his cat. Thor agreed to the challenge and as soon as he had a monstrous cat sprang from underneath Utgard-Loki's throne. Thor grasped the mighty feline tightly around the waist and tried to lift it to no avail. Its paws were still firmly planted on the floor. He then got underneath the cat and tried to push it off the floor using his legs. His muscles were stretched almost to their breaking point and yet only a single paw was raised above the floor.

Frustrated that he had failed at this test as well, Thor challenged Utgard-Loki to provide him with a suitable wrestling partner. The giant King said that most of his fellow giants would feel it beneath them to wrestle one so puny as Thor, but agreed to see if his elderly mother Elli would consent to the fight.

Elli came to the great hall and accepted Thor's challenge. Thor threw himself at the old hag but found that she was far stronger than he had ever imagined an elderly giant could be. He could barely get her to move one foot out of place. Finally, without warning Elli switched her center of gravity and threw Thor off balance, forcing the proud god down on one knee.

At this point Utgard-Loki called a halt to the contests as it was getting late. He had food and drink brought to the weary travelers as well as soft bedding. Soon the four were fast asleep. They woke the next morning to see a wonderful breakfast table in front of them with Utgard-Loki at the head. They feasted as well as they had the night before. Then Utgard-Loki led them outside the walls of Utgard where he turned in his tracks and faced the party with a look of utmost sincerity on his face. He told Thor that never again would the god of thunder be let inside Utgard's walls. Thor had expected this; considering how poorly he had fared in each and every contest, Thor felt he had disgraced himself. Then Utgard-Loki told Thor the real reason for his banishment.

It had been he, Utgard-Loki, who had disguised himself as Skrymir and led the travelers to Utgard. Skrymir's bag, which had proved impossible to open, had actually been sewn shut with iron wire. He pointed to a series of three deep valleys, each one deeper than the one before it, which were made when Thor had tried to brain Skrymir with Mjolnir. At this point Loki couldn't help but crack a smile at the giant king's inventiveness.

Utgard-Loki went on to explain that the being Loki had competed against in the eating contest was none other than wildfire, which indiscriminately eats everything in its path. The man Thialfi ran against was none other than pure thought, impossible to outrace. Thor's countenance turned a bit when he learned that the horn he had tried to drain had been connected to the ocean itself and that now the ocean was visibly lower than it had been. The cat he had tried to lift off the ground was in actuality none other than Jormungand, the child of Loki, the gigantic serpent that encircled Midgard. Finally, Elli, the apparent old hag, was in fact, old age herself. Utgard-Loki expressed to Thor his deep-

est admiration since never before had one been able to fend off old age as Thor had done the previous day.

When Thor realized he had actually frightened the giants with his various deeds, he swung Mjolnir high above his head, ready to brain Utgard-Loki for his deceptions. But when the hammer came down the king of the giants had vanished, as had Utgard itself. Thor's wrath was to have no outlet that day.

Soon Thor, Loki, Thialfi, and Roskva were on their return voyage. Thor reclaimed his chariot and goats from the farmer he had visited earlier, and soon was happily back in Thrudheim with the knowledge that the giants in Jotunheim were so terrified of him and his terrible power that they would never attempt to invade Asgard.

These three objects, which were found in Trendgaarden, Jutland, are (from left to right): an early cross; a mold for making crosses; and an amulet in the shape of Thor's hammer. Thor's hammer, a symbol of strength, was widely portrayed in Norse artifacts; of course, it is closely related to the cross, which was also widely portrayed in Iceland following the advent of Christianity there.

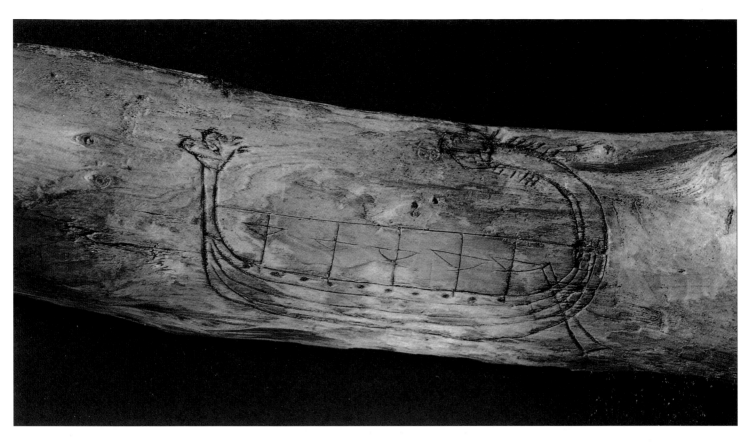

would become so revered a weapon that an oath sworn upon its blade could never be broken, by god or man. Pleased with the creations, Loki thanked the brothers and began his return trip to Asgard.

On the way to Asgard Loki came across two other dwarven brothers, Brokk and Eitri. The two expressed great interest in the treasures the Trickster was carrying, boasting that their skills at metallurgy far exceeded those of the sons of Ivaldi. Loki disagreed with the two and offered up a contest to test their skills. Loki bet his own head that the two wouldn't be able to fashion better gifts than the ones he now held. Brokk and Eitri jumped at the challenge, confident in their skills. Also, they thought, it would not be a bad thing to rid the world of Loki once and for all.

They sat Loki down in a comfortable chair in a luxurious room, with a full horn of mead, and retired to their smithy. With Brokk working the bellows and Eitri manning the hammer and anvil the two soon fashioned three magnificent items. They made the

golden-haired boar Gullinbursti for Frey, which was capable of carrying its rider anywhere in the world, even into the darkness of the underworld, since its hair radiated a brilliant light by which to navigate. For Odin they made the arm ring Draupnir, which when worn would self-replicate. Their greatest accomplishment, though, was the hammer Mjolnir, which they made for Thor.

With these latest gifts now finished, Brokk and Loki set off for Asgard to place the treasures before Odin, Thor, and Frey, and have them decide which pair of craftsmen was the more talented.

The three gods were more than pleased with everything Loki had brought back, but agreed that of all the gifts there was none finer than Mjolnir, since it alone would be able to defend Asgard from the giants. Brokk cackled with glee when he heard the Aesir's decision. He immediately demanded that Loki make good on his bargain and relinquish his head.

Loki agreed that he had promised his head if he lost the wager, but reminded Brokk that their bet had said nothing about his neck, which would have to be cut through for Brokk to get his prize. Grudgingly Brokk relented. The Trickster had outthought his opponents. But then, having a glimmer of insight as to how the Trickster's mind worked, Brokk demanded that he be allowed to sew Loki's lips together, since technically he did now own Loki's head. No fault could be found with this and so, taking Eitri's finest awl in hand, Brokk carefully and tightly sewed Loki's lips together. If he couldn't kill the god, at least the dwarf could silence him.

After Brokk left Asgard to return home Loki ripped the stitching out. The voice of the Trickster was free once again and the fabulous weapons and treasures of the gods had been made, all because of Loki's practical joke. But just as Loki could be unintentionally helpful he could just as easily cause massive amounts of damage and mayhem without any malice aforethought.

LOKI AND ANGRBODA

Loki often took trips to Jotunheim to visit the giantess Angrboda. With her he produced three of the world's most hideous monsters. The oldest of the three was Fenris the wolf, a monster so terrible that only Tyr, the god of war, was able to imprison it. The middle child was Jormungand, the serpent that encircled Midgard, lying at the depths of its oceans. Their last child was Hel, who became the goddess of the underworld, the resting place of those who died of illness or old age. Hel was depicted as fairly normal-looking from the waist up, but hideously decayed and rotting from the waist down. She fed on the corpses of those who had died straw deaths; hence her realm was filled with the stench of decay.

Loki's most despicable act, the one that caused him to be banished from Asgard alto-

This soapstone artifact from the late Viking period was found on a beach in Denmark. Incised on the stone is Loki's face; note that the Trickster's lips are here sewn shut.

He is usually depicted as a well-built, muscular god with only one hand. In this hand could always be found his sword, which he never let out of his sight. He was the patron god of swords, and his name was inscribed on many Norse blades.

It is unclear if Tyr had his own palace in Asgard, as no mention of one is ever made in the texts available today. Whether he had one or not, the other gods were always more than ready to accommodate him as a guest. The episode Tyr figures the most prominently in is that of the binding of Fenris, the monstrous wolf-child of Loki.

One of the hideous brood that Loki produced with Angrboda, Hel fed on the corpses of the ignoble. She was herself more corpse than flesh from the waist down.

THE BINDING
OF FENRIS

Soon after Loki and Angrboda produced Fenris, Jormungand, and Hel, the Aesir learned of the monsters' existence. These were three of the most frightening creatures that had ever lived in the universe, and therefore it was not without cause that Odin questioned the Norns, the three goddesses of fate, as to what to do. They told Odin that all three creatures were the living embodiments of evil and should be dealt with as soon as possible to avoid any trouble they might cause.

At Odin's command a group of Aesir sneaked into Jotunheim one night and overpowered Angrboda. With the giantess incapacitated the Aesir kidnapped her three children and brought them back to Asgard, where the gods hoped they could figure out what to do with the atrocities.

Odin quickly banished Hel to Niflheim, where she would live out her days as the goddess of those who died natural, and therefore dishonorable, deaths. The dark realm of Niflheim suited Hel very nicely. She was a particularly hideous being, her lower half decayed and rotting. In her kingdom she feasted on the corpses that were sent to her, cracking their bones and licking out the marrow with her tongue. Her appetite for such delicacies was never sated.

Jormungand, the serpent, was thrown by Odin into the circle of ocean that surrounded Midgard. The snake quickly sank to the bottom, where he lived on, growing so long that eventually his head met his own tail, completely encircling Midgard.

When it came to Fenris, Odin was hesitant to banish him. He seemed like an ordinary wolf in every respect, and since Odin was fond of wolves he granted the young Fenris free reign over the fields and woods of Asgard.

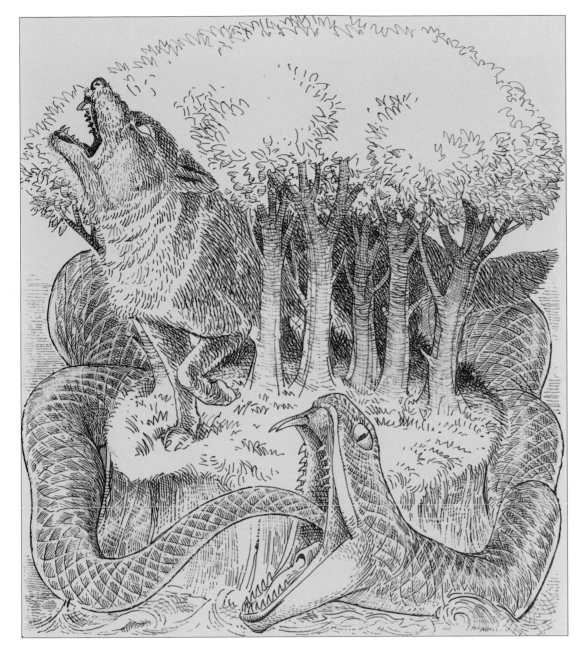

Hel's brothers Fenris
and Jormungand
were two of the most
potent agents of evil
in the Norse canon.
They would prove
particularly
dangerous during
Ragnarok.

This soon proved to be a problem, since Fenris' growing hunger caused him to bellow and howl, disturbing all the Aesir. Tyr took it upon himself to regularly track down the wolf and feed him huge haunches of meat to quiet him. Because of these feedings, Tyr was the only Aesir that Fenris even remotely trusted.

One day Odin noticed that Fenris was growing noticeably larger with every passing day. He then remembered the Norns' prophecies, especially the one in which they had foretold that Fenris would eventually slay him. Odin knew it was impossible to change what the Norns had foreseen, but at the same time he didn't want to hasten his demise. He ordered that Fenris not be killed but instead bound tightly.

The first binding implement they employed was called Laeding, a massive iron chain that intimidated even Thor. They approached Fenris and asked him if he would consent to be bound. After carefully sniffing the chain and trying it between his teeth, Fenris allowed the gods to bind him with it. The Aesir tied Laeding around the wolf, but as soon as they were finished, Fenris stretched his muscular body and popped the iron links apart as if they were paper.

The mighty Odin,
here depicted with
both eyes, takes stock
of the nine worlds as
Hugin and Munin, his
raven familiars, bring
him news of the
doings of god and
human alike.

The Aesir tried a second time to immobilize Fenris, this time using an enormous chain called Dromi. It was twice the strength of Laeding, with links so large that no one on Midgard would have been able to move even one. The chain was secured around Fenris, but, as with Laeding, the wolf broke Dromi with relative ease.

Odin realized that drastic measures were going to have to be employed. He sent Skirnir, Frey's messenger, to Svartalfheim to convince the dwarves to create an unbreakable fetter for the terrible wolf. Only after being promised unbelievable amounts of gold did the dwarves consent to make the item. Into its making went six ingredients that only the magic of the dwarves could isolate—the sound of a moving cat, the beard of a woman, the roots of mountains, the voices of fish, the sinews of bears, and the spit of birds. All of these things, invisible to the eye and impossible to find, went into the construction of the magical ribbon Gleipnir.

Skirnir returned to Asgard, Gleipnir in hand. The gods once again set out to find Fenris and convince him to let them tie him up. The wolf took one look at Gleipnir and immediately suspected a trick. The ribbon was so thin it seemed it would snap in a light wind. With a vicious growl Fenris made it clear that he would not allow himself to be bound with the obviously magical ribbon. The gods then tried to bargain with him, telling him that if he was unable to break free of Gleipnir they would release him. Fenris did not believe the gods in the slightest and another fierce growl convinced them to keep their distance. Seeing as how this situation was going nowhere, Tyr alone approached the wolf and offered up a gesture of faith that he hoped would change Fenris' mind. If Fenris consented to be bound by Gleipnir, Tyr would place his hand in Fenris' mouth to ensure that the word of the gods would be kept when it

came time to untie him. Hesitantly Fenris agreed. If anyone else besides Tyr had put forth the proposition he would have bitten them in two, but he remembered the god who had been kind enough to feed him when he was a hungry pup.

Tyr placed one of his hands between Fenris' dripping jaws as the Aesir wound Gleipnir round and round the massive wolf. After they had finished, Fenris tried to move and found it impossible. The fur on his back bristled with anger and he demanded to be let free. When none of the Aesir made the slightest move to free the wolf, Fenris clamped down his jaws, biting off Tyr's hand.

Fenris remained bound by the magical ribbon until the time of Ragnarok, when Gleipnir succumbed to the evil in the air and limply fell to the earth. Fenris then took his revenge on Odin, the god who had suggested the wolf be bound in the first place. On the battlefield of Vigrid the enraged wolf devoured mighty Odin in one massive gulp.

Here, Odin and company bind Fenris with Gleipnir, the remarkably strong dwarvish ribbon. Tyr, on the right, has just lost his hand.

FREY—GOD
OF SUNSHINE
AND THE ELVES

rey was the son of Njord, the god of the winds and seas, and Skadi, daughter of the storm giant Tjasse. Frey, who came to Asgard with his father and sister, was of Vanir descent. Frey was the god of good weather and sunshine—things invaluable to the beleaguered Norsemen, who spent a good deal of the year in dusky blackness and freezing cold. Because of his life-giving nature, Frey was held in high regard. Hence it was natural that Frey was depicted as a very handsome god.

**Frey and Gerd travel over Midgard, led by
Gullinbursti, the magical golden boar.**

After the war between the Aesir and Vanir, Frey was granted a seat in Gladsheim and given rule over the realm of Alfheim, the land of elves and fairies. This was a suitable kingdom for the lord of sunshine.

Frey also possessed the most feared weapon (with the exception of Mjolnir) in all the universe. When he was accepted into Asgard the gods furnished him with a sword that, when unsheathed, would fight an opponent under its own power.

Frey's trusty steed was the golden boar, Gullinbursti. On occasion Frey was known to travel in his magnificent ship Skidbladnir, which when not in use could be conveniently folded up and kept in his pocket.

As Frey was the god of sunshine, it is significant that his most prominent myth deals with his courtship of Gerd, the daughter of the frost giant Gymir. This myth is symbolic of the brief merging of frozen earth with nourishing sunlight that constituted the fertile, short-lived summer season the Norsemen so depended on.

FREY'S COURTING OF GERD

One day while Odin was otherwise disposed Frey climbed atop Hlidskialf. If Odin had known of this Frey's punishment would have been quick and harsh, but Allfather was nowhere to be seen; hence Frey had no qualms about sitting in the seat from which all was visible. It was only a few moments until he spied, deep in Jotunheim, a lovely giantess emerge from her father's castle. Her name was Gerd, and Frey found it impossible to take his eyes off her. She was surrounded by an ice haze that enhanced and magnified her beauty. From that moment Frey knew that he must have the gorgeous giantess, but had no idea how to go about courting her since such involvement with the giants would be severely frowned upon in Asgard.

The constant ache of unrequited love began to take its toll on Frey. He ate less and less and barely touched his mead. Soon his father Njord took Skirnir, Frey's assistant, into his confidence. He asked Skirnir to find out what was troubling his son and take whatever measures were necessary to remedy the situation. Frey told his trusted aide of his desire for Gerd and his frustration at the fact that a relationship between them would never be allowed, by Aesir and giants alike.

Then inspiration hit Frey. He told Skirnir to travel to Jotunheim and tell Gerd of the god's love, in return for which Frey would grant Skirnir whatever treasures he had at his disposal. Skirnir agreed to go, requesting Frey's sword as payment for the service. He also asked the use of Frey's magical horse, Blodughofi, who was able to see clearly in the dark and was unafraid of flame.

Although hesitant to part with his fabulous sword, Frey couldn't resist the possibility Skirnir was offering. He accepted his friend's terms and for a moment was filled with joy, thinking only of Gerd's wondrous countenance. But he soon fell back into despondency, slumping in his throne and sighing heavily. Meanwhile, Frey's sword at his side, Skirnir mounted Blodughofi and headed towards Jotunheim.

Riding full speed Skirnir soon approached Gymir's castle. The closer he got the more clearly he heard the howling of Gymir's guard dogs, which were the fierce winds of winter itself. Up in the distance he saw the flaming circle that enveloped the castle, but since Skirnir knew Frey's steed was unafraid of flame, he

dug his heels into the horse's sides and plunged headfirst through the blazing barrier.

Luckily Skirnir arrived during a time when Gymir was out hunting. The messenger located Gerd with little difficulty and told her of Frey's great love for her. Gerd responded with indifference. She wanted nothing to do with a god whose occupation dealt with the warming of the land—she was a frost giant and had her loyalties. So fierce was her rejection of Frey that Skirnir became overcome with rage. He brandished Frey's mighty sword above his head and warned the giantess of what might befall her if she continued to refuse the affections of one so powerful.

Still the giantess rebuffed Frey. As a last resort Skirnir pulled out his own staff, which was covered in runes. With it, he told her, he would be able to make her into the loneliest person in the universe. He threatened to transport her to the edge of the world, where her only view would be that of the gates of Niflheim. There she would grow so old and haggard that no man, giant, or god would ever want anything to do with her, save for the giant Hrimgrimnir, who lived near Niflheim. Hrimgrimnir was the vilest of the frost giants. His caresses would be like death itself.

After hearing Skirnir's threat and realizing that he indeed had the power to follow through on it, Gerd realized she had no choice but to accept Frey. Skirnir was delighted to hear Gerd's decision and was all set to ride back to Alfheim when she stopped him. She told him that she would meet with Frey in the forest of Barri after nine nights, claiming that she needed the time to prepare herself mentally for the change her life was going to take. After their woodland meeting, she would consent to be his wife.

Upon his return Skirnir told Frey the good news, but Frey did not see it as such. He wailed and howled in despair, complaining that nine nights was too long for his desire to go unfulfilled. As he had no choice, however, he resigned himself to wait. And, after the nine days had passed, the two met in the forest of Barri and consummated their relationship, making the barren forest sprout to life with the merging of cold, wintry earth and brazen, life-giving sunlight.

FREYA—GODDESS
OF LOVE

Freya was the Norse goddess of fertility and physical love. Whereas Odin's wife, Frigga, oversaw the marital side of love, Freya's job was to make sure the reproductive urge never died. She was the sister of Frey and the daughter of Njord, and, like her relatives, was of Vanir descent. After the war of the Aesir and Vanir, she, along with her brother and father, agreed to live in the realm of the Aesir as a peace offering. Among the goddesses Freya was by far the most beautiful. Her hair was more lovely than Sif's, her features more

---

This is a romantic depiction of Freya, Frey's sister, the Norse goddess of fertility and physical love.

Freya spies the dwarves forging Brisingamen. In return for the magnificent necklace, the underworld creatures demanded sexual favors from the goddess of love.

handsome than Frigga's. Despite her attractive countenance, however, the other goddesses held little jealousy toward her. As she was the goddess of physical love, her palace, called Sessrymnir, which was found in the realm of Folkvang in Asgard, was home to the wives and concubines of the Einheriar.

Since Freya had close relations with the chosen dead, it was only natural that Odin would choose her to become the leader of his elite force of warrior maidens, the Valkyrs. Some might think that being the queen of the battle maidens might compromise Freya's position as goddess of love, but one must remember that the Norse were a hearty race who found strength and physical prowess to go hand in hand with beauty.

As Valfreya, as she was known when leading the Valkyrs, Freya led her maidens down to the fields of battle, and by herself chose half of the slain who would be transported across Bifrost, the rainbow bridge, into Valhala. Because of this duty Freya is often represented as being dressed in battle armor: corselet, shield, helmet, and spear. Other depictions of her show her as being garbed in

the most feminine of flowing robes and dresses. Each personification is quite fitting to her character.

Freya was the proud owner of two fantastic objects, the necklace Brisingamen and her cloak of falcon feathers. Once, while she was visiting the land of the dwarves, Freya spied a number of the little people creating the most wonderful necklace she had ever seen. Her vanity was as elevated as her libido, and she immediately coveted the object. She pleaded with the dwarves for it, but they steadfastly refused it to her unless she would offer herself to them as payment. With a grimace, Freya accepted their proposal and, after an unpleasant few minutes, was the owner of Brisingamen, which would come to represent either the stars in the night sky or the undying fertility of the earth, depending on the version.

Freya's falcon cloak had the power to give its wearer the ability to fly. On a number of occasions Loki borrowed this magnificent object to help him out of whatever trouble he had gotten himself into at the time. Since she was such a beloved goddess the Norse dedicated a day of the week to Freya. Freya's day, or "Friday," is still held in great regard throughout the civilized world.

THE RELATIONSHIP OF FREYA AND ODUR

In some areas of the world, Freya was considered not only the goddess of love but the goddess of the fertile earth as well. Given this it is only natural that she would become attracted to Odur, who, like her brother Frey, was a personification of the nourishing sun. In some parts of the northern world he was also considered to represent the intoxicating power of pure love. In this respect it makes sense that he should be aligned with Freya.

Soon after they met they had two daughters, named Gersemi and Hnoss, who were so beautiful that the people of Midgard soon took to using their names as synonyms for anything lovely. For a while this family of four was quite content to live in Asgard, lazily whiling away the days, content with each other's company.

Then, as the summer sun is known to do, Odur began to wander throughout the world, looking for adventure. When Freya discovered that her husband was missing she broke down and began to weep, her tears falling to the earth. So warm and passionate were these tears that they soaked deep into the very rock of the earth, where they were transformed into gold.

After searching throughout Asgard and not finding her husband anywhere, Freya resigned herself to a long journey. She gathered up her falcon cloak, left Asgard, and began to scour the world, intent on finding her beloved husband. Along the way she flew over every known land and even some unknown lands, leaving behind her a trail of golden tears. It is for this reason that gold is to be found throughout every corner of the earth.

After a long and arduous search, Freya eventually found her wandering husband in the southern lands. She found him leaning against a myrtle tree, lazily relaxing in the daylight. She crept up behind him and fashioned a wreath out of the myrtle's flowering branches and placed it upon her head. She then emerged from her hiding place looking as lovely as the day they were wed. (For this reason it was customary among the Norse for brides to wear wreaths of myrtle.)

Freya asked no questions and held no grudges about what Odur might have been up to during his absence—she was simply pleased

to have him once again by her side. For his part Odur was more than happy to see his wife again since on his many travels he had never come across one so enchanting and lovely as Freya. Hand in hand, they took their own sweet time traveling back to Asgard, lingering in whatever land they happened to fancy at the time. As they went, the forces of nature celebrated Freya's return to happiness by creating the magnificent flowers and vegetation of summer in the couple's wake.

BRAGI—GOD OF POETRY AND IDUN—GODDESS OF YOUTH

The Norse god of poetry and music was named Bragi. He was the son of Odin and the giantess Gunlod. Not surprisingly, he was the prime deity of the scalds, the bards and poets who preserved the many tales of the Aesir in the compositions and poems that were later collected by the likes of Sturluson. Bragi is usually depicted as an old man cradling a golden harp in his arms. His grey hair and his long beard are typically seen flowing around his body, mimicking the waves of music and song that he personifies.

Bragi explains some musical point to his wife, Idun. She is balancing a bowl of the apples of immortality, which kept the Aesir young and vital.

was accustomed to. As Odin never ate, this proposal was simply a ruse to uncover the true natures of the men.

Immediately Odin was besieged with invitations to dinner, each man trying to outdo the others in the size and selection of the supposed menus. Allfather recognized the greed in the men's eyes and, instead of accepting any of the offers, threw the whetstone high into the air. The men, all wanting to be the one to catch the stone when it returned to earth, scurried around, vying for the best position. In their hurried scuttle they ended up slicing open each other's throats with their scythes. Odin smiled, realizing that these deaths could easily be used to his advantage. He tucked the whetstone back into his cloak and began walking in the direction of Braugi's palace. When he arrived he found the giant sulking. Odin introduced himself as Bolverk and asked Braugi what the trouble was.

Braugi told the stranger that that very day all nine of his field hands had been killed, and now it would be near impossible to complete the harvest in time. Seizing the opportunity Odin volunteered to harvest the entire field, saying that he easily had the strength of nine men. When Braugi asked what type of payment he would require for such a service, Bolverk demanded a draught of Suttung's treasured mead as his salary.

Braugi reluctantly agreed to the terms, doubting if this lone man would be able to complete all the harvesting in one single summer. The season came and went and at its end the field stood bare, completely harvested by

Bolverk. Keeping true to his bargain, Braugi took the stranger to Hnitbjorg, Suttung's palace, where he asked his brother for the payment Bolverk required. Suttung scoffed at his brother's request, unwilling to part with even a drop of the mead.

Hearing this, Odin decided to it was time for trickery to come into play. When he and Braugi were outside Hnitbjorg, he took an auger from his belt and told Braugi that with it he would be able to drill a hole straight through Suttung's mountain palace.

Not believing Bolverk, Braugi grasped the auger and pressed it into the side of the mountain and began turning. The sound of the tool slowly grinding into the depths of the mountain made Odin's teeth rattle but the god didn't complain, knowing full well that the gullible giant would succeed in boring all the way through.

As soon as Braugi withdrew the drill and inspected the hole he had made, which did go completely through the mountain, Odin changed himself into a snake and slithered down the tube until he came to the room in the center of the mountain where Gunlod, Suttung's daughter, kept guard over the three vessels containing the mead of Kvasir.

When Allfather appeared in the chamber he turned back into the form of Bolverk, surprising the lonely giantess. Gunlod was soon overtaken with desire and the two of them lay together for three days. After this time Gunlod was so in love with the disguised Odin that she showed him where the three containers of mead were kept.

In three hearty draughts Odin emptied Odrorir, Bodn, and Son, holding the liquid in his mouth. He then changed into an eagle and flew out of the mountain and back to Asgard, spilling a small amount of the precious liquid in Midgard. This small amount became the inspiration for poets and bards all over the northern lands.

These tenth-century Viking coins, featuring an unidentified hero, were found in England.

Back inside Hnitbjorg, Gunlod couldn't restrain her tears. The man she had fallen in love with had fled after betraying her trust, leaving her alone and with child. She soon gave birth to the infant Bragi. Some dwarves who were fond of Gunlod gave the newborn a magnificent harp and sent him out of the dark realm beneath the earth on one of their dwarven boats. The infant was thus shielded from the wrath of Suttung, who was outraged that his treasure had been stolen and his daughter defiled.

When the infant, who until this time had remained very still and lifeless, passed into the world above ground, his eyes opened and he picked up the harp and began playing beautiful music, the likes of which had never before been heard. The boat soon came to rest and Bragi took to his feet, walking among the many lands of Midgard, bringing song and joy wherever he went. Eventually he came across Idun, the goddess of youth, and the two deities fell in love; together, they were warmly welcomed into Asgard.

THIAZI AND THE THEFT OF IDUN'S APPLES

One day Odin, Loki, and Vili were struck with wanderlust. They left Asgard, hoping to find a bit of adventure. All day they walked throughout Midgard, but found little to pique their interest. When night began to fall and the earth began to quiet down they realized that the disquieting noises they heard were the rumblings from their empty bellies. Moving on ahead, Loki spied a herd of oxen. He quickly killed one of the beasts and returned with the fresh meat to the others, who had built a suitable fire.

They relaxed under the dusky sky as the meat cooked. The delicious smell of the roasting only increased their hunger. When their dinner looked fully cooked Odin pulled a joint out of the fire, but, biting into it, realized that it was still raw and cold in the middle. He put it back in the flames, thinking that his hunger must have made him impatient.

After more time had passed Odin again picked out a joint and took a bite, but still the insides were cold and red. Realizing that some form of trickery was afoot the three looked around their camp, searching for anything that might give a clue as to their bizarre situation. Their eyes soon came to rest on a massive eagle, sitting atop a tree, staring down at them. The eagle said he knew the solution to their problem but would only help them if they would let him have a portion of the meat. The gods agreed as their stomachs were doing their thinking for them.

The eagle flew down and stole away with both shoulder pieces and both rump pieces, the majority of the meat. It landed back on the tree and proceeded to feast. Incensed at the bird's gluttony, Loki picked up his staff and thrust it deep into the eagle's breast. With

Like the Aesir, the tribes of the North were famous for their wanderlust. This detail from a twelfth-century tapestry from Baldishol Church in Norway depicts a warrior in full battle gear as he roams in search of adventure.

BRAGI—GOD OF POETRY AND IDUN—GODDESS OF YOUTH 185

a loud squawking the bird flew up into the air, taking the surprised Loki along with it, as his staff was too deeply imbedded to come out.

The eagle dragged the hapless Trickster all over Midgard, scraping him across rocks, dunking him into lakes and freezing streams, and slamming him against the faces of cliffs. Through all of this Loki held on, for he found that through some form of magic, his hands were stuck to his staff.

After hours of the bird's torturous flight, Loki had no choice but to plead with the eagle to stop battering him. The eagle looked down at Loki with dark eyes and said he would relent if Loki promised to bring him both Idun and her golden apples.

Loki knew from the request that the eagle had to be a giant in disguise and that the magic that glued his hands to the staff had to be of the giant's concoction. Loki didn't answer the request, since he knew that sacrificing Idun and her apples would bring old age, senility, and eventually death to the gods, himself included.

Frustrated, but determined to get the prize it sought, the eagle swooped down to earth at a frightening pace, smashing Loki's kneecaps and shins against a crag of brutally sharp rocks. Screaming in pain, the Trickster agreed to the bird's demands, and promised to bring Idun and her apples of youth out of Asgard in seven days.

As soon as the promise passed his lips his hands became unstuck from the staff and Loki found himself on the ground, bleeding and swollen and faced with an unpleasant task. After seven days of deliberation on how best to trick Idun out of Asgard, Loki paid the goddess a call at her palace. She received him with all the warmth and hospitality that one would expect from one who was never troubled. Loki immediately broke into his rehearsed speech. He told Idun how he had recently come across a tree in Midgard that produced apples that

looked very similar to the ones she always carried in her basket. And if the apples contained the same magic as hers the tree should be brought to Asgard and put under her protection. Idun agreed with Loki and asked to be shown the tree so a comparison could be made. She took her basket of apples with her so as to compare the fruits.

As soon as Idun and Loki set foot in Midgard the giant eagle rose up from a hiding place and grasped Idun and her basket in its talons. Off the eagle flew towards Jotunheim, just as Loki had suspected it would. The Trickster watched until he saw the bird land at the palace of Thrymheim, home of the giant Thiazi. There the bird transformed back into the giant and welcomed the befuddled Idun to her new home.

It didn't take long for the gods to feel the lack of Idun's youth-sustaining fruit. They began to age. Thor, once strong and powerful, now had trouble lifting Mjolnir. Freya's skin began to sag, causing her once-beautiful face to resemble that of a hag. Bragi found that he could no longer remember all the words to his wonderful songs. And even mighty Odin was having trouble keeping his mind focused. He also began to experience trouble holding his bladder.

Realizing that something must be done to remedy their situation, Odin called a meeting in Gladsheim. It took a while, but eventually all the Aesir hobbled in and took their seats. Odin shook his head, for the once-mighty Aesir now resembled a pitiful group of elderly fools. All, that is, except for Idun and Loki, who were not in attendance.

With the absence of Loki the gods immediately knew who was behind their troubles. Odin ordered that all of Asgard be searched until the Trickster was found. Loki was found relaxing in Idun's garden, incriminating him all the more. He was hauled before Odin and forced to reveal what had happened.

When the story was finished Odin decreed that Loki would travel to Jotunheim and retrieve Idun and her apples or he would be killed in a manner most fitting those who consorted with eagles. He would be spread out on a rock, face down. Incisions would be made down the length of his spine and then his entire rib cage would be pulled, intact, from his back, sprouting from his body like a pair of ghastly wings.

Loki immediately agreed to retrieve Idun. He asked Freya for her falcon cloak, and, donning it, took to the air, headed for Jotunheim. When he came to Thrymheim, Loki was lucky to find Thiazi out hunting and Idun unguarded in a little room. The Trickster spoke the runes that Odin had given him and Idun was turned into a nut. Loki then wrapped himself in Freya's cloak and, keeping a firm grip on Idun, took to the air once again, flapping furiously to get home before Thiazi returned and realized what had happened.

Thiazi returned shortly after Loki's departure and, finding Idun missing, realized that only the Aesir could have stolen her. He looked to the sky and saw Loki flying away. He quickly donned his eagle disguise and took to the air, determined to catch the god before he returned to Asgard.

From his seat on Hlidskialf, Odin could see Loki and Thiazi approaching. He noticed that Thiazi was gaining rapidly on the Trickster. Odin ordered that a massive pile of kindling be made just inside the walls of Asgard and that torchbearers stand at the ready. When the falcon-Loki passed over Asgard's wall Odin ordered the kindling to be lit. The dry twigs and branches caught fire immediately, flaring up to great heights and singing Thiazi's wings. With a flaming crash Thiazi fell to the ground inside Asgard, where he was quickly killed.

Having landed, Loki gently placed the nut on the ground and spoke the runes that would return Idun to her natural form. In a puff of mystical light the goddess appeared. She took one look at the old, haggard faces of her beloved friends and lost no time in distributing her apples to all of them. Soon, everything was back to normal in Asgard.

These gilt-bronze bird figurines of Swedish origin may have been brooches or harness mountings.

HEIMDALL—GUARDIAN OF ASGARD

One fine day, soon after the creation of the world, Odin was taking in the sea air along the beach. The wandering god came across nine giantesses relaxing in the cool sea air. He was so entranced by this nonet of gargantuan beauties that he decided to lie with each one, right then and there. So powerful was the passion generated among Odin and the giantesses that the nine women magically combined into one being, who subsequently gave birth to a son named Heimdall.

This detail from the Heimdall Cross slab is
a tenth-century Viking artifact from
the Isle of Man. Heimdall is pictured here
blowing Gjallar on the eve of Ragnarok.

BALDER—GOD OF LIGHT AND TRUTH AND HODUR—GOD OF DARKNESS AND SIN

B alder, the god of light and truth, was the son of Odin and Frigga. He is typically depicted as the handsomest of all the Aesir. His flowing blond hair was thought to be the radiant beams of the summer sun, which warmed the earth and spirits of the northern races. His skill with runes and his tremendous knowledge of healing herbs made him a prominent deity during times of illness in Midgard. Of all the gods in the Norse canon, Balder was by far the most beloved.

Here, Balder and Nanna are resplendent in the sunshine that nurtures Midgard and symbolizes their innocence and beauty.

His palace was called Breidablik, where he lived with his wife, Nanna, a goddess of vegetation. Breidablik's most astounding feature was its golden roof, supported by towering pillars of solid silver. It was said that no untruth could pass through its doors.

Hodur, Balder's twin brother, was the exact opposite of his sibling. Where Balder exemplified light Hodur personified darkness. Where Balder personified innocence Hodur was the epitome of sin. Where Balder was able to see with the utmost clarity Hodur was totally blind.

One of the most important myths in the entire Norse canon concerns these two brothers. The myth tells of Balder's murder and how that event foreshadowed Ragnarok, the apocalypse.

THE DEATH OF BALDER

There came a time when Balder's sleep became terribly troubled. Night after night he lay in his bed in Breidablik, tossing and turning in a half-sleep, visited by terrible visions of dark and distasteful things. These dreams persisted for so long that Balder began to dread even the idea of going to sleep. Eventually, the lack of rest and the memories of the nightmares began to take their toll. The god who was usually the brightest and most joyful of all became dour and depressed, moping around Asgard, barely speaking to anyone.

It wasn't long before the Aesir took notice of the change in Balder's disposition. When asked about it he told them of his nightmares. The gods became greatly distressed. The dreams the god of light was having had to be

portents of great evil, they thought, since no untruth (and therefore no false visions) could pass through the walls of Breidablik. The gods knew that Balder's life was in great danger and that some method of forestalling his fate must be discovered.

They gathered in Gladsheim to discuss the problem. The Aesir racked their brains trying to think of every possible way in which Balder could meet his doom. They named every possible situation, weapon, disease, and being that could conceivably kill the most beloved of the gods. This catalog grew to astonishing proportions. When it was finished Frigga took it upon herself to travel to every corner of the nine worlds and get assurances from everything listed that they would never harm her son. She completed this task with little trouble.

Upon her return the gods again gathered in Gladsheim, this time for a celebration. It wasn't long before toasts to Balder's health and the crashing of drinking horns could be heard throughout Asgard. Soon, drunk with celebration and with mead, the Aesir decided to put Frigga's safeguards to the test. Picking up a tiny pebble, one of the gods flicked it at Balder's forehead. When asked if it stung, Balder responded that he had felt nothing. The pebble, remembering its oath to Frigga, had withheld its weight.

Growing in confidence the Aesir began experimenting with different weapons. From a pebble they graduated to a stone, then a boulder, then a dagger, then a sword, on and on, until even mighty Thor was hurling enormous axes at Balder. All of these items bounced off his skin, harmless as feathers.

Sulking in a dimly lit corner of Gladsheim, Loki determined to find something that could truly harm the god of truth. His eyes glowed with evil intent, a plan forming in his mind. With his characteristic slither, Loki left Gladsheim to mull over the possibilities.

Found in Sweden, this striking Viking spearhead—made of bronze with an incised silver hilt—demonstrates the synthesis of beauty and savagery common among the ancient Norse.

A few days later Loki had his plan. He transformed himself into a haggard old woman and made his way to Fensalir, Frigga's palace. When he got there he found the queen of the gods alone, taking a break from the ongoing celebration in Gladsheim.

Loki barged in, trying to be as obnoxious as possible. He made the long, warted nose he'd given himself run, creating quite a disgusting mess on the grungy frock he was wearing. In his grizzled voice he asked Frigga what all the commotion was throughout Asgard, referring to the cacophony emanating from Gladsheim. Frigga told the annoying hag that the revelers were celebrating the health of the god of truth. If this was the case, the old woman asked, why was someone there being tortured with all manner of weapon? Frigga then explained how she'd traveled the nine worlds, seeking assurances from everything that no harm would ever come to her son. With a wrinkled, bony finger, Loki picked at a boil and asked Frigga if she was certain she'd gotten such an assurance from everything. Now, being quite disgusted, and simply wanting the hag out of her sight, Frigga told her that there was in fact one thing she hadn't asked. That thing was the mistletoe, a shrub so young that she hadn't even bothered since she'd been certain it wouldn't have been able to understand her.

Loki kept up his revolting guise until Frigga rather forcibly asked the old woman to leave. Complying with her demands, the old woman left, heading in the direction of a patch of forest where mistletoe grew. Loki changed back to his original form, broke off a sizable branch, and sharpened one end into a fine point. With this in hand he walked back to Gladsheim.

Coming into the hall Loki made a beeline for Hodur. The blind god was standing over in a corner, propping himself up rather clumsily on a wall. He was not taking part in the fes-tivities due to his blindness. Loki, pretending to be kindhearted, told Hodur that it was a shame he had to be left out of the celebration. He offered not only to provide Hodur with a formidable-looking weapon but to guide his aim as well. Thanking Loki for his kindness, Hodur let himself be guided by the Trickster over to where the others were positioning themselves for the next throw. Grasping the mistletoe spear firmly in his hand, he let Loki guide his arm. He threw with all his strength. The staff pierced Balder through the chest, and without so much as a groan the god collapsed on the floor.

Having caused Balder's death, Loki sneaks away from the tumult, grinning maliciously.

The other gods were stunned. No one said anything; they simply looked at each other in befuddlement. But when they noticed the Trickster standing behind Hodur, still grasping his throwing arm, the Aesir knew the whole story. With a coward's speed Loki fled the great hall.

Then the lamentation began. The gods and goddesses could not restrain their grief. Where once Asgard echoed with the sounds of revelry, now there was the sound of mourning. Of all the gods only Odin knew the true consequences of this event, and because of this his mourning was the most soulful of all. He knew that with light and truth gone from the world Ragnarok could not be far off, when evil and death would gain hold, shaking the stability of the universe. The nine worlds would soon be nothing more than a smoldering pile of ashes.

Frigga, in her distress, called for some brave soul to travel to Hel's domain and ask for Balder's return to the land of the living.

Hermod, son of Odin and the messenger of the gods, offered his services. To aid him in his journey Odin lent him the use of the eight-legged Sleipnir. Without any goodbyes Hermod mounted Odin's steed and began the long journey to Niflheim.

As the sound of Sleipnir's hooves faded in the distance Odin ordered that Balder's body be taken to Breidablik and prepared for the funeral. He also ordered a great many trees felled so that a funeral pyre worthy of the slain god could be built. Down to Ringhorn, Balder's dragonship, the gods hauled their massive tributary gifts. On the ship's deck the pyre was built. When it was completed the bathed body was brought, dressed in the finest battle clothes, and placed atop the mountain of wood.

In keeping with tradition the ship was outfitted with the most luxurious worldly goods. Ornate tapestries, magnificent weapons, blazing golden objects—all were laid next to Balder's corpse. As the gods drew

The Vatnajokull
glacier in Iceland
is typical of the
forbidding environ-
ment that informed
the myths and legends
of the ancient Norse.

ULLER—GOD OF WINTER

The son of Sif and an unnamed frost giant, Uller was to the Norse not only the god of the winter months, but the god of hunting and archery as well. Since the winter months usually proved to be the time of many deaths for the Norse, Uller also held the position of god of the straw death.

Given his frost-giant lineage, it was only natural that Uller would feel most comfortable in the dreaded winter months that blanketed the northern regions for most of the year. During this time, it was believed that he took over command of Asgard from Odin, who would return to power when the first rays of sunlight warmed the earth. On one hand, the northern people considered him second in importance to Allfather. On the other hand, since Uller was not a very benevolent god—bestowing only ice, cold, and suffering upon Midgard—he was never as popular or beloved as Odin.

NJORD—GOD OF THE WINDS

After the war between the Aesir and the Vanir, the Vanir Njord, the god of summer, and the Aesir Vili exchanged places in accordance with the war pact. Njord and his children, Frey and Freya, took up residence in Asgard, and Vili moved to Vanaheim. Njord was thought to be a very handsome god, usually wearing a green tunic, which represented the growth of the summer months. As the god of calm, friendly weather, it was Njord who was typically invoked when a particularly fierce winter storm hit or an equally violent tempest blew in from the sea. His palace, Noatun, was

This detail from the Bryggen stick depicts an entire Viking fleet. Note the dragon heads and weathervanes that decorate the prows of the longships.

located near the seaside, supposedly so he could keep the temper of Aegir, the god of the oceans, in check.

Swans were considered sacred to Njord, because they first appeared each year at the beginning of summer. The playful seals that lived by the coast were also considered to be favorites of Njord, as they seemed to personify, with their playful nature, the pleasantness of the summer months.

VIDAR—THE SILENT GOD

Odin once lay with the giantess Grid. Together they produced a son, named Vidar, who was characterized not only by his magnificent strength but by the fact that he rarely, if ever, spoke. He represented the sheer force and quiet power of nature. He was destined to survive Ragnarok and be essential in the creation of the second universe. Vidar was de-

picted as a tall, handsome man, clad in armor, and always sporting a finely honed sword. He was also depicted wearing a sturdy pair of shoes, made of either iron or leather, that would protect his feet from the sharp teeth of Fenris, whom he would meet at Ragnarok to avenge his father's murder. It was believed that every piece of scrap leather that went unused in Midgard became part of Vidar's shoes, and hence Norse leather workers usually discarded their scraps with a very solemn and religious attitude.

AEGIR—GOD OF THE SEA

Aegir was the omnipotent lord of the oceans of the world. He was unique in that he belonged to neither the race of Aesir nor Vanir. He had existed long before those races came into being and would survive long after they had died.

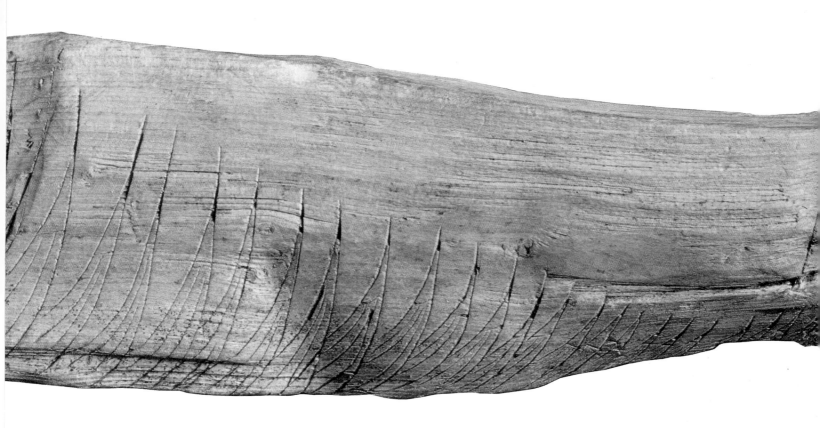

Aegir was thought to be an old man, with long white hair and gaunt, tight skin stretched over his bony frame. He was not a kind god, but rather one who took perverse delight in overturning ships and drowning their crews. He and his wife, Ran (who was also his sister), lived for the moment when a ship, laden with men and treasure, would unknowingly pass above them, easy prey for their cruel and malicious hearts.

These two ornaments, which date from the late Bronze Age, were found in a funeral boat at a burial site in Denmark. It was a common practice among the ancient Norse to bury powerful warriors in a boat (or a boat-shaped plot) well equipped with weapons and valuables for the journey into the next world.

RAGNAROK—THE APOCALYPSE

W ith Balder dead and Loki shackled, Odin knew the time of Ragnarok

was not far off. Light and truth had been destroyed. And while evil had

been imprisoned, Allfather knew that this shaky stability could not be

maintained for long. He could feel the balance of the worlds shifting.

· He knew the end was near.

For too long the Aesir had tolerated Loki in their midst. Too often they

had taken his advice and had had trouble because of it. Now, with Loki

---

This seventh-century artifact, called Sigurd's Helmet, comes from a pre-Viking grave site at Vendel, Sweden. A mortal hero, Sigurd was a favorite of Odin's, and in fact rode a steed (Greyfell) that was descended from Sleipnir.

banished to Midgard, Odin was certain Loki's evil was slowly seeping into the hearts and minds of men. With Balder dead, there was nothing with which to keep the spread of evil in check. Portents of doom were all that reached the eye of mighty Odin.

All too soon the malignant forces began to manifest themselves in Midgard. High on Hlidskialf Odin saw the men of earth wage war on each other, their hearts overtaken with evil and malice. He saw fathers cut down sons in fits of rage, sons slay their families under the blanket of night, brothers and sisters lie together, fathers and daughters bear children, mothers lust after sons. It was a time of metal on metal, sword blade on sword blade. Hatred and anger ran freely. Midgard ran red with blood. During this stage, mankind forgot the civilization it had created and reverted back to an earlier, more monstrous state.

After this age of weapons and blood came the time of Fimbulvetr. For three years the earth was blanketed in unending winter. The cold was unbearable. Ice and frost covered the world as far as Odin's eye could see. All of the creatures of the world starved. The lucky ones froze to death before starvation gripped them in its throes. It was a barren, desolate age, when the sun refused to shine and the earth refused to warm. During this hideous winter all that remained of people's humanity was discarded. The men of earth turned into little more than snarling, savage beasts, more akin to brutes than men. When the winter finally ended, all love and compassion was gone from the fields of Midgard. Only the blackest and most savage of hearts remained.

After the age of metal and the age of winter came the age of the wolf. The giantess Angrboda diligently fed Skoll and Hati, the wolves who pursued the sun and moon every day. Into their snarling jaws were thrust the bodies of those men who had killed their families and members of their clans. The bodies

of those who had taken liberties with their kin also found their final resting place between the jaws of these tremendous wolves. As the past years had been full of such brutality, Hati and Skoll never went hungry. In fact, they grew to such fantastic size and strength that they soon caught the heavenly orbs they had been chasing for so long. Skoll overtook the sun, chomping the chariot and its driver in his massive jaws, covering the Midgardian

snow with bright red gore. Hati likewise devoured the moon. After these losses, the stars lost their will to shine and the earth was covered in blackness.

This all-pervasive darkness not only killed the will of the stars, but destroyed the integrity of all magical bonds as well. All those imprisoned quickly found themselves free. Fenris felt Gleipnir drop around him, limper than unwoven flax. Loki felt his bonds dissolve and his freedom restored. The fires of vengeance flooded through these two evil beings, and their eyes glowed red with hate.

This darkness also gave Nidhogg, the serpent that lay deep in Niflheim curled around the root of Yggdrasil, the strength he needed. Nidhogg bit through the root, shaking the mighty ash tree to the heights of Asgard. The moment his teeth bit through, cocks crowed, alerting all to the fact that the end was near.

The age of blood and the age of winter, as described in the Norse canon, rendered the normally daunting Icelandic landscape completely uninhabitable by human and horse alike.

In Niflheim, Hel's blood-red rooster crowed its warning. Gullinkambi, the cock of Asgard, screeched his signal at the same time. From his perch high above Valhala, Gullinkambi could be heard throughout the realm of the noble Einheriar.

Apart from Odin, however, the only other Aesir to hear Gullinkambi's terrible portent was Heimdall. Like Odin on Hlidskialf, Heimdall was able to see all that went on in Midgard given his position on Bifrost, the bridge that separated the two worlds. After having seen the terrible age of blood and the blinding white age of Fimbulvetr, Heimdall knew the time had come for him to finally blow the sacred horn Gjallar. He did not do this lightly, for the music from Gjallar would rouse not only the Aesir but also the noble Einheriar for one final, valiant battle. Upon hearing the call to arms the Aesir and Einheriar quickly drew their swords, axes, and hammers and left the warm tables of Valhala. Through each of the five hundred and forty doors of the palace eight hundred noble souls emerged ready for

battle. They crossed Bifrost to Vigrid, the field where they all knew the final battle would take place.

The residents of Asgard were not alone in hearing the call to arms. Deep in the depths of the ocean, Jormungand, the serpent that encircled Midgard, heard the call and began to writhe and twitch, causing massive tidal waves and storms. Jormungand's movements brought the terrible ship Nagilfar to the surface. This ship was constructed of the nails of dead men, whose families had forgotten to clip them before entrusting their corpses to the flames of the funeral pyre.

As soon as Nagilfar broke the surface of the water, Loki, free from his torture, landed on its deck and steered it towards Vigrid. Along the way he was joined by his children, Fenris and Jormungand. The two evil brothers flanked the ship, Fenris devouring everything that came his way and Jormungand spewing poison everywhere. Where Nagilfar went only desolation was left in its wake. As the ship neared Vigrid, Loki caught sight of another

ship, sailing from Jotunheim, packed to the brim with giants, all of them armed and ready for the final battle. This second ship was steered by the hideous giant Hrym. Loki also saw, coming from Asgard, where they had just destroyed Bifrost, the flame giant Surtr and his children of fire, their eyes ablaze with the flames of wrath.

Loki beached Nagilfar on the shores of Vigrid and was delighted to see that his daughter Hel had emerged from a crack in the earth, bringing with her the terrible demon dog Garm. Nidhogg crawled out of the crack as well, bits of Yggdrasil's root still hanging from his reptilian jaws. It was a terrible sight when Nidhogg spread his wings and took to the air, letting fall to the earth the countless corpses previously tucked away inside his leathery wings.

The forces were assembled. The final battle, the melee of Ragnarok, was about to begin. The two sides stared at each other for a long time. The Aesir, Einheriar, and the Vanir carefully studied the evil forces that stared back at them across Vigrid. Likewise, Loki, his minions, the flame giant Surtr, and the frost giants glared at the forces of good with hate and loathing in their eyes.

The field of Vigrid was soon filled with the cacophony of battle cries as the forces of good and the forces of evil commenced their attack. Odin fought Fenris. Thor faced Jormungand. Frey met Surtr. Tyr met Garm. Heimdall clashed with Loki. The Einheriar and the Vanir valiantly met Hel's undead army and the frost giants.

Odin's battle with Fenris was long and fierce, but eventually the terrible child of Loki

RIGHT: In some versions of the apocalypse, Thor survives Ragnarok and is the creator of the new world. In the most common versions, however, Thor perishes and his sons Magni and Modi are the architects of the new universe.

OPPOSITE: During Iceland's brief summer, the landscape becomes quite verdant. Here, moss and lichens are thriving on a glacier-worn bed of rocks.

life. Yggdrasil, which survived Ragnarok, grew green and fruitful once again, its roots implanted deeply in this new and fertile earth, creating a cosmic stability that far surpassed that of the old universe. When they noticed the world turning green once again the eyes of the two surviving humans peeked out from their hiding place within Yggdrasil. The woman was named Lif, the man Lifthrasir. The pair climbed out of their sanctuary and began building their lives anew in a world that had been reborn from the ashes of the old order.

Lif and Lifthrasir were not the only beings to survive the fires of Ragnarok. Vidar, the slayer of Fenris, and Vali, the avenger of Balder, somehow escaped Surtr's flames. These two personifications of the indefatigable spirit of nature were met by Magni and Modi, the sons of Thor, on the plain of Idavoll, where once stood Asgard. Magni and Modi had salvaged their father's hammer from the fires of Ragnarok, and with their strength, Mjolnir's power, and Vidar and Vali's energy they built a new heaven. They were joined there by the twin brothers Balder and Hodur, who had been given new life, resurrected in the new world with their past differences resolved. There would be no place in this new universe for spiteful grudges and vendettas among the few remaining deities. The two reincarnated brothers met each other and embraced.

The only other Aesir to survive was Vili, brother of Odin, who had, along with Odin and Ve, created the first world out of Ymir's gigantic corpse. These seven gods sat on Idavoll and remembered their dead kin with

the honor due fallen heroes. They soon discovered, much to their joy, that the gaming fields of the old gods had survived the ravages of the apocalypse. In some versions these fields contain magnificent golden chessboards; in others, they are where the Aesir used to throw their golden dice in games of

chance. Either way, the new gods' discovery of this treasured field would be a constant reminder of the glory and honor of their fallen brothers and sisters.

The seven deities soon restored what once was Asgard. The finest palace they called Gimli. It was built higher than any palace of old Asgard had ever been. Here the gods would reside, overseeing the goings-on down below. The old evils had been destroyed. The world was fresh again, unspoiled, unstained. While the ending of the old world had been bathed in fire and fury, the beginning of the new world was awash in sunshine and the promise of a bright future.

PART 3

THE CELTS IN MYTH

& LEGEND

and brutal carnivals of blood, the *Halloween* movies. Even the holiday of Halloween traces its origins back to the yearly ancient Celtic celebration of Samhain, a time when the Celts believed the worlds of the dead and of the living became one.

Somewhat less dramatically, every time you use a handsaw or file, wash with soap, or eat bread made from flour that was ground in a rotary mill, you are using the inventions and technology of the Celts. The pioneers of North America rolled westward on iron-rimmed wagon wheels and harvested their wheat with a rotary reaper—again, both inventions of the Celts. Later, the standard track gauge of North American railroads was set at four feet eight and one-half inches—the structurally sound distance between the wheels of a Celtic chariot.

On a literary level, the legend of King Arthur, from Malory to the movies *Camelot* and *Monty Python and the Holy Grail*, is taken from an ancient Celtic source and still has the power to fascinate us. On the lighter side,

Albert Uderzo and Rene Goscinny's comic book series *Asterix* entertains millions with the adventures of the Celtic hero Asterix and his bumbling friend Obelix as they confound the Roman Army. A testament to its popularity is the fact that the comic is published in twenty-two languages, including Icelandic, Afrikaans, and Welsh. For the truly erudite or aggressively archaic, the comic book is even published in Latin.

On a more visual level, one of the most important contributions of the Celts has been their art; in a purely aesthetic sense, Celtic art stands out stylistically among the arts of ancient cultures. Unlike their Roman contemporaries, the Celts felt no need to record the practical or the real in their art. Roman art was the ultimate in realism; a man or woman was sculpted with loving attention to his or her flaws—scowls, pimples, and even moles were faithfully recorded. A painting of a tree or an animal (to judge from the few that have survived) was a faithful and exact copy of the real thing. Not so with Celtic art. The Celtic artist

This mythological animal, perhaps a representation of an elephant, adorns the lid of a bronze flask found at Durnberg, Austria. It was common practice for Celtic nobles to decorate the lids and handles of their drinking vessels with whimsical animal designs.

delighted in the abstract and the fantastic. Renderings of foxes, ducks, horses, and people were fanciful and fun, stylized and full of motion. On the Basse-Yutz flagons from circa 300 B.C., for example, the handles are abstractions of foxes chasing a duck up toward the spout. A vase from Nord Bavay, France, bearing a lifelike relief of a bearded man staring straight ahead seems to be an exercise in realism until one notices two more heads sprouting from his ears. And the Gundestrup Cauldron, a silver-plated bowl that was dredged out of a peat bog in Denmark, is covered with whimsical people and creatures cavorting on its inside and outside surfaces. One figure holds two deer by their hind legs, while on another part of the bowl a woman in what looks like a miniskirt dances with a dog. Elsewhere on the cauldron's surface a naked figure rides a fish, and a man wearing antlers holds a snake with a duck's head. We can only guess at what fascinating mythological stories lie behind these images.

The most well-known sources of Celtic art are the famous illuminated manuscripts of the European Dark Ages, which, while they reflect a Christian background, nevertheless continue the traditions of whimsical, and even comical, Celtic art within a technical framework that is truly amazing. For instance, *The Book of Kells* and the *Lindisfarne Gospels*, which date from the eighth century, contain hundreds of drawings and designs that illustrate the stories of the Christian Gospels. Often, the initial letter of a passage is formed of a mythical animal with an elongated body that runs down the entire page and legs and claws that range out and away from the animal's body and evolve into separate and equally fanciful designs. If the artwork were not so painstakingly rendered and laboriously colored, these initial letters could be mistaken for artists' doodles. Upon reflection, an artistic kinship between these medieval illustra-

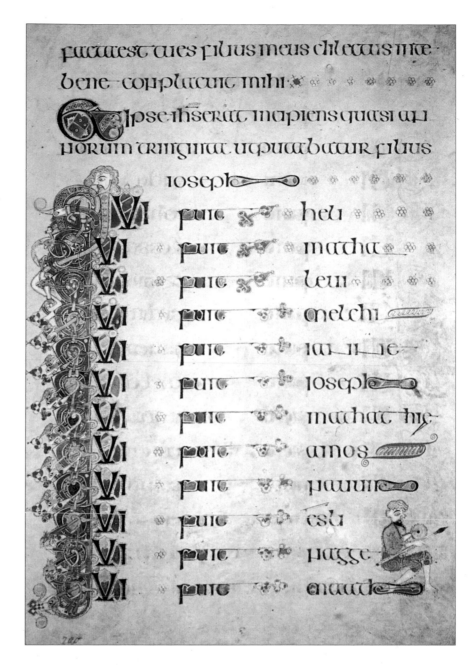

tors and modern abstract painters becomes apparent—neither strives for an exact reproduction of a subject but for an expression of vitality and an outpouring of emotion.

The Romans and early Christian writers have left us a vivid account of the people who created this lively and unusual art. The Romans—who spent the first three hundred years of their recorded history fighting the Celts, until Julius Caesar beat them decisively at Alesia, Gaul, in 52 B.C.—painted a dark and terrifying picture of them. To the Romans, who seldom topped five and a half feet (1.6m), the Celts, who were generally at least

A page from *The Book of Kells* (c. A.D. 800), now housed in Trinity College, Dublin, Ireland, depicting Celtic art adapted to represent part of the Gospels (Luke 3:23–26). The Latin *Qui* ("who") on the left side of the page is repeated over and over again as part of the elongated body of a fierce-looking Celt whose body evolves into the heads and limbs of fantastic animals as it descends the page.

Bronze swords of the early Hallstatt period (c. 800 B.C.). Their blades decorated with battle scenes, these Irish-made weapons were probably placed in the tombs of Celtic nobles.

six feet (1.8m) tall, were almost giants. They painted and tattooed their bodies with strange designs, used lime to stiffen their long hair into spikes, and wore long, drooping mustaches that caught pieces of food when they ate. They fought sometimes in brightly colored, checkered tunics and pants, sometimes completely naked, wearing only the bizarre designs they had painted on their bodies—a practice the puritanical Romans found especially disturbing.

Despite the alarming portrait they painted of the Celts, the Romans nevertheless held a certain grudging admiration for these "primitives," for the Celts were great warriors, a trait the Romans respected above almost any other. In battle, the Celts fought with frenzied abandon, frothing at the mouth and swinging huge double-edged swords. Indeed, it was this frenzy that often defeated the Celts, for once their leaders launched them into battle, there was no way to maneuver them or control their actions. The more disciplined Romans, with their carefully trained armies, beat their more enthusiastic opponents time and time again. At Alesia, Caesar was able to defeat vastly larger numbers of Celts even though his Roman troops had to fight on two fronts at once. Also, Celtic courage was legendary. The Greek historian Posidonius (135–51 B.C.) once told the story of Alexander the Great asking a delegation of Celts what they most feared. They replied, "Only that the sky might crack open and fall on our heads."

When the Celts were not fighting Romans or Greeks, they fought one another in a bewildering number of wars and raids that were conducted as much for personal glory as for territorial expansion and financial gain. Even times of peace were not truly peaceful, for social occasions often degenerated into brawls. Each warrior at a banquet was seated by precedent, according to his skill and renown as a warrior, and anyone could challenge that precedent either by bragging about his military prowess until everyone agreed to a new seating arrangement or, as happened more often, by pulling out his sword and fighting for a new seat. Once the seating was settled, the next cause for concern was who would receive the "hero's portion." The favorite food of the Celts was roast boar, and the rear haunches of that animal were, by custom, reserved for the bravest warriors. Bravery was determined, of course, not by an official scorekeeper but by an ongoing series of challenges. A good portion of Celtic mythology is, in fact, built around these "beer hall brawls."

In the myth entitled Mac Da Tho's Boar, three heroes, along with their retainers, attend a great feast given by King Mac Da Tho of Leinster. The centerpieces of this feast are a collection of seven huge cauldrons filled with meat, and a boar of such prodigious size that forty oxen were required to haul the carcass to the feast hall. The common warriors are given the meat from the cauldrons, and the heroes are awarded the boar. The warrior Cet of the kingdom of Connacht, assuming that he is entitled to the boar because he is the greatest warrior present, steps forward with drawn knife to slice off a choice portion. He is immediately challenged by Loeguire of Ulster. Cet reminds Loeguire of their last meeting in a border skirmish, during which Loeguire lost his chariot, horses, and driver. When Cet resumes his slicing he is once more interrupted, but this time it is Oengus who challenges Cet's right to the hero's portion. Cet wins this exchange by reminding Oengus that he once cut off Oengus' father's hand in battle; Oengus sits back down. Before Cet can resume cutting, another warrior, Eogan the One-eyed, challenges Cet. But when Cet reminds Eogan that he is one-eyed because of Cet's skill with the spear, Eogan thinks better of his challenge and sits down. In quick succession, three more heroes challenge Cet; Cet reminds each that he bears an infirmity caused by battle with Cet—one has lost a foot, another has lost his testicles, and still another has damaged vocal cords and so must speak in a high, squeaky voice unbecoming to a true hero.

By now the rest of the feasters are enjoying the verbal give-and-take of Cet and his challengers. Cet himself is also enjoying the exchanges, and after verbally defeating each challenger he yells, "Another challenger or I begin the cutting!" Finally, when everyone has had his chance, Cet puts his knife to the flesh only to be interrupted once again—this time by a new arrival to the feast, Connall

This small bronze figure (now in the Hungarian National Museum in Budapest) represents a boar, the favorite food at most Celtic feasts. These dinners were lavish affairs that often degenerated into brawls as warriors argued over who should receive the hero's portion.

Cernach of Ulster. Connall claims the right to carve the haunch because he has killed so many of Cet's fellow Connacht men that he has had a fresh head for a pillow every night for a year. That argument impresses even Cet, who acknowledges Connall's right to carve. However, as a parting shot, Cet says, "You would not be the carver if my brother Anluan was here, for he is a greater warrior than I am." Connall laughs and replies that Anluan is indeed present, for, he says, "I killed him this morning and here is his head to prove it!" He then throws the head at Cet with such force that it knocks Cet down. Connall then begins the carving and takes the whole animal, leaving nothing but the knuckles for Cet and his Connacht men. This stinginess, however, proves too great an insult, and the Connacht men spring to their feet and attack the other guests; the feast quickly becomes a bloodbath in which parts of bodies float out the door on rivers of blood.

The argument over the hero's portion was a constant element of Celtic society. Roman, Greek, and early Christian writers report similar incidents during their five hundred years of contact with Celtic groups throughout Europe. War, killing, and violence were the constant trademarks of the Celts. They decorated their homes with the heads of their defeated enemies and preserved the heads of the most famous in honey, keeping them so that they could, when the occasion merited, be taken out and exhibited to honored guests.

However, the same records of the "civilized" Romans, Greeks, and early Christians that recount the violence of Celtic society also present a picture of a people with some very positive attributes. The Celts were not simple raiders of the lands around them. They had a well-developed agricultural economy, created wonders of metallurgy, and built an extensive commercial empire centered in locations that developed into such great modern trading

LEFT: Detail of a gold bracelet found near Lasgraisses, France. According to tradition, this bracelet, now in the Bibliothèque Nationale in Paris, was stolen from the Greek sanctuary of Apollo at Delphi when the temple was raided by the Celts in 279 B.C. The fearsome Celts are said to have fled in terror from Apollo's temple when the god appeared at the head of a ghostly band of Greek warriors.

OPPOSITE: A statue of a Celtic warrior dating from the sixth century B.C. Celtic warriors often went into battle wearing only a gold torque, a conical cap made of metal or leather, and a leather belt. While the sight of male genitals was said to inspire terror in the enemy, there was in fact a medical benefit to be derived from this lack of clothing—wounds could not become infected, as they often did, by cloth fibers getting caught in them. This stone figure, now in the Wuerttembergisches Landesmuseum, Stuttgart, Germany, is from a burial barrow at Hirschlanden, Germany.

centers as Bonn, Trier, Frankfurt, Würzburg, Augsburg, Geneva, Lyons, Toulouse, Verona, Budapest, Belgrade, and Leiden.

The Celts also created their own coinage and traded as equals with the Romans, importing wine and luxury goods while exporting grain, horses, and metallurgical crafts. Gaius Julius Caesar fully expected the wealth of Gaul—once he had captured it—to allow him to compete for control of the Roman world against Marcus Lucinius Crassus (112–53 B.C.), reputed to be the wealthiest man in Rome, and Gnaeus Pompeius Magnus (106–48 B.C.), who had recently stolen the treasury of Mithridates Magnus, one of the richest potentates of the eastern Mediterranean. Caesar was not disappointed—he returned from his eight years of conquest in Gaul with enough money to pay off his 75,000,000-denarii debt and bribe the whole Roman electorate (spending approximately 20,000,000 denarii), with enough left to treat the citizens of Rome to

the most expensive gladiatorial combat in the city's history. He did all this with the money he stole from the Gauls, funds that also allowed him to pursue his lavish lifestyle. While there is no way to estimate the actual amount that Caesar took from the Celts in Gaul, it must have been incredible, for he flooded the market with so much gold that its value fell below the value of silver.

Gaul continued to be a wealthy province even after the Roman conquest, and the Romans continued to milk the area for years. According to the Greek historian Dio Cassius, when the mad emperor Caligula (A.D. 12–41, emperor A.D. 37–41) exhausted the Roman treasury in A.D. 39, he immediately set off for Gaul to replenish his finances from its "overwhelming wealth." Another historian of that time, Strabo, writing in A.D. 23, described a shrine at Tolosa (modern Toulouse) in which the Celts stored 100,000 pounds (45,000kg) of gold and 110,000 pounds (49,500kg) of silver.

ABOVE: In addition to their long, double-edged swords, the preferred weapon for Celtic warriors was the battle-ax. These bronze axes, from about 700 B.C., were excavated at Hallstatt sometime during the nineteenth century.

OPPOSITE: This ford on the Vltana River was once guarded by Celts garrisoned at the Trisov *oppidum*, a fortress situated on a nearby hilltop. The warriors stationed here also guarded the trade route between the Rhine and Danube rivers.

THE ORIGINS
OF THE CELTS

The Romans, who at the same time were scared, fascinated, and repulsed by the Celts, had their own legends about Celtic beginnings. According to these legends, the Celts were descended from Hercules, who, on his way to steal the Golden Apples of the Hesperidae and the Cattle of Geryon—two of his famous twelve labors—paused often on his journey to mate with various local princesses. The true origins of the Celts are unfortunately not so titillating.

The Celts did not emerge as a distinct group until 800 B.C. Before that, their ances-

tors were an indistinguishable part of the swarm in central Europe. Linguists, however, have built a theory about their origins that leads from the Russian steppes, through several migrations, to their first firm date in the ninth century B.C.

About 3000 B.C., a group of people whose language, called Old European, would someday evolve into Sanskrit, Iranian, Hittite, and Hellenic, which would in turn evolve into Indian, Persian, Greek, Latin, Welsh, and Gaelic, lived in the area of what is now Russia where the Volga River empties into the Caspian Sea. Archaeologists who deal with tangible objects such as pots, spear points, and bones, instead of vocabulary and syntax, call these people the Kurgan culture. *Kurgan* is Russian for "mound," specifically the burial mounds that these Volga dwellers built for their high-ranking dead.

By 2400 B.C. the Kurgan people had domesticated horses and learned to make bronze weapons and beautiful jewelry of gold, silver, and turquoise; they had also started to migrate to the west and south. By 2000 B.C. one branch, which archaeologists now call the Indo-Europeans, had moved into the area that is now Turkey. By 1600 B.C. they were recognizable as the Hittites. Another branch of these people had begun to filter into Greece at about the same time, eventually becoming the Mycenaeans, while still another group—the one of interest to us—had by this time entered the lower Danube River Valley. There Danubian invaders, called by archaeologists the Corded Ware People or the Battle Ax People, slowly continued their move to the west and north into the areas that today are Denmark, Sweden, Norway, Britain, and Bohemia. By 1200 B.C. they were firmly settled, but sometime around 1000 B.C. they received some unwelcome attention from the Scythians, another group from the Russian steppes. The Scythians gave to the people who

The Celts at one time dominated all of western Europe, with the exception of Scandinavia. By the first century B.C., however, they had begun moving north and west toward the British Isles because of attacks by Germans and Romans. Today the Celtic population of Europe is largely confined to Wales, Cornwall, Brittany, and the western edge of Scotland.

would someday evolve into the Celts an artistic addiction to fantastic, stylized animal forms, plus innovative ideas in horse paraphernalia, like snaffles and reins. These last elements allowed a man to maneuver and control a horse more easily, thereby improving mobility and the ability to fight on horseback. The Scythians also gave to these "Proto-Celts" the custom of taking heads as war trophies, as well as the grooming customs of combing the hair of the head straight up and stiffening it with lime into a kind of cockscomb, wearing mustaches, and strutting around in brightly colored, checkered plaids.

By 800 B.C. a culture that most scholars and archaeologists agree was Celtic was flourishing north of the Alps all the way to the Baltic and Atlantic shores. Historians and ar-

chaeologists, whose audiences demand neat names and dates, have chosen to call this earliest Celtic culture Hallstatt, after an especially rich archaeological site in Austria. The same people have determined that the Hallstatt culture flourished between 800 and 600 B.C.

This site was discovered in 1846 by an Austrian civil servant, Georg Ramsauer, in the little Austrian town of Hallstatt. Hallstätters had been mining salt from beneath the local mountain for thousands of years and burying their dead in neat mounds on that same mountain for an equally long time. On his own initiative, Ramsauer had begun excavating those graves, and he eventually convinced the Austro-Hungarian government to take up the task. There were 2,500 graves in all, and it was these graves that provided the world with its first good view of the early Celts. The grave goods—sword hilts, fibulae (large, highly decorated safety pins designed to hold cloaks around the shoulders), and numerous bronze castings of animals—have given the world an art style known as Hallstatt. This style, which between 800 and 600 B.C. was found all over western Europe from Ireland to Spain to Hungary, combines elements from Scythian, Roman, Greek, and Etruscan art. Stylized animals, ornate whorls, and geometric designs predominate. There is a feeling for design and proportion, but little concern for accurate representation of animal or human forms. One feels that the Hallstatt artists could certainly have portrayed anything in absolutely accurate detail, but preferred to experiment with design and shape for the fun of it.

Probably the most dramatic collection of Hallstatt art comes from the tomb of a Celtic princess, a woman whose name is lost but whom art historians have chosen to call the Princess of Vix, after the modern French village near where she was found. The site is six hundred miles (960km) from Hallstatt and is near the source of the Seine River (called the Sequona River in Celtic), on the slopes of Mont Lassois, where in the seventh century B.C. a Celtic fortress sat across a trade route that ran between the English Channel and the Rhône River. The treasures from the tomb, which are now in a museum at nearby Châtillon-sur-Seine, are rich and varied. They include a golden crown adorned with stylized Scythian horses, bronze bowls of exacting workmanship, Attic black-figured pottery imported from Greece, and Etruscan pitchers and bowls. The prize of the museum is an immense bronze krater (a bowl for mixing wine and water) thirteen feet (4m) in circumference, five feet (1.5m) high, and weighing 460 pounds (207kg). In the ancient world, wine was seldom drunk in its unadulterated form—people were astounded, for instance, when Alexander the Great drank his wine "neat." The krater was manufactured south of the Alps, probably in Singidunum (modern Belgrade), by Greeks anxious to win the favor of the Celts, who controlled the movement of tin and iron into the Mediterranean Basin. The krater was a rich gift; clearly somebody from the south felt that the Celts were people whose favor was worth cultivating.

The Hallstatt culture, however, was merely one stage in the development of the Celtic culture. By 600 B.C. Europe north of the Alps was dominated by hundreds of Celtic *oppida*, fortified cities that controlled trade routes. From 600 B.C. until nearly the beginning of the Christian era, the Celtic world was

This bronze representation of a goat, which dates from about 300 B.C. and is now in the Moravian Museum in Brno, Czech Republic, was once affixed to the side of a wooden pitcher.

The beginning page of
the Gospel of Mark as
found in *The Book of
Durrow*, which dates
from about A.D. 650
and is now stored
at Trinity College,
Dublin, Ireland.
Although this book
is from an earlier era
than *The Book of Kells*
(see page 227), it also
shows the characteris-
tic Celtic style. The
famous Celtic spiral
designs, called the
"Trumpet Pattern"
by historians, are
clearly visible in the
design of the first two
letters in INITIUM
EVANGELII IHN XPI
("The Beginning
of the Gospel of
Jesus Christ"). The
"Trumpet Pattern"
is also found on
artifacts from
Hallstatt, Austria,
that date from
1,200 years before
The Book of Durrow.

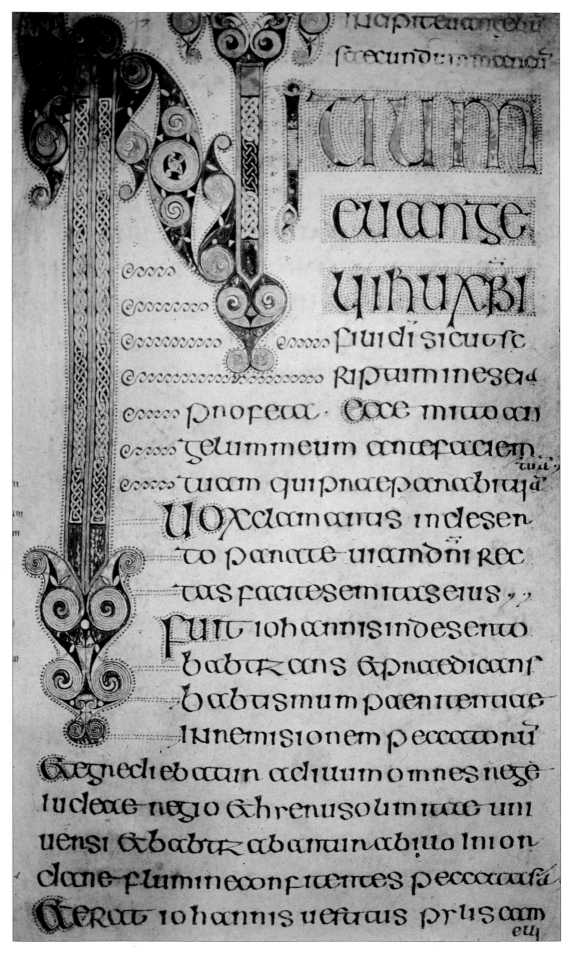

central Anatolia (modern Turkey), where they founded the kingdom of Galatia. In A.D. 55, after about three hundred years—a period of time during which the Galatian Celts "settled down" and became "civilized"—Saint Paul introduced the Galatian Celts to Christianity.

THE CELTIC MENACE: A ROMAN PERSPECTIVE

If there is one thing the authors of the ancient sources agree on, it is that the Celts were Rome's worst nightmare for over three hundred years. Titus Livius, Gaius Julius Caesar (who, besides being the architect of the Roman empire, was also an accomplished historian), and Marcus Annaeus Lucan, who all wrote about the Celts, pay tribute to their courage and their deep religious feeling, but also stress their barbarism and brutality.

Of all the peoples Rome fought in her long history, only the Celts were able to extract a bribe as the price of peace from the Romans. In 391 B.C., a group of Celts, hungry for land, came over the Alps and down into the Po River Valley. Five years later, a Celtic chieftain named Brennus attacked a Roman army near the Allia River and destroyed it; even worse than the defeat itself was the apparent cause—it seems that this Celtic victory was due more to Roman cowardice than to superior strategy on the part of the Celts. The Romans were so shaken by the defeat that they did not try another attack on the Celts in the open, but retreated up into the Capitoline fortress in Rome itself. The defeated soldiers did not pause to close the city gates, and they even abandoned their older citizens to the enemy.

When the Celts entered the city, they discovered the oldest, most distinguished members of the Roman Senate sitting calmly outside their homes, apparently too proud to follow the safest course of action (which to them seemed cowardly): running. When one of the Celtic warriors tugged at the beard of Senator Marcus Papirius, the Roman official struck him on the head with his senatorial staff. This action precipitated a wholesale massacre, and the Celts burned the entire city to the ground. To this day, when archaeologists excavate sites in Rome, they can find a thick layer of ash that separates the city of Rome as it existed before the invasion from the city built afterward.

The eastern side of the Cross of the Scriptures at Clonmacnoise, Ireland. Dozens of these stone crosses, which are usually over seven feet (2.1m) tall and decorated with interlaced Celtic designs surrounding depictions of events in Christ's life, can be found throughout Ireland. At the center of this cross is a figure of Christ wearing a crown and holding a cross.

This representation from the inside of the Gundestrup Cauldron (see page 237) shows a religious ceremony and procession in which a priest or god seems to be plunging a victim head-first into a cauldron. According to some scholars, the figure being dipped into the cauldron may not be a victim at all, but the lucky recipient of a second lease on life. Magical life-giving cauldrons are an important feature of many Celtic myths. The members of the procession include warriors carrying shields and wearing helmets, horsemen with animal crests on their helmets, and a group of musicians playing ram-headed trumpets.

people were forced into huge human-shaped wicker cages that were then set on fire. Supposedly, condemned criminals were the usual victims, but if the supply of felons was inadequate, innocents were also used. So fearsome were the Druidic sites that Caesar's soldiers, tough legionnaires that they were, refused to enter one such place near Marseilles until Caesar entered first.

Roman writers also stated that the Celts took the heads of enemies slain in battle or during raids and decorated their homes with them, held funerals during which wives and slaves were burned alongside the corpse, and enforced their laws through torture and mutilation. In one source it is claimed that sacrificial victims were stuck head-first into huge cauldrons and drowned. Certainly there seems to be a representation of just such an event on the side of the Gundestrup Cauldron. Knowing this, it is not hard to imagine the great cauldron from Vix, France, also being used for just such a purpose.

Were such atrocities actually practiced? If so, were they truly as common in the Celtic culture as these writers claimed? We must re-

member that most of these grisly accounts were written by the Romans, who had fought the Celts for centuries—often with disastrous results. Stories like these are just the kind to inspire fellow Romans to resist a dangerous foe. Since the Celts left no written records of their own, it is questionable how far we should trust these hostile sources—the best we can say about such stories is "perhaps."

THE CONTINENTAL MYTHS: WHAT HAS BEEN LOST

Even though the Celts dominated Europe for nearly a millennium, we know very little about their mythology, quite simply because so little of it has survived. On the one hand, the mythology of the continental Celts died out after the Roman conquest, as the Celtic culture became Romanized; on the other hand, the Celtic mythology of that part of

beacorum apRy

Europe the Romans did not conquer—Ireland and Wales—survived only after passing through the sieve of Christian scribes who wrote down these tales but sometimes removed "offensive" pagan elements.

At one time there must have been a rich mythology surrounding the Celtic people of continental Europe, for the names of hundreds of deities survive in inscriptions and place names. Surviving archaeological treasures, such as the Gundestrup Cauldron, and sculptured pieces show Celtic deities in what one can only assume are representations of various myths. It is maddening to realize that the details of these myths will never be known. The Gundestrup Cauldron, for instance, preserves a picture of a being commonly believed to be Cernunnos, the Celtic god of the dead, who is shown holding a snake in one hand and a torque, or collar, in the other; he has antlers and is sitting in the midst of wolves and reindeer. On the other side of the cauldron, a female figure wearing a short skirt dances with what looks like a dog. We would like to know what these figures represent, what story out of Celtic mythology

they refer to. But there is no way to know, for the myths themselves are lost. What gruesome tale is represented by the so-called Monster of Noves, France, whose jaws hold the head of a man and whose claws rest on the tops of two human heads? What delightful story is concealed in the tiny bronze statue of what may be a goddess offering a bear a basket of fruit? Barring the unlikely discovery of a previously unknown Druidic holy book, we will probably never know. Historians are able to piece together only the barest outlines of the Celtic pantheon.

At the top of the Celtic divinity heap is the god Lugh, whose widespread appeal can be inferred from the names of various modern European cities that seem to have been derived from his name: Lyons, Laon, Leiden, Leignitz. According to several Roman writers, his feast day, which seems to have been August 1, was called Lugnasad. His sacred symbol was the spear and he was always accompanied by ravens. In some representations he is shown with only one eye. The spear, raven, and single eye are also attributes of the Germanic god Wotan, and it is certain that the Germans grafted aspects of Lugh onto their chief god. The Irish also had a god named Lugh, whom the Christian monks converted into a sort of super-hero who excelled in every art and defeated his enemies with a magic spear.

Another god of the continental Celts was Teutates, a god who reveled in sacrifices of human victims drowned in cauldrons. Caesar, whose statements about such things are no more reliable than those of other Roman writers, claimed that Teutates was given credit for inventing all the crafts of mankind. In statues and stone reliefs of Teutates, he is depicted wearing a long, flowing mustache and sideburns. The Gundestrup Cauldron shows a figure that meets this description holding two stags by their hind legs. Whatever legend this

Almost all of what we know of Celtic mythology comes to us secondhand through Christian monks who copied the myths from local *filids*, or storytellers. It seems likely that these Christian brothers "sanitized" the myths as they wrote them down. Here a monk sits at his desk under an oil lamp, illustrating a manuscript.

monuments depict an old man carrying a club, was apparently a Celtic version of the Greek hero Hercules. But unlike Hercules, who was exceptionally stupid, Ogmios was depicted as wise—it was Ogmios, according to the Greek historian Lucan of Samosata, writing in about A.D. 150, who invented *ogham*, the system of writing developed by the Celts. Another deity was Epona, the goddess of horses, who is known from numerous European sites. She is usually depicted sitting sidesaddle, and there are often sheep in the representation; this combination of sheep and horse obviously refers to some now lost myth. In some sculptures, she is seen with a male figure behind her, which has been interpreted by some as a representation of Epona leading the souls of the dead to the realm of Cernunnos. Belenus was a healing god often identified with the Greek god Apollo. Belenus is associated by the Roman poet Decimus Magnus

Ausonius (c. A.D. 310–395) with a number of healing temples in Aquitania. He is also associated with the sun, not as a sun god per se, but in reference to the healing aspects of the sun. Sucellos, the god of alcoholic beverages, was apparently popular, to judge from the numerous representations scattered throughout western Europe that depict him carrying a small beer barrel suspended from a pole; he is often shown carrying a hammer, but the significance of this is unknown.

The frustration Celtic scholars experience due to their lack of knowledge about the Celtic pantheon is compounded by the fact that many of Europe's rivers are named for Celtic deities about whom nothing is known—the goddess Sequona gave her name to the Seine, the goddess Matrona to the Marne, and Souconna to the Sâone. Certainly it is unfortunate that such a rich mythological heritage has been lost.

THE
IRISH MYTHS

While much has been lost, a great deal of Celtic mythology survives—albeit in a somewhat corrupted form—in the mythology of Ireland, which begins, logically enough, with the peopling of the Emerald Isle. These "origin myths" are preserved in a twelfth-century manuscript written by Christian monks entitled *The Book of the Conquest of Ireland*, which is usually referred to simply as *The Book of Invasions* (*Leabhar Gabhala* in Irish Gaelic). It is important to remember that dozens of Irish myths survive only

With the coming of the Christians, Celtic society was thrown into disarray and its hierarchy disrupted. Because of this, Irish *filids* such as this one often found themselves in dire straits—the audience for their stories was greatly reduced.

Aerial view of Tara, County Meath, Ireland. Tara was the legendary capital of the Tuatha de Danu under King Nuadha the Silver Hand. Tara remained the seat of the high king of Ireland until the English conquest of the island. There has been a settlement at Tara since 2000 B.C. At the top of the hill on the left is the famous Stone of Fah, which, according to myth, will cry aloud when a true king touches it.

the Formorians. He not only supervised the construction of wonderful weapons, but taught the court Druids incantations to weaken the Formorians by making it impossible for them to urinate. In addition, Lugh and Cian prepared a magic well in which the Tuatha dead could be brought back to life.

Finally, the great day arrived and Lugh led the Tuatha out to battle, which took place on exactly the same site where they had earlier beaten the Fir Bolg—Magh Tuiredh. As is usually the case in mythological battles, the slaughter on both sides was immense. Lugh magically transported himself around the battlefield, lending aid and encouragement wher-

ever the Tuatha troops wavered, and finally came face-to-face with his grandfather, King Balor of the Formorians. Balor possessed a huge, death-dealing eye, the lid of which was so heavy that four men were needed to lift it. Wherever Balor turned this gruesome eye, men died, and the outcome of the entire battle, Lugh realized, hinged on destroying that baneful organ. Lugh gave a mighty shout to attract Balor's attention, and as Balor and his four lid-lifters slowly turned toward Lugh, the young king launched a stone from his sling with such force that it tore through Balor's eye and out the back of his head, killing a dozen Formorians standing behind their king. When

Balor toppled to the ground, the Formorian host fled the field in panic. (In another account of the battle, Balor's horrible eye was pushed out the back of his head by the stone and fell to the ground, where the sight of it killed the Formorian troops standing behind him.)

The Formorians were gathered together and exiled from Ireland forever. Some of them sought to make a private deal with the Tuatha de Danu by promising magic spells that would guarantee four harvests a year, but Lugh rejected this offer and the Formorians departed Ireland for their original homeland to the north.

There was, however, a cloud over the great victory at Magh Tuiredh, for Lugh experienced a vision in which his father, Cian, was killed in the battle. This proved to be true—Cian had been brutally murdered by three Tuatha brothers, Brian, Iuchar, and Iucharba, the sons of Tureinn.

In the collections of Irish myths, the story of the murder of Cian always accompanies the account of the second battle at Magh Tuiredh, even though it has nothing to do with the victory there. To a modern reader, the sudden appearance of the story of Cian's murder and Lugh's vengeance seems to be a violation of the rules of literary organization. To the ancient Irish, however, it would have seemed quite normal, since the great myth cycles were designed to be recited by professional bards who earned their livings by reciting these legends before members of the Irish nobility. The more evenings a bard took in reciting a tale, the longer he enjoyed the hospitality of the noble's home. Therefore a strategic "aside" could prolong a stay at a comfortable stop for an extra day or two.

Lugh had assigned Cian the task of recruiting soldiers in Ulster for the coming bat-

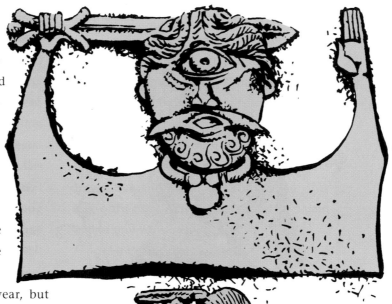

tle. On his way back from this mission Cian was waylaid by the three sons of Tureinn, whose family had long ago sworn vengeance against him for an earlier insult. Realizing his vulnerability, Cian tried to avoid the confrontation by magically changing himself into a pig and joining a nearby herd of swine. Unfortunately for him, however, the eldest son of Tureinn, Brian, saw the change and ran into the midst of the pigs and began spearing them indiscriminately in an attempt to kill the one that was really Cian. Wounded by a spear, Cian asked for time to change back into the shape of a man. The Tureinn brothers agreed, but once the transformation was complete, Cian laughed and said they had been tricked. Now, Cian said, when the murder was discovered the brothers would have to atone for the death of a man, not that of a pig.

At the famous battle of Magh Tuiredh, King Lugh of the Tuatha de Danu saved his army from certain defeat by casting a stone from his sling and putting out the eye of Balor, King of the Formorians. This eye was endowed with powerful magic— Balor was able to kill men with a mere glance. In another version of the story of this battle, Lugh did not put out Balor's eye, but hit him so hard on the back of his head that the Formorian king was turned around to look at the Formorian army, who died when they saw his terrible eye.

After Lugh
discovered who had
killed his father, he
told the murderers
that he would not
have them killed,
as was his right, but
that in order to atone
for their base deed
they had to complete
a series of tasks.
The final task was to
give three shouts
from the top of the
Hill of Miodhchaoin.
This task was not,
however, as it easy
as it seemed: King
Miodhchaoin's sons
were friends of the
murdered Cian, and
the king refused to
allow the brothers
to climb the hill to
shout. This refusal
led to a battle in
which the Tureinn
brothers killed the
sons of Miodhchaoin,
but not without
themselves receiving
mortal wounds.

and thus be free of obligation. There now remained only two tasks: to acquire the cooking spit and to give three shouts from the hill of King Miodhchaoin. To gain the spit, Brian made a magical suit out of water lilies, descended into the sea between Ireland and Britain to find the island of Fianchuive, and so charmed the 150 maidens who guarded the spit that they gave up their virginity as well as the spit. That completed, the three went to the Hill of Miodhchaoin to give their three shouts. But King Miodhchaoin's three sons had been friends of the murdered Cian, and the king refused to give the sons of Tureinn permission to ascend the hill. A fierce battle ensued that ranged the length of Ireland before the villainous brothers triumphed. Despite being badly wounded, the brothers crawled to the top of the hill and gave the requisite three shouts, then immediately returned to Magh Tuiredh to report their success to Lugh and to be healed by the magic pigskin that they had already given him. Remembering the brutal murder of his father, Lugh refused their request and the three died in great agony to the immense pleasure of the young king.

THE COMING OF THE GAELS: THE LAST MYTHOLOGICAL INVASION OF IRELAND

The victorious Tuathans enjoyed their good fortune for only a few years. On May 1—again the sources neglect the year—a new and strange race landed on the southern coast of Ireland at a place called Ihbhear Sceine. These people were known as the Sons of Mil or, more simply, the Gaels. Supposedly, they came from Spain, which at that time was called Iberia. Some linguists believe that the name Mil is a rendition of the Latin word *miles*, which means "soldiers," and that these soldiers also named their new home Iberia, which gradually evolved into Hibernia—the name by which Ireland was known in the ancient and medieval worlds. Whatever the evolution of Ireland's name, this mythical

This terra-cotta head, which is now in the Museo Civico, Bologna, Italy, was originally part of a temple frieze in Bassoferato, Italy.

Gaels realized they had been tricked, and Amhairghin invoked still more powerful magic; the contrary wind died, and the invaders once more stormed ashore, angry at this treachery. The Battle of Tailtiu followed, and the warriors and magic of the Tuatha proved no match for the Sons of Mil. The two sides agreed to a treaty, but the Tuatha proved untrustworthy, harassing the Gaels by stunting their crops of wheat and reducing the flow of milk from their cows.

Under duress, the Tuatha accepted a new treaty by which they withdrew underground to live in the *sidhs*, the Neolithic burial mounds that can be found throughout Ireland. There the Tuatha de Danu lived a wonderful life in perfect harmony with one another. The sidhs were said to have their own sky, green grass, trees, and brooks. Inside them was constant feasting, song, and sport, as well as an endless supply of beautiful women. The residents were ageless and free from disease. Each sidh had its own magic cauldron that produced an inexhaustible supply of food, and the inhabitants spent their time feasting, making love, and fighting (the fighting produced no permanent wounds). It is to the sidhs that the dead traveled to join in this eternal happiness. The living could also cross over into this sidh world and enjoy both the women and the food. While there, they stopped aging, but when they returned aboveground, to the real world, they immediately reverted to their true age, adding on the time they spent in the sidh. This happened to Oisin, the son of the Irish hero Finn mac Cumhail, who was lured into a sidh to be the lover of the beautiful Niamh. Oisin stayed with Niamh in her father's sidh for years, but eventually began yearning to return to the world above. Niamh warned him that he should not set foot on the earth and gave him a horse to ride out of the sidh. When Oisin returned to the world of mortals, he realized, to

account is no doubt the pale reflection of the historic arrival of some Celtic group in Ireland from the European continent.

The invaders were under the leadership of the warrior-poet-magician Amhairghin, who led his troops to the gates of Tara and there demanded the submission of the Tuatha de Danu. The Tuatha played for time, asking the Gaels to withdraw to the sea, or as they put it, "past the ninth wave from the shore." The ninth wave off shore was a magical barrier, and once the Gaels had passed beyond it, the Tuatha were certain their magic could raise a great wind that would prevent the attackers' return. But once beyond the ninth wave, the his surprise, that he had been away for three hundred years and immediately turned his horse around to reenter the sidh. Unfortunately, at that moment he fell off his horse, aging three hundred years the minute he touched the ground. He died a disfigured, wrinkled, and bent old man with whom the eternally lovely Niamh wanted nothing to do.

The Tuatha in their sidhs were ruled by the Daghdha, a hero god who waged war with the last Formorians. He carried a huge club, one end of which killed while the other healed any wound. The Daghdha was said to wander in and out of the sidhs, apparently immune to the aging process, wearing a tunic that was too short to cover his bottom. He was an odd combination of hero and buffoon with a huge sexual and gastronomic appetite. For instance, he was once captured by the Formorians and forced to eat a huge porridge made of eighty gallons (304L) of meal, eighty gallons of fat, and equal amounts of milk and wine, to which had been added eighty goats and eighty sheep. He attacked this mass of food with a spoon that needed four mortal men to lift it. When he had easily eaten it all, he seduced all the Formorian women, including the dread war goddess Morrighan, who, in gratitude for his attention, promised from then on to use her magic against her own people.

By and large, the Tuatha and the Gaels got along well after the establishment of the second truce, although the Tuatha occasionally returned to their old mischievous habit of stunting the Gaels' crops. There were numerous occasions of intermarriage between Gael men and Tuathan women, but comparatively few marriages between Gael women and Tuathan men.

Gael men were wise to treat the beautiful sidh women with great care and respect, for they possessed powerful magic. Once, for instance, Crunniuc mac Agnoman, a prince of Ulster, fell in love with a Tuathan beauty named Macha, daughter of Sainrith. She agreed to marry Crunniuc, but only if he swore never to tell anyone that she was the fleetest creature in the world. He promised, they married, and she soon became pregnant. From the size and shape of her belly it was clear that she would bear twins. Soon after, Crunniuc decided to take Macha to the fair, to show off her great beauty and to advertise his virility (as shown by her obvious pregnancy). At the fair they watched a chariot race in which the chariot of the king of Ulster took first place. Everyone said that the king's chariot was the fastest in the world, but Crunniuc, by this time full of beer, declared that he knew of someone faster. He immediately realized his slip and tried to cover it up, but upon close questioning by the king was forced to admit that the someone

When the Gaels invaded Ireland they drove the Tuatha de Danu underground, into the *sidhs* (the burial mounds that dot the Irish landscape). The sidhs were underground paradises, similar to the mortal landscape but more beautiful. Here the Tuatha indulged in endless feasting, drinking, and fighting, experiencing no pain or unhappiness and remaining forever young. Each year on the night of November 1, the Tuatha are said to leave their sidhs and move freely among mortals.

British representing the huge forces of Queen Maeve, and the Irish Republican Army (IRA) as the modern descendant of Cuchulainn standing against the horde.

The Connacht army moved east and Maeve soon showed her evil, unbalanced nature. One evening she saw that the Leinster contingent of her army had set up camp more quickly than the men of her own country. Jealous of their performance, Maeve contemplated sending them home, but then decided, arbitrarily, that it would be better to kill them. Her husband was shocked and pointed out the negative effect that this action would have on the troops, recommending that the Leinster group instead be broken up and the men distributed throughout the rest of the army. Maeve reluctantly agreed.

Shortly after this, the Connacht men had their first encounter with Cuchulainn at a ford, and this encounter was a harbinger of the problems this boy would cause. Scouts found a wooden horse hobble on which ogham characters had been carved. The carved characters spelled out a challenge stating that no one could cross the ford unless there existed in the army of Maeve and Ailill a man who could carve such a hobble with one

hand. (Apparently, Cuchulainn's hands were so large that he was able to perform this trick.) Since no one could do this (try carving anything with one hand!), the army, under the rather formalized rules of warfare that seem completely out of step in today's brutal world, was forced to find another ford to cross.

At the next ford Cuchulainn killed four scouts and cut off their heads; with a single stroke he sliced off a tree branch as thick as a man's thigh, then mounted the heads on the stick, placing this grisly trophy in the middle of the ford. Cuchulainn covered the branch with ogham characters stating that no Connacht man could cross at that ford unless there was a man in the army who could cut a similar tree branch with one sword stroke. The Connacht army once more turned aside, for they could not meet this challenge. As they marched down the road, they again found the way blocked, this time by a huge downed oak bearing an ogham inscription forbidding use of the road unless the Connacht men had someone who could jump the oak in his chariot. While the attention of the army was fixed on this obstacle, Cuchulainn sneaked up and killed Orlam, the son of Maeve and Ailill, in a duel.

The goal of Cuchulainn was to slow down the invaders until the Ulstermen could recover from their illness. He adopted terror tactics, slaughtering soldiers at long range with his sling and even shooting Maeve's pet squirrel off her neck and Ailill's pet bird off his head. Cuchulainn took to aiming stones at Maeve with such unerring accuracy that she was unable to appear anywhere in camp save with a bodyguard of shield men surrounding her on all four sides. By now the army was completely terrified and many men demanded an explanation of who this incredible boy was. Only one man, Ferghus mac Roich, could tell them. Ferghus was a friend of Cuchulainn and an exile from Ulster. His

These small statues—one of an elk, the other of a wild boar—date from the second century B.C. They are now in the Landesmuseum, Veduz, Liechtenstein. The holes in the body of the elk probably held semiprecious stones.

friendship with Cuchulainn prevented his fighting the young man (another of the customs of war at that time), even though the Tain leaves no doubt that he could have done so with a reasonable chance of success. Ferghus was a giant with the strength of seven hundred men and could eat seven deer, seven boars, and seven cows, all washed down with seven tubs of beer, at one sitting.

Ferghus explained that Cuchulainn was the son of Lugh mac Ethnenn, the hero who had led the Tuatha de Danu to victory over the Formorians; he was also the son of Sualdam the Smith. (In Irish mythology there is no impediment to a hero having two fathers, one divine and one human; this merely adds to his strength.) His mother was Deichtine, the sister of King Conchobar of Ulster. At the age of seven the young Cuchulainn, who at that time bore the name Setanta, left home to seek his fortune at the court of King Conchobar. During his journey to the court, the boy entertained himself by hitting his ball with his bat, then throwing the bat after the ball so that it hit the ball while it was in the air, driving it farther, and then hurled his spear so

that it struck the bat, pushing it after the ball. He then sprinted ahead to catch the ball, the bat, and the spear before they hit the ground, repeating the process all the way to the royal residence at Emhain Macha.

When Setanta reached the vicinity of the palace, he saw 150 boys—the sons of the noblest warriors of Ulster—practicing for war. Since he was a stranger, they decided to rough him up a little, and they threw their spears at him. To their surprise he caught or deflected every one of the spears with his shield, and when they threw their clubs at him he dodged them. By this time the youngster was angry, and he rushed the group, beating fifty of them so badly that it took them three years to recover. The rest of the boys ran to the safety of the king. Standing boldly before King Conchobar, Setanta identified himself as the king's nephew, and the king invited him to join the boy troop and become its leader.

Later, Setanta was attacked by a huge dog that belonged to the blacksmith Culann, and had to kill the dog in self-defense. When Culann complained that he now had no one to guard his forge and tools, Setanta volunteered to stand in place of the dog: "I will be your hound and guard your forge until another dog can be trained." In gratitude, Culann renamed the boy Cuchulainn, which means "hound of Culann."

Soon after this, he single-handedly killed the three sons of the outlaw Fer Ulli and rode back to Emhain Macha with their heads dangling from his saddle. During this fight, he had been seized with a berserker rage in which he changed physically, growing in stature while his hair stood on end. His right eye shrank to the size of a pin and his left eye grew to the size of a saucer, his lips turned back in a deathly grin, and his body temperature increased to such a level that his mere presence ignited nearby trees and dwellings. In this altered state he was unable to tell friend from foe and sought to kill everyone within reach. His charioteer ran back to Emhain Macha, where he told the king of Cuchulainn's changes. Conchobar, apparently experienced in these matters, sent all the women in court out to meet the returning hero with their breasts exposed—this apparently was the time-honored way to deal with a hero's berserk frenzy. Still, it required three baths in ice-cold water to return the boy's temperature to normal.

When Ferghus had finished his tale of Cuchulainn, it required all the forcefulness of Maeve's personality, plus aspersions cast on their manliness, to get the army to remain in the field. In the succeeding days, Cuchulainn challenged various individuals to single combat. Either by magic, cajoling, or the promise of sexual favors, Maeve was able to find individual champions to fight Cuchulainn almost daily. When all these challengers failed, Maeve sent men to attack him at night, even though this was a serious breach of etiquette. It made no difference, however, for Cuchulainn met this treachery and effortlessly defeated all comers. When the hero Nad-

cranntail came against him with nine spears of holly, the youngster deflected each spear easily and without ceasing his activity of trying to catch birds. Later, when Cuchulainn was practicing his trick of walking along the length of a spear in flight, the warrior Cur mac Calath attacked him with a spear and Cuchulainn threw an apple core he was eating at the man, splitting Cur's head open. Only once did he come close to defeat, when Gail Dana and his twenty-eight sons attacked him all at once, using poisoned weapons. This was so unfair that one of Maeve's own soldiers, an exiled Ulsterman named Fiachna mac Fir Febe, came to the aid of Cuchulainn, helping him to kill all twenty-nine attackers.

Finally, despite repeated successes, after almost a month of daily single combat punctuated by pauses only long enough for the

This collection of Irish spearheads, all of which were found in Irish rivers, may have topped some of the spears thrown at Cuchulainn by the 150 sons of the noblest warriors of Ulster.

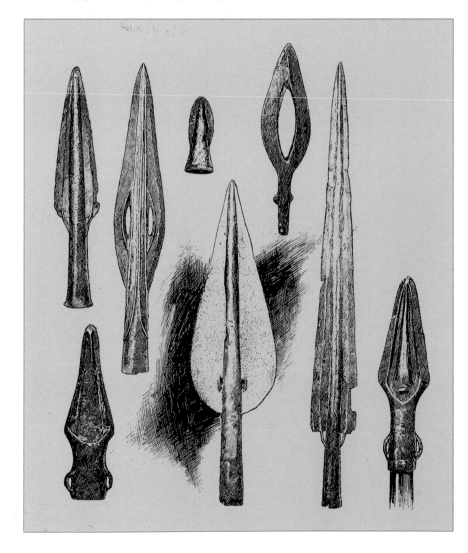

Connacht men to clear their own dead away so that fresh attackers could attack, Cuchulainn began to tire. He had not slept all this time and had caught only a little rest by standing up leaning on his spear. In Cuchulainn's time of need, however, his father, Lugh mac Ethnenn, came back from the land of the dead to take up the challenges and allow his son to get three days of sleep. While his son slept, Lugh treated his wounds so that the young hero awakened refreshed and ready for battle. Lugh also left his son a chariot and horse, both armored with spikes, plus special body armor made of twenty-seven layers of cowhide. Thus equipped and rested, Cuchulainn went on the offensive, taking the battle to the enemy. He underwent the berserker rage and physical changes that had first happened in his youth, and in a single attack killed five hundred nobles, including 130 kings, and an unspecified number of commoners. In a towering rage, he slaughtered women and children, too. By the time Cuchulainn's berserker rage had passed, the bodies were piled up six deep. This rampage came to be called Seisrech Bresligi, the Sixfold Slaughter.

At last the wicked Maeve found a champion to match Cuchulainn—his own foster brother, Ferdia mac Damain. Ferdia had stayed away from the fight out of respect for his brother, but Maeve used a combination of ridicule and the promise of marriage to her beautiful daughter Finnebair to persuade Ferdia to take up the challenge. The duel was titanic and lasted four days. Each day, the two fought with different weapons: on the first day, darts and shields with razor-sharp rims; on the second, spears and shields; and on the third, short stabbing spears. At the close of each day, the warriors rested, making camp together and treating one another's wounds. Finally, on the fourth day, Ferdia allowed Cuchulainn the choice of weapons; the hero chose to fight with his own personal weapon, the *gae bolga*, a spear with five points, each of which would spring open into a clump of seven barbs once it entered the body, making it impossible to pull out except by cutting away huge clumps of flesh. The gae bolga was always launched with Cuchulainn's right foot, and was known to never miss its mark. The valiant Ferdia was wounded, and died with Cuchulainn expounding on his dead brother's courage and skill with arms.

Following this four-day battle, the Ulstermen recovered from their ailment and began to march to support Cuchulainn. They were goaded into action by Cuchulainn's mortal father, Sualdam, who had gone to Emhain Macha to plead with King Conchobar for aid. Unfortunately, while delivering his plea,

LEFT: An artist's interpretation of the Seisrech Bresligi (the Sixfold Slaughter), a pivotal battle in the Tain Bo Cuailnge in which Cuchulainn killed so many men that the bodies lay six deep on the battlefield. During this battle, Cuchulainn went into his famous berserker rage, during which he experienced profound physical changes—he grew to an enormous size, his left eye expanded to the size of a plate, his right eye shrank to the size of a pinprick, and his hair stood on end.

OPPOSITE: This close-up of the ornamental disk on a horse harness is a fine example of the artistic detail with which the Celts invested even their most mundane articles. Dating from about the fourth century B.C., this item is now in the Musée des Antiquités Nationales, St. Germain-en-Laye, France.

The Tain Bo Cuailnge climaxes with an incredible battle between the two great bulls—the white bull Finnbennach and the brown bull Donn Cuailnge. The battle rages across the plain of Muirhevra, with Donn Cuailnge emerging victorious (though he later succumbs to mortal wounds incurred during the battle) and Finnbennach's body parts and internal organs scattered across the landscape.

Sualdam had tripped, fallen against the razor-sharp edge of a shield, and cut off his own head. To the amazement of everyone, the severed head had continued its appeal on Cuchulainn's behalf, pleading that the Ulstermen, even if not completely recovered, needed to begin marching to Cuchulainn's aid. Twenty great companies marched; so great were their numbers that the breath of so many men was confused for morning fog.

The final battle between Cuchulainn and the Ulstermen, on one side, and the forces of Queen Maeve and King Ailill, on the other, was one gigantic melee in which the war chariots and infantry were packed so tightly together as they fought that one could drive a chariot over them from one end of the battlefield to the other without touching the ground. The exiled Ulsterman Ferghus mac Roich, who had been with the Connacht army throughout, now joined the battle but sought to avoid a confrontation with his friend Cuchulainn. At one point Ferghus came close to killing King Conchobar of Ulster, but Conall Cernach restrained him in midstroke by telling him that killing the king would earn him too many enemies. "But how

then will I vent my anger?" cried Ferghus. Conall Cernach suggested that he use his strength to slash off the tops of three nearby mountains. Ferghus did so in three mighty hacks and felt much relieved.

In this last great melee, even Maeve waded into the battle, killing one hundred men with her spear before withdrawing from the field. In the last moments of the fight, Cuchulainn actually came face-to-face with Maeve and briefly toyed with the idea of killing her. He decided not to, exclaiming, "I do not kill women," apparently forgetting the women and children he had slain during the Sixfold Slaughter.

The last act of this great epic comes about when the objects of it all, the great bull Finnbennach and the brown bull Donn Cuailnge, meet to fight. The struggle between these mighty beasts lasted all night, and at dawn the Ulster army saw Donn Cuailnge wandering across the plain of Muirhevra with the bones and internal organs of Finnbennach hanging from his horns. The great bull, mortally wounded, staggered about looking for water with pieces of his beaten enemy dropping off his horns. To this day, the poet of the

Tain tells us, Ath Luain (Loin Ford) marks the place where the great testicles dropped off, Finn Lethe (Shoulder Blade River) the spot where Finnbennach's shoulder blade fell off, and Tromma (Liver) Spring the site where the great bull's liver came to rest. Finally, Donn Cuailnge lay down and died at Druim Tairb, or Bull Ridge.

There is a final irony in the ending that seems typically Irish. Heroes and armies struggled for a month, and thousands died over the silly whim of a wicked woman only to see the object of that whim—the great bull—die unclaimed by either side.

BRICRIU'S FEAST

While much of Irish mythology deals with war, as illustrated by the Tain Bo Cuailnge, a good portion of it has to do with Irish social life—although even there fighting and violence seem to have been the norm. One of the most famous of these tales has to do with Bricriu Nemthenga and the great feast he gave for the Irish heroes. This story is found in Maelmuiri's twelfth-century *Book of the Dun Cow*, but dates from at least five hundred years earlier. Something of Bricriu's personality is apparent from his cognomen, for Nemthenga means "Poison Tongue."

Bricriu Poison Tongue was a man who enjoyed controversy. He loved witnessing disputes and he enjoyed causing them even more, especially if they ended in bloodshed. One year he decided to work a great mischief that he hoped would bring the greatest heroes in Ireland into conflict with one another. He planned carefully. First, he built a huge feast hall at Tech Midchuarta that was grander in size than the royal palace of King Conchobar at Emhain Macha, and certainly more resplen-

dent with gold and silver overlay than any palace in the world. The dining room alone was a huge chamber surrounded with thirty elaborate pillars so tall that seven men and a team of oxen were required to place each one, and thirty Druids were needed to plan each placement. The hall included private apartments for each guest, but the most fascinating room in the the place was a secret chamber from which Bricriu Poison Tongue could watch the goings-on in the dining room and not be seen—he planned to use this room to observe with delight the disputes he would engineer among his guests.

When at the end of a year the hall was finished, Bricriu traveled to Emhain Macha to

This stone head, which dates from the second century B.C. and was found at the Celtic sanctuary of Msecke Zehrovice near Prague, Czech Republic, is another classic example of Celtic art.

invite King Conchobar and the heroes to a feast. He described the preparations and the food, told the nobles of the accommodations they would enjoy, and promised not to bring about any discord. But Ferghus mac Roich did not believe him, and he warned the nobles that no good would come of attending this feast for, he said, "Bricriu cannot help but be himself and longs to set warrior against warrior, servant against servant, and wife against wife." At this, Bricriu became angry and swore that while he would promise not to use his poison tongue at the feast he would certainly use it if the court did not attend! He threatened that he would use his evil gift of lies and deceit to set father against son, brother against brother, and mother against daughter. He further claimed that he possessed a magic incantation that would set the right breast of every woman in Ulster rubbing against the left one until both were so badly chapped and sore that every woman in the kingdom would be miserable and would make her husband miserable, too. Faced with these threats, the Ulster nobility agreed to come, but they demanded certain guarantees: Bricriu would have to provide hostages to guarantee his good behavior and was forbidden to attend the feast itself, the assumption being that if Bricriu knew he could not observe dissension he would not want to cause any. None of the nobles, however, knew of the secret chamber Bricriu had built above the dining room.

Hardly had Bricriu extracted the nobles' promises to attend before he started to sow trouble. He approached each of the three greatest warriors—Loeguire Buadach, Conall Cernach, and Cuchulainn—separately and said, "You are the greatest warrior in Ireland and so you deserve the champion's portion at the feast." He described what the champion's portion would be, and it was truly amazing. A seven-year-old boar that had eaten nothing but oatmeal, milk, nuts, and wheat all its life

had been stewed in a cauldron big enough for three men to sit in, along with a seven-year-old cow that had been fed the same diet as the boar. This meaty broth had been simmered with wine until the meat was fit for the gods. Each hero, thinking he alone had been asked by the host to take the champion's portion, agreed to claim it when the servants brought it in. Bricriu hoped to watch the resultant battle from the safety of his hidden room. He was not disappointed.

Within minutes of being seated, all three heroes had claimed the champion's portion, and had fallen to blows to enforce their claim. Their brightly polished swords clashed so swiftly that witnesses claimed it looked as though lightning were in the house. Conall Cernach and Loeguire Buadach quickly turned their attention to Cuchulainn, and the unfairness of two on one caused King Conchobar and Ferghus mac Roich to intervene and separate the three. The king declared that no one would get the champion's portion that night, but all would share equally. The next night, according to the king, they would all make a judgment as to who would receive the next champion's portion.

Now, however, Bricriu saw a further opportunity to cause trouble. He left his room and went secretly to the wives of each of the three heroes, who were preparing to enter the hall to sit with their husbands. First to Fedelm, Loeguire's wife, then to Lendalair, Conall's wife, and finally to Emer, Cuchulainn's wife, Bricriu made the following statement: "You are clearly more beautiful than the wives of your husband's rivals and your spouse is clearly the best of the three, therefore you and your retinue should by right enter the feast hall first. In fact, I insist on it!" Impressed with Bricriu's statement, the three women, each with fifty attendants, began marching toward the hall, all determined to get there first. At first, the three groups moved

As the argument over who will get the champion's portion continues, the heroes undergo a series of tests. In attempting to complete the first test, Loeguire Buadach and Conall Cernach are defeated by a giant who steals their swords, armor, and chariots. Cuchulainn later confronts and defeats this giant in the misty forest, and retrieves his rivals' possessions.

with stately pomp, but when they caught sight of one another, they gradually increased their speed to arrive first at the door. Within moments, 153 women were running hell-bent for the door with their skirts hitched up well past the point of modesty. Inside, the warriors felt the tremor of this advancing horde and, fearing an attack by enemies, ordered the door shut. The women reached the door and began yelling for admission. Each man, hearing his wife's voice, strove to force open the door, but King Conchobar, disgusted with the lack of dignity, forbade his warriors to do so. Nevertheless, Loeguire and Conall smashed holes in the walls of the hall and pulled their women inside. Cuchulainn merely bent down, worked his hand under the wall of the feast

hall, and raised one side of the hall high enough so his wife could come inside. Needless to say, the rest of the women streamed in through the opening, and complete chaos reigned at the feast.

By now, Bricriu should have been helpless with laughter, but Cuchulainn's stunt had toppled Bricriu and his wife out a window and down into the garbage pit outside the hall. Covered with muck, Bricriu ran to the door and demanded admission to his own hall. At first the gatekeeper did not recognize him because of his foul covering, but Bricriu pushed past and angrily claimed the feast was over unless he who had tilted the hall set it right. Cuchulainn grasped the tilted wall and easily set the hall straight again. Nevertheless, for that night the feasting was ruined, and everyone retired.

The next morning King Conchobar suggested that each warrior prove his right to the champion's portion by performing a great deed; the three heroes—Loeguire, Conall, and Cuchulainn—immediately set out to find suitable adventures. Loeguire went first, but was stopped by a mist and a giant with a club who stole his chariot and sword and then ran him off. Next, Conall came along, found the same mist, and was also deprived of chariot and sword by the giant. Last was Cuchulainn, who also met the mist and the giant. He not only killed the giant, but brought back the possessions of both Loeguire and Conall. The assembled nobles wanted to declare him the winner of the champion's portion for that night, but Loeguire and Conall whined that the mist and the giant were tricks of the people of the sidh, who were known to be friends of Cuchulainn. King Conchobar, who wished to be completely fair, refused Cuchulainn the victory and declared that there would be no award of a champion's portion for that night.

In the morning the three men once again set out. This time they traveled to Connacht to let King Ailill and Queen Maeve decide who would receive the portion. Although there is never a clear chronology in Irish mythology, this event must have taken place before the Tain Bo Cuailnge because Ailill and Maeve appeared happy to see Cuchulainn and soon decided that he deserved the champion's portion. The young hero had defeated a giant cat that tried to steal his meal, hurled a chariot wheel through the palace roof, and tossed one hundred needles into the air one at a time in such a way that each needle went through the eye of the needle just thrown. When all the needles had been thrown, they fell to earth in an interconnected chain. As if that was not enough, Cuchulainn cleared the palace of the ghosts who had sent Loeguire and Conall running in fright. After performing these deeds, Cuchulainn was quickly deemed the most worthy.

However, Maeve and Ailill did not publicly declare their choice. Instead, they called each hero to them separately, gave each a cup, and declared him the winner secretly. Loeguire got a bronze cup, Conall a silver cup, and Cuchulainn a cup of red gold. Apparently, Maeve and Ailill did not want to declare a winner for fear the losers would wreck the palace. To prevent this, they obtained a promise from each to return to Bricriu's feast hall before he showed his victory trophy. Once the three returned, Cuchulainn's cup made it obvious to all that he was the winner, but Loeguire and Conall again planted a seed of doubt in King Conchobar's mind by swearing that Cuchulainn had bought the cup instead of earning it. Once again the champion's portion went unclaimed.

The next day the three contestants set off for the lake where the great Druid Uath son of Imoman lived. After the warriors told Uath why they had come, the Druid made all three promise to undergo a certain ordeal and to

abide by his decision as to who deserved the champion's portion. Uath declared that each hero would cut off the Druid's head and on the following day Uath would get to cut off the hero's head. Loeguire, who went first, accepted the challenge because he was certain that Uath could not live without his head. He sliced off Uath's head and was horrified to see the Druid stand, pick up his head, and walk off. The next morning, Uath was at the lake with his head firmly on his shoulders, but Loeguire was nowhere to be seen. It was now Conall's turn, and he, thinking that perhaps Loeguire had botched the job, struck off the Druid's head with a mighty whack. Again, the headless body stooped, picked up the head, and stalked off into the forest. The next morning, Conall was nowhere to be seen, but Uath was there waiting for Cuchulainn to cut off his head. Cuchulainn easily struck off the head and watched the Druid leave. The next morning, however, unlike his two cowardly predecessors, he duly laid his head on a tree stump and awaited Uath's blow. Uath took a

The Celtic fascination with decapitation is further exemplified by this 4-inch (10cm) silver plaque, which dates from the first century B.C. and is now in the Museo Romano, Brescia, Italy.

large ax and swung it high above his head as if to cut off the hero's head, but at the last moment he reversed the blade so that the flat side struck Cuchulainn's neck. Uath then declared Cuchulainn the winner and truly worthy of the champion's portion. To the amazement of many, Loeguire and Conall nevertheless protested the decision since, as they pointed out, no one had been there to witness the exchange between Uath and Cuchulainn, and without witnesses the decision was invalid. Again the champion's portion went unclaimed.

The next morning, the members of the court set out for the castle of Cu Rui mac Dare, where, without much trouble, Cuchulainn triumphed over a sea giant, twenty-seven attackers, and a fifty-foot (15m) monster. Loeguire and Conall, needless to say, ran at the first sign of danger. This time, however, Cuchulainn could prove his contention, for not only was the court there to witness, but he had the

head of the sea giant, twenty-seven other heads, and the heart of the monster, which he had ripped from its body through the creature's throat. Faced with this indisputable evidence, Loeguire and Conall could not deny Cuchulainn's prowess, but they convinced King Conchobar that since the deeds were done outside Ulster, they could not apply to the naming of an Ulster champion.

By now Cuchulainn was disgusted with the whole sorry mess and withdrew from the contest. But fate took a hand, for as the king and his court sat at Emhain Macha, a truly hideous ogre shambled into the audience hall. His head was huge and had such a growth of tangled, dirty hair that thirty calves could have found shelter there from winter storms. His yellow eyes were the size of cauldrons, each finger was thicker than a man's wrist, and he carried an ax that twenty oxen could not pull. The ogre made the same challenge that Uath the Druid had made. When no one took up the challenge, the honor of Ulster fell under question, and the king ordered that Cuchulainn be summoned. Rather than see his country dishonored, Cuchulainn accepted the challenge. He sliced off the ogre's head and, just as he had suspected, watched the monster stoop, pick up the head, and leave the hall. The next morning, the creature was back, and true to his word, Cuchulainn put his head on the block to await the blow. The ogre made as if to cut off the head, but in the midst of the downward stroke reversed the ax and brought the flat end down onto the hero's neck. At that moment the ogre changed shape and became Uath, who was still angry that his decision had not been honored. The king, shamed by his poor judgment, declared that henceforth Cuchulainn would be acknowledged as the greatest warrior in all Ireland, and with that everyone returned to Bricriu's feast hall to watch the hero eat his champion's portion.

THE FINN CYCLE—THE "OTHER" IRISH HERO

Cuchulainn is not the only Irish hero. Existing side by side with his legends are those of another hero, Finn mac Cumhail. To place Finn in his proper context, it is best to describe him as a mercenary captain of a band of roving soldiers, called a *fianna* in Irish Gaelic. Admission to this band of adventurers was difficult, for each *feinnidh*, or new recruit, had to pass two tests: He had to stand in a pit while every member of the Fianna threw a spear at him; if he flinched he was not acceptable. And he had to run through the forest with the whole fianna chasing after him; if they caught him he could not join the group. During this run the feinnidh could be disqualified if his hair caught on a branch or if a twig broke under his foot. Needless to say, everyone in the fianna was an exceptional warrior.

Finn himself was the most exceptional of the group. He had first shown his courage at the age of eight. At that time he had traveled to Tara just before the Feast of Samhain and noted the sad demeanor of the people. When he asked the meaning of this, an old Druid told him that every year at this time a giant wizard named Aillen mac Midna came to Tara and burned the place down. "Why don't the warriors just kill him?" asked the precocious eight-year-old. "Because Aillen mac Midna possesses a magic spell that causes everyone in Tara to fall asleep just before he comes, so there is no one awake to stop him," replied the old Druid. Finn laughed and said that he could easily kill this wizard. When the Druid reported the boy's comment to King Cormac mac Airt, he called Finn before him and asked how a mere child could hope to defeat such a

powerful wizard. Finn would not divulge his plan, but he extracted a promise from the king that should he defeat the wizard he would become the most honored warrior in Tara. The king readily agreed.

On the day that the evil wizard was to arrive, Finn set his plan in motion. It was really quite simple—to prevent himself from falling asleep, he placed his sharp spear against his neck so that it would cut him slightly each time he began to doze off. Thus, when Aillen mac Midna cast his spell, the pain of the wound kept Finn awake even though everyone else in the city was in a deep sleep. As Aillen mac Midna prepared to burn down Tara, Finn got up and ran the giant through the back. It was not a particularly heroic attack, but it was courageous enough for an

A detail of the Witham Shield, which is now in the British Museum, London, England.

eight-year-old. The court was overjoyed to awaken the next day with a roof over their heads, and the king made Finn his champion.

As champion, Finn practiced constantly with weapons, but also set aside time to develop his intellect. He asked the court poet, Finnegas, to teach him poetry and other intellectual skills. One day as the two were fishing, Finn caught a huge fish that Finnegas recognized as the salmon of all knowledge. Finnegas and Finn cooked the salmon and ate it, thus gaining knowledge of all things. From then on, Finn was as liable to defeat an enemy through guile as by brute force.

Once, for instance, Finn used trickery to defeat a huge Scottish giant, in the process creating three famous geographical landmarks: the Giant's Causeway off the northern coast of Ireland near Rathlin Island, the Isle of Man in the Irish Sea, and Lough Neagh in the center of present-day Northern Ireland. Finn had heard from traveling bards that a Scottish giant was making fun of Finn's fighting ability and courage. Angered by this, Finn wrapped a challenge around a rock, took his sling, and cast the missile fifty miles (80km) across the Irish Sea to Scotland. The Scot got the message and also got "cold feet." He replied—by messenger, not by sling—that he would like to come to Ireland to take up the challenge but was unable to swim across the sea. Rather than give the giant an easy out, Finn pulled out his huge sword and hacked the great chunks of basalt that littered the coast of Ireland into five- and six-sided pillars. He then stuck these upright in the sea side by side so as to form a causeway from Scotland to Ireland. Now the giant had no excuse, and reluctantly he came across.

When the giant arrived at Finn's house, however, the Irish hero was nowhere to be seen. Finn's wife, the beautiful Sava, invited him in and said that Finn was away. She asked him to take a seat by the cradle. The giant sat

A portion of the Giant's Causeway, located off the northern coast of Ireland. The six-sided basalt columns are natural, but look so perfect and artificial that people have always suspected they were man-made. During World War II, a German U-boat commander, thinking that they were British coastal fortifications, went so far as to shell them.

down beside the cradle and the huge baby, who was over eighteen feet (5.5m) long, that was in it. The longer the giant sat there and looked at the huge baby, the more fearful he became, for, he reasoned, if this was Finn's baby—and Sava assured him it was—then how big must Finn be? As he sat pondering this, the baby reached out of the cradle and took the giant's hand. He stuck one of the giant's fingers into his mouth and bit it off! The baby chewed the finger well and swallowed it with a grin. That was too much for the giant, who jumped up, ran across the causeway, and never again made any comment about Finn's prowess as a fighter.

The baby, as it turned out, was really Finn in disguise. As soon as the giant left, Finn jumped up, ran to the coast, and began hurling huge clods of earth after him. The hole created by the removal of the largest clod, which Finn had torn up from the center of what is now Northern Ireland, filled with water and became Lough Neagh, the largest lake in Ireland. The chunk of earth fell into a shallow part of the Irish Sea, where it became the Isle of Man. To this day, geography teachers all over the world comment to their students on the similarity between the shape of Lough Neagh and that of the Isle of Man.

However, Finn was not always so clever. As he grew older, he began to have doubts about his physical prowess and, like so many aging men, decided to fortify and reassert himself with a young and beautiful wife. (Sava had died by this time.) He selected Grainne, the daughter of the High King of Ireland, and she—much against her will—accepted him because her father told her to. But she did not like him and resented her noblewoman's duty to marry for political considerations. Consequently, at her wedding feast she was bold with her glances, finally noting a handsome young man at the end of the table who was obviously of noble background. He was not only strong and virile, but had an intelligent mien, something that was lacking in many of the young warriors, who thought only of killing, drinking, and making love. She asked her nurse who he might be and the old woman scurried off to find out, returning soon after to announce that he was named Diarmaid ua Duibhne and that he was not only a fine warrior and poet but also had been blessed by the love god Oengus so that no woman could resist him. However, the old nurse went on to say that he was fickle, as befitted someone who could have his pick of women. This last bit of news made Grainne desire him all the more, and she decided to use him to escape her unhappy marriage as well as to satisfy her basic lust for him—for he was marvelously handsome in her eyes.

Grainne made a plan. With the help of her nurse she concocted a powerful sleeping

This ceremonial helmet from the La Tene era is made from gilded enamel and bronze over iron. Triumphs of Celtic metalwork, helmets like this one were highly valued trade items, and consequently found their way far outside the area normally occupied by the Celts. This helmet is now in the Musée des Antiquités Nationales, St. Germain-en-Laye, France.

potion and secretly had the old woman slip it into the drinks of all the people at the banquet except Diarmaid. When everyone except Diarmaid fell asleep, Grainne approached and blatantly propositioned him. To her consternation he refused, saying that he was a member of Finn's fianna and could not dishonor his pledge to his lord. Grainne first tried to shame him by calling him a coward, but when this did not work she threatened him. "When everyone awakes tomorrow I will tell them you raped me, and who do you think they will believe? Who could doubt the truthfulness of a young bride?" Diarmaid, stuck for a solution, agreed to leave with her, still hoping he could find a way out of his predicament. The two fled into the forest.

The next morning, Finn awoke to find his bride missing. He finally shook the truth out of the old nurse, who had unaccountably

According to myth, the Isle of Man was formed when Finn mac Cumhail tore up a clod of earth to throw at a Scottish giant who had come to test Finn's fighting prowess. In another story, it is said that the Isle of Man was named for Manannan mac Lir, son of the Irish sea god Lir.

Toward the end of the Finn Cycle, Finn's beautiful young wife, Grainne, tricks the valiant hero Diarmaid, a member of Finn's *fianna* (his band of mercenaries), into sneaking off with her. Believing that Diarmaid has abducted his wife, Finn pursues them, and the two are aided by the Irish love god Oengus, who gives them an enchanted spear that grows in length when its wielder so chooses and a magical cloak that makes its wearer invisible. In this scene Finn and the other members of his fianna corner the lovers, but the two are able to escape as Diarmaid pole-vaults over the warriors and Grainne, wearing the cloak, sneaks quietly past her husband's troops.

stayed behind. Finn swore vengeance and pursued the couple with the whole fianna. The pursuit lasted seven years and ranged over all of Ireland and parts of Scotland. The first year, Diarmaid honorably resisted the sexual advances of Grainne, still hoping to find some way out of his dilemma and return her to her husband a virgin. He left signs at each of his campsites to show Finn that Grainne was still unsullied—a spotless white cloth, an uncarved haunch of venison, an unbroken loaf of bread, a jug of wine with the clay stopper intact. Still Finn pursued the two. At the end of the year, try as he might to avoid it, Diarmaid succumbed to her taunts. This pleased Oengus, the Irish love god, and he came to the aid of the two young fugitives. He gave them a magic cloak that conferred invisibility on whoever wore it, and a magic spear. Several times in the ensuing year these items saved the lovers. Once, when the two were trapped in a fortress, Diarmaid covered Grainne with the cloak and she easily slipped away unseen

through the very center of her husband's army. Diarmaid, meanwhile, used the spear, which could be magically lengthened, to pole-vault over the encircling enemy and thus make his escape.

After years of pursuit, Finn gave up, and the two lovers settled down, raised four children, and reached a reconciliation of sorts with Finn. Finn even allowed them to return to Tara, where the three lived in uneasy peace for a few years. But all the while, Finn, still worrying about his virility, plotted revenge. Finally he got his chance. One afternoon the fianna was out hunting and a huge boar gored Diarmaid, spilling his intestines out through a great hole in his belly. As he lay on the ground surrounded by the fianna, some of its members begged Finn to save Diarmaid. (Finn, it seems, had the magical ability to cure injuries by taking water in his hands—where it was magically changed into a healing balm—and then letting it flow over a wound.) Finn realized that he had his enemy in his power, but he also had the fianna looking on. He went to a nearby spring, took water in his cupped hands, and began to return to the wounded Diarmaid only to stumble purposely and let the water fall from his hands. He returned to the spring again to get more water, but once more stumbled and lost it. He then repeated this act once more. By this time, poor Diarmaid had lost too much blood, and while Finn was returning to the spring for a fourth try, the young man died. Everyone in the fianna suspected that Finn had allowed the young man to die, and this cast a shadow over the organization.

Grainne mourned for a year and then decided to make the best of things. To the disgust of all, she returned to Finn. Yet even in this seeming triumph, Finn was uneasy, for while he finally had Grainne, her past actions and flirtatious nature never allowed the old man a moment's peace. He was always imagining an affair between Grainne and a member of the fianna, or seeing meaningful and suspicious glances cast between his wife and some younger man. He became desperate to prove his strength and virility and tried to keep up with the youngest members of the fianna. One day during a jumping contest, he tried to leap the River Boyne, but fell in and drowned. Grainne remarried within the year.

The entrance to a sidh, or burial mound, in New Grange, County Lough, Ireland. This mound was built about 2500 B.C., long before the Celts arrived in Ireland. Each ruler of the Tuatha had his or her own sidh in which there was a tree that always bore fruit; a pig that, once slaughtered, was magically reborn the next day, so there was never a lack of meat; and a magic vat that always remained filled with beer.

She took the word *mabinogi* ("the early years"), mistranslated it as "the children's story," and added an *on* (which she thought was the correct plural ending) to make it "the children's stories." That was not the correct plural ending, but the name has stuck. And there is room for more confusion, for only the first four stories in the collection—Pwyll Lord of Dyfed, Branwen Daughter of Llyr, Manawydan Son of Llyr, and Math Son of Mathonwy are identified as mabinogi in the text. It would be most correct to title the collection *The Mabinogi and Other Myths*, but it is too late to do that after 160 years.

Equally vexing to scholars of Celtic mythology is the question of how long ago these myths were composed. The earliest copy of *The Mabinogion* that has survived is *The White Book of Rhydderch*, which was written about 1300, and that must have been many years after some bard first told the myths it contains. But there is no earlier source, or mention of an earlier source, to give a clue as to the myths' true age. Still, they must be ancient because they contain so many classic, early Celtic elements: the love of feasting and the emphasis on the otherworld (the sidh of Irish Celtic tales), to name only two. These early elements, however, sit beside much later medieval elements, such as chivalry, knights, ladies in distress, and jousting, all of which are products of continental literature that

developed long after the Celts. It is all very confusing, and many scholars have simply given up trying to sort it out.

Still, given what survives, scholars have been able to create a theory about how *The Mabinogion* came to combine Celtic and late medieval elements. Originally, the eleven myths in the collection traveled to France via Brittany, where they picked up some elements from the chivalric tradition before they once more crossed back over the English Channel to Wales. Hence these myths are different from the Celtic tales from Ireland, which never had the "advantage" of a continental experience. For instance, Irish myths are almost exclusively confined to Ireland, while the Welsh myths take place in Ireland, Wales, Scotland, France, and Italy. Irish myths describe combat in the classic Celtic style, with chariots, spears, and strange, fanciful weapons, but rarely armor. In the Welsh myths, there are armor, lances, jousting, tournaments, and warhorses, but never a mention of a chariot. Finally, the dialogue in the Irish Celtic myths is short and to the point, while that of the Welsh myths uses the flowery and polite conversation of the French nobility in the courtly love epics of the Continent.

One of the major literary elements of *The Mabinogion* that has long fascinated scholars is the book's preservation of the earliest attempt to portray King Arthur. This Arthur is far from the courtly king created by Chrétien de Troyes or William of Monmouth, yet he is certainly no crude Celtic chieftain; he is something in between.

Four of the most interesting myths in *The Mabinogion* are Lludd and Llevelys, Pwyll Lord of Dyfed and Rhiannon Daughter of Herveyd, Branwen Daughter of Llyr, and Gereint and Enid. If one can suggest a relative chronology for these four myths based on their content it would be as follows: Lludd and Llevelys is certainly the earliest, since it has the purest Celtic elements and exhibits the least continental influence. The action is presented in a direct, no-nonsense fashion and includes a liberal sprinkling of magic and mythical monsters; it could be Irish. At the other extreme is Gereint and Enid, which is certainly the latest myth simply because it has the most chivalric atmosphere and clearly owes much to French literature. Pwyll Lord of Dyfed and Branwen Daughter of Llyr come somewhere in between. There is certainly Celtic magic and mystery in Pwyll's visit to the otherworld, and in the magical, regenerating cauldron that is part of Branwen's dowry, but there is also a good dose of courtliness and chivalry in these tales. Still, the best plan is not to overanalyze these stories, but simply to let them speak for themselves.

LLUDD AND LLEVELYS

Very early in the history of Britain there was a great king named Beli mac Mynogan who ruled wisely and well and had four sons: Lludd, Casswallawn, Nynnyaw, and Llevelys. They were all fine men and great warriors, but Lludd and Llevelys exceeded the other two in wisdom. Even as children, the two other brothers came to these two for advice and help. For this reason, when King Beli knew he was about to die, he sent for Lludd and invested him with the kingship of Britain. He chose Lludd over Llevelys because Lludd was older, not because he was wiser. Yet soon after Beli's death, Llevelys got a kingdom of his own. When the king of Gaul died, leaving only a daughter to succeed him, his regent sent an ambassador to Britain asking that one of Beli's sons marry the princess and become king of Gaul. Lludd was happy to choose Llevelys, and Casswallawn and Nynnyaw did

A typical late-medieval battle of heavy cavalry against massed infantry armed with pikes. The Celtic inhabitants of Wales are portrayed in *The Mabinogion* as fighting on horseback, but in reality probably only the Celtic leaders rode horses.

not object, for they were enjoying a war against the Irish in which they were gaining great success and much fine booty. So Lludd ruled in Britain and his brother ruled in Gaul, and so things stood for many years.

But happy times do not last forever, and one day three great evils overtook the British. First there came to the island a group of beings called the Corannyeid. Although they looked human, these creatures were really demons. They immediately began causing all kinds of misfortunes throughout the land, not the least of which was cheating people in business transactions—when they bought something they paid for it with coins that looked real, but that overnight turned to dust, leaving the seller with nothing. When the people of Britain tried to do something about the Corannyeid, they discovered yet another nasty aspect, namely that no matter where or how softly the British spoke, the Corannyeid could hear them talking and so know their plans. Even if two Britons went to the most remote spot on the island and spoke in whispers during a windstorm, the Corannyeid still

heard them. Try as they might, the Britons could never rid themselves of these evil beings because they could never make plans that their unwelcome guests could not overhear and consequently foil.

The second problem was even worse. At times, a loud, piercing shriek would, without warning, rend the peace of the realm. It was so loud that the stained glass windows in the churches would crack, pregnant women would miscarry, and people would temporarily lose their hearing. Try as he might, Lludd could not discover what caused these terrible shrieks, but the uncertainty of when the shrieks would occur caused great concern throughout Britain, and people demanded that King Lludd do something.

The third problem was not as great as the first two, but it was still of great concern to Lludd. Every time Lludd planned a feast, the victuals would be set out the night before, as was the custom, and the next morning everything would have disappeared. No matter how many guards were set over the food, the results were the same. Lludd soon gained the reputation of being a stingy king, and his subjects began to talk among themselves, saying that perhaps they needed a new king.

Now Lludd realized how unhappy his people were and determined that there was only one person in all the world who could help him: his brother Llevelys. He therefore announced that he was going to visit his brother, the king of Gaul, but so as not to arouse the suspicions of the Corannyeid, he told everyone it was a purely social call. Lludd fitted out a fleet that was worthy of the visit of one king to another, and sailed across the Channel to Gaul. When the fleet was still far offshore, Llevelys saw it and joyfully set out in his own royal ship to meet his brother. The two brothers met in the middle of the Channel. Llevelys asked his brother why he had come and Lludd replied in a voice that he knew the Corannyeid could hear that it was a social call. At the same time he signaled his brother for a piece of parchment, on which he briefly wrote a description of his problem and drew a diagram of a long tube that he thought could provide the solution. Without saying a word, Llevelys signaled his men to make the tube.

Once the tube was ready, Lludd put one end in his mouth and signaled for his brother to put the other end in his ear. When this was done Lludd began to speak. But when Lludd spoke into his end, "My brother, I have come to ask your help in solving a great problem that besets my country," Llevelys heard, "You are a poor leader for Gaul and I have come to tell you that your father was not my father but a low-born swineherd." Llevelys yanked the tube from his ear and glared at his brother. "Have you come all this distance just to insult me?" he asked angrily. Bewildered, Lludd spoke again into

the tube, "What do you mean, brother? I have come to ask your help!" But all Llevelys heard was his brother calling him a drunken lout. It was a mystery to both brothers, for while each spoke with affection to the other without the tube, any message sent through the tube became corrupted and was certain to raise the anger of one brother toward the other.

Finally Lludd figured it out. "Brother," he said, "I have an idea that a demon is inhabiting this tube. If we pour wine down it, then the demon will flee." This soon proved to be true, for when wine was poured through the tube, the demon fled and the two brothers could talk clearly and, most importantly, without being overheard.

Lludd then explained his problems, and, just as he had expected, his brother had a solution. "Take this bottle full of insects," said Llevelys. "They are a special kind that inhabit the land where the Corannyeid come from. When you get home, kill them and crush them into a fine powder. Mix this powder with water until it is completely dissolved.

A representation of the scene in the myth of Lludd and Llevelys in which Lludd orders the construction of a tube through which he can communicate with his brother Llevelys without the Corannyeid overhearing the conversation. The concept of Llevelys as a king of France and Lludd as a king of Britain is an invention of the later Middle Ages that has been grafted onto the older Celtic legend.

Then call all the people of the kingdom together, including the Corannyeid, for an important announcement. When everyone has gathered together, unstopper the bottle and throw it on the throng. It will do no harm to the normal people, but even the faintest whiff of the mixture will cause the Corannyeid to fall down, writhe in agony, and then die." Lludd thought that was a fine solution and said he would do it. Then he asked his brother if he could help with the second problem.

"Indeed I can," replied Llevelys. "Your kingdom is beset with two dragons that are mortal enemies. The shrieks you hear, brother, are the sounds they make when they fight. To get rid of these beasts you must have your scholars measure the longest distances in your kingdom from north to south and from east to west. Where those two measurements intersect you are to dig a deep pit. In the bottom of that pit you are to place a huge vat of beer—the finest that you can brew in Britain. Then you must cover the vat with a fine silk cloth and wait. The pit and the beer will quickly attract the dragons, for they are curious and great drunkards. Once they both appear at the pit they will begin to fight over the beer in the bottom of the pit, and they will fall, struggling, into the vat. Once they are in the beer they will change into pigs, and at that moment, brother, you must jump down into the pit, draw the four corners of the silk cloth around the pigs, and then have your men pull them out of the pit. Quickly put the pigs and the cloth in a large iron chest and bury the chest as deeply as you can. That will end the problem of the dragons." Lludd liked that idea and told his brother he would do it.

"But can you help me with my third problem? For my subjects think I am a stingy king and do not like to share food with them," said Lludd. And Llevelys told him, "Your problem is a gigantic wizard who owns a magic bag that never becomes full, no mat-

ter how much is put into it. Every night, prior to a banquet, this creature comes and stuffs his sack full of your food. He knows a great many spells, one of which can make everyone in your castle fall asleep. When they awake the next morning, everything is gone. When you return to Britain, and after you deal with the first two problems, you must lay out a great feast just as before. But in order that you may resist the spell, have brought from Mount Snowdon ice, and put it into a tub of water so that the water turns icy cold. Throughout the night, as the wizard's spell takes effect, step into the icy tub to wake yourself up. Then when the wizard appears you will be able to kill him easily, for he is not a good fighter and will beg for mercy."

Lludd thanked his brother through the tube and then announced loudly to his retainers that the visit was over and it was time to leave. He boarded his ship, and two days later he was home, ready to put his brother's advice into practice.

First he ground up the insects, dried them, and added water to make a solution. Next, he invited all the people to a meeting. When everyone was there he suddenly threw the water-insect mixture at them. Nothing happened to the Britons, but the Corannyeids fell to the ground writhing in agony and quickly died. The people cheered and declared Lludd the greatest king ever. Thereafter the place where this occurred was called Caer Llundein—Lludd's Castle—a name that has evolved into London.

His first problem solved, Lludd turned to the second problem: ridding Britain of the dragons. His scholars carefully measured the length and breadth of Britain and found that the spot where the line of the longest east-west measurement crossed the line of the longest north-south measurement was near the town of Carmarthen in western Wales. Llevelys dug the pit as instructed and placed

During his conversation with Llevelys, Lludd is told that in order to rid himself of the dragons wreaking havoc in his kingdom, he should dig a deep pit at a certain location and fill the pit with beer, to which the dragons will immediately be attracted. Llevelys tells Lludd that the beasts will fight over the beer, fall into the pit, and be transformed into pigs. The pigs can then be buried in an iron chest and thus vanquished forever. The point at which this pit would have been sited is somewhere near Carmarthen, Wales—the meeting point of a line drawn from the northernmost tip of Scotland, near the Orkneys, to the tip of Cornwall, and another from the easternmost point of land in East Anglia to a point of land west of St. Davids. Dragons are a common element in Welsh mythology, and it is not surprising to find them in Celtic legends.

in it a huge vat of the finest beer. He then covered the vat with a silk cloth. In no time at all, he heard the sound of great leather wings and saw two huge angry dragons descending. They met over the pit and immediately fell to fighting each other. They both tumbled from mid-air into the pit and down into the beer vat, carrying the cloth in with them. Just as his brother had predicted, the vile beasts were transformed into squealing pigs. Lludd jumped down into the pit, grabbed the corners of the cloth, and tied them together. Then he called for his men, who helped him draw the wiggling burden up out of the ground and put it in a great iron chest that they then buried. Lludd was pleased with himself and so were his subjects, who again called him the greatest king ever. He immediately began to prepare for ridding the kingdom of the food-stealing wizard.

He sent runners in relays to bring ice from Mount Snowdon and chilled a great vat of water. He then ordered a great feast laid out on the tables of his banquet hall. Finally, he hid in the shadows and waited. Several times during the night, his eyelids began to droop and he almost fell asleep. Each time this happened, however, he stepped into the vat of ice water and was jolted to full awareness. Finally, just before dawn, a huge man entered the hall carrying a great leather bag. Lludd watched as the man quickly gathered up all the meat and drink off the table and stuffed them into his bag. Lludd was amazed to note that no matter what the wizard put into his sack, it never seemed to expand or to become anywhere near full.

At last, when the wizard had put everything into the bag and was about to leave the banquet hall, Lludd jumped out from behind

A view of Llyn Trawsfynydd, east of Harlech Castle. This area was part of the ancient post-Roman kingdom of Gwynedd, one of the wealthiest Celtic kingdoms in Wales because it controlled the island of Anglesey, where grain was grown in abundance.

a pillar, grabbed a bench, and, swinging it high over his head, brought it firmly down on the wizard's skull. The wizard fell to the floor and Lludd drew his sword for the kill. "Spare me, warrior," cried the wizard. "If I do, what can you do for me, beast?" countered Lludd. "I will replace threefold everything that I have stolen all these months and be your faithful follower from then on," came the reply. Lludd

agreed to spare the wizard, and with the surplus food that the sorcerer gave him, he held a feast for every subject in Britain to celebrate freedom from the three terrible things the country had endured for so long. All the people then praised Lludd, saying that he was not only the greatest king the Britons had ever had, but also the greatest king they would ever have.

The dragons do battle before falling into the pit dug by Lludd and being transformed into pigs.

saddled and waiting on the hill, and when the mysterious beauty rode by he jumped into the saddle and set off in pursuit. Yet even his foresight did not help, for the woman kept far ahead of him no matter how fast he drove his horse. In desperation, he cried out for her to wait, and surprise of surprises, she did. He approached, confident that this woman had something to do with his destiny. He asked her where she was going, and she replied that she was seeking Pwyll Lord of Dyfed, for she had a favor to ask him. "Indeed, lady, I am he, and I will grant you any favor you may ask," replied Pwyll.

The woman identified herself as Rhiannon, daughter of Herveyd the Old, and told Pwyll that she would soon be forced to marry a man she did not love, a man named Gwawl mac Clud. Rhiannon hated Gwawl, who was not only stupid but also brooding and sullen. She requested that Pwyll come to her father's court and ask for her hand; Herveyd the Old would grant his wish, she said, for Pwyll was a great king while Gwawl mac Clud was a comparative small fry. Much taken with the woman's beauty, Pwyll agreed to come to her father's court and ask that he be allowed to marry her.

Without delay, Pwyll went to the house of Herveyd the Old, arriving amid all the pomp and splendor that Herveyd could muster, and was ushered into the great hall. He was given the seat of honor and made the lord of the banquet. After being served great amounts of food and wine, Pwyll was about to make his request when a young man, who was blond, handsome, and sullen, made his way into the hall, stood before Pwyll, and said he had a boon to ask of Pwyll. In a half-inebriated state, ignoring the frantic tug on his sleeve from Rhiannon, Pwyll said, "Speak! For I will give you whatever I can."

"I am Gwawl mac Clud," the young man proclaimed, "and I ask that tonight you grant

me permission to marry Rhiannon and proclaim a great wedding feast for my men." Pwyll knew he would have to grant this request because he had given his word, and Rhiannon—who was neither retiring nor bashful—asked him, "What will you do now, you great country clod?" Pwyll told Rhiannon

to hold her tongue, for although he may have been caught off-guard once, he was not without resources and he had thought of a very good plan. Giving Gwawl his most winning grin, Pwyll said, "I cannot give away what is not mine, friend Gwawl, for the food and drink of this feast are not mine to give as they are the gift of Herveyd the Old. But should you return here in a year, I will grant both your wishes."

Later that night, after dinner, Rhiannon asked Pwyll to tell her of his plan. He informed her that he had good relations with the people of the otherworld, whose magic was great, and that they would help him. He was thinking, of course, of Arawn of Annwvyn, who, when Pwyll explained his problem, gave the mortal king a certain magic bag. This bag was small—no bigger than a man's head—but it had the odd characteristic that no matter how much you put into it, it never became full. "I am sure, Lord Pwyll," said Arawn, "that you can find a way to use such a special resource."

"Be assured, King Arawn, that I will find a use for the bag," said Pwyll, who was already hatching a plan.

At the end of the year, right on schedule, Gwawl mac Clud returned to Herveyd's great hall, and Pwyll was ready for him. Pwyll was not in the feast hall when Gwawl arrived. Instead, he had disguised himself as a beggar, and he entered the hall only after the feast was well under way and Gwawl was filled with beer. Pwyll approached the high seat, where Gwawl sat as guest of honor, and said that he came as a suppliant seeking a favor. "And what is that, beggar?" asked Gwawl. "To fill my little bag with food, good lord," replied

In the myth of Pwyll and Rhiannon, Gwawl mac Clud is tricked into a bag by Pwyll and then ingloriously beaten by the king's one hundred retainers. Magic bags and cauldrons frequently play important roles in Celtic myths from both Ireland and Wales.

Pwyll. "Easy, that," laughed Gwawl, and ordered a servant to fill the bag to capacity. Yet no matter how much was put into the bag, it never became full. "What churlish trick is this?" roared Gwawl. "Oh, great Lord," answered Pwyll, trembling as if terrified at his audacity, "the bag cannot be filled until a good and noble man steps into it and begins to stamp down its contents." Immediately Gwawl got up, came down off the high seat, climbed into the bag, and began to stamp on its contents. Pwyll jumped forward and, seizing the bag in one hand and Gwawl's head in the other, pushed the poor, stupid fool deep into the bag and tied it shut. Though he struggled like a champion, Gwawl was unable to break free.

Pwyll, gloating over his victory, added insult to injury by hanging the bag from a rafter and encouraging his retainers to strike the bag with sticks, joking that it was like playing badger-in-the-bag (a Welsh children's game). Since Pwyll had brought nearly one hundred men with him, this proved quite painful. Gwawl, overcome with pain, begged for mercy, stating that this was an undignified death for a person of noble birth. Rhiannon agreed and persuaded Pwyll to release him on the condition that Gwawl accept her marriage to Pwyll and promise not to seek revenge. Gwawl agreed, and Pwyll and Rhiannon celebrated their nuptials at the court of Herveyd the Old, returning afterward to Pwyll's court at Arberth. But this was not the end of their adventures.

After Pwyll and Rhiannon had been married for two years, Pwyll's retainers became worried, for Rhiannon had not produced a male child, or any child for that matter, to carry on the royal line. They went to Pwyll and asked him to take a new wife for the good of the kingdom. Pwyll recognized the legitimacy of their concern but refused the request, asking for an additional year in which to produce an heir. At the end of that time, he promised, if Rhiannon had not produced a fine baby boy, he would divorce her and find another wife. Exactly nine months later, Rhiannon gave birth to a boy. Joyfully, the entire kingdom celebrated the birth. Yet the very first night after the birth, a tragedy struck. The serving women who were charged with caring for mother and child drank a little too much wine, and when they awoke in the morning they discovered that the infant was missing. There was no way to explain the disappearance, and the women knew that they would be severely punished for losing the child.

To escape punishment the servants concocted a cruel plan. First, they killed a puppy and tore it to pieces so that it was unrecognizable as an animal; then they smeared Rhiannon's face with the blood as she slept, and scattered a few bones around the bed. When this was done, they began to scream and tear their hair, wailing that Rhiannon had murdered the infant in the night and eaten it. Certainly, the evidence was convincing, and even poor Rhiannon believed herself guilty of this terrible crime. The women told the court that Rhiannon had awakened during the night, spoken with a voice that was not her own, and—before their very eyes—devoured the baby, reveling as she spread the baby's blood over her body. The court was horrified, and Rhiannon, having no way to deny the story, wanted to kill herself.

She was brought to trial and would have been executed had not Pwyll intervened, out of his love for her, and demanded a lesser sentence. Instead of death, the court determined on a truly humiliating punishment for the noblewoman—for seven years Rhiannon was to sit outside the castle gate at Arberth and recount the story of her crime to anyone who entered; she was also to offer to carry anyone, regardless of his or her station in life, into the castle on her back.

The marriage of Pwyll Lord of Dyfed to Rhiannon, daughter of Herveyd the Old. Rhiannon is the ideal Celtic wife, accepting the dictates of her husband but using her beauty and brains to mold him to her will.

Submitting to her fate, Rhiannon went out through the castle gate, built a small lean-to against the castle wall, and began to suffer her punishment. Everyone coming to Arberth heard her story, and most turned their heads away for the shame of it. Strangely, the people who seemed to revel in her misfortune were the very serving women who had created the tale—they often demanded rides into the castle on the back of their former mistress. So things stood for two years.

At the end of that time, about forty miles (64km) to the east in Gwent Ys Coed, a dependency of King Pwyll's, the local lord, Teirnon, had an adventure that would have an important impact on poor Rhiannon. Lord Teirnon owned a mare, which most people said was the finest in all of Wales, for on May 1 of every year for the last seven years she had given birth to a fine colt. Yet just as regularly for those same seven years, the newborn colt disappeared the night after it was born. These disappearances were a great mystery, and the

wisest men in Wales could not discover the reason. In the eighth year, Teirnon determined to discover what was happening.

After the birth of the newest colt, he hid himself in the stable and waited quietly to see what would happen. Just before dawn, he was startled to see the roof of the building suddenly tilted back by a huge clawed hand with no more effort than a man might use to lift the lid of a box. Then another clawed hand reached through the opening and plucked the colt away from its mother. Without stopping to consider the risk—the hands were huge and belonged to a monster that was certainly many times larger than a man—Teirnon leaped out of his hiding place and swung his great sword, cutting off the hand that held the tiny colt. With a cry of terrible pain, the mutilated stump was jerked back and the roof crashed back down on the stable. Teirnon felt the ground shake as the huge thing ran off roaring with pain. He ran outside the stable and there, to his surprise, he saw seven horses ranging from a yearling to a stallion seven years old that the monster had left behind—these were certainly the horses that had been taken from him in past years. But of more interest to Teirnon was a handsome two-year-old boy with so noble a bearing that Teirnon knew immediately it must be the child of Pwyll and Rhiannon.

The next morning, Teirnon and his retinue set out for Arberth. When they reached the royal castle, they saw Rhiannon sitting at the gate, and as they passed into the courtyard they heard her piteous tale. Teirnon's wife, a kind woman, wanted to stop and release the poor woman from her misery, but Teirnon stopped her, saying, "Woman, only Pwyll can free her. Let us go quickly and tell him." Because the rules of hospitality demanded that Teirnon attend a feast in his honor before discussing business, hours passed before it was proper to tell Pwyll the news.

When Teirnon at last told his tale, Pwyll was overjoyed. They brought the child forward and everyone agreed that the lad must be Pwyll's son, as he had the king's features. Only then did someone remember to summon Rhiannon, who immediately recognized her child, and the family was at last reunited in the happiness they should have been enjoying for two years. Teirnon became a trusted advisor to King Pwyll and foster-father to the boy, who was named Pryderi and grew up to be one of Wales' greatest kings.

B R A N W E N
D A U G H T E R   O F
L L Y R

King Bran, also known as "the Raven," ruled well and wisely over all of Britain. Bran was so large that he had never lived in a house because there had never been one big enough to hold him. His advisors were his two brothers, Nissyen and Evissyen. These two had extremely divergent personalities, and when Bran asked their advice he always found that the middle course between their opinions was the best one to follow, for Nissyen always counseled moderation and forgiveness while Evissyen always argued for vengeance and brutality. As a result, Bran gained the reputation of being the wisest king in Europe, but his two brothers hated each other because it seemed they were always in competition.

One day when King Bran, Nissyen, and the members of the court were sitting on the high hill at Harlech in northern Wales, they saw a huge fleet coming toward them from the direction of Ireland. The ships in this fleet were well fitted-out and each carried a shield tied to the mast just under the yardarm to announce that theirs was a peaceful mission.

King Bran immediately sent messengers to the landing to ask to whom this grand fleet belonged and to bid them welcome. He found that the fleet was that of King Mallolwch of Ireland, who had come to ask for the hand of King Bran's sister, Branwen White Breasts, in marriage. King Bran was happy to hear this and so was Nissyen, who advised the king to accept, for this would create a firm alliance between two powerful countries. Evissyen was not there, but Bran felt that his brother could not possibly object to so fine a match.

Bran ordered a great feast, and many men made many fine speeches. The eating and drinking lasted all night and into the next morning. Happily, King Mallolwch was much taken with Branwen, and she with him.

Everything would have been fine if it had not been for Evissyen, who, on his return, took exception to King Bran's decision to allow the marriage. Secretly, Evissyen thought the marriage was a fine idea, but he nonetheless raised many objections to it, for he was angered that Bran had made the decision without asking his advice. When Bran would not change his mind, Evissyen set out to ruin the arrangement.

He sneaked off to the stable where King Mallolwch had stabled his horses and mutilated the poor animals with a knife. He cut away the lips of the poor beasts so that their teeth showed, cut their ears off, and peeled back their eyelids so the animals could not blink. When Mallolwch found his horses so brutally maimed, he had to kill them, and he swore to leave Wales immediately and seek vengeance on his Welsh hosts. He did marvel, however, that a people who had feted him and betrothed a princess to him in the same day could turn around and insult him the next day.

King Bran did not want the Irish to leave, and he sent a delegation to Mallolwch to persuade him to stay. The delegation apologized and swore to pay compensation: to each man whose horse had been maimed, a finer horse than the one that had been lost, and for King Mallolwch, a rod of silver as tall as a man and a plate of gold as big around as the king's face. As further incentive to peace, Bran offered Mallolwch a huge, magical iron cauldron that had the power to raise the dead; when a man was killed in battle and afterward thrown into this cauldron, he immediately emerged completely healed save that he had lost his power of speech. This was a truly valuable item for a king and Mallolwch forgot his anger and asked Bran how he had gotten the cauldron, for he had once seen one just like it. Bran replied, "Indeed you have, sire; it is probably the very one, for I got it from two people who came originally from Ireland, Llassar Llaes Gyngwyd and his wife, Kymidei Kymeinvoll."

"Indeed I know those two, King Bran," replied Mallolwch, "for I once had them as guests, and a dirtier, viler pair have never yet been born. The man, Llassar Llaes Gyngwyd, was a braggart and a drunk, and the woman was a lustful slut who attempted to seduce my nobles although none would lie with her because of her stench and foul breath."

"Then," asked King Bran, "why did you let them stay with you?"

"Because they were too big and too dangerous to force out easily, and because the woman gives birth every six weeks to a fully armed and fully grown warrior. I tolerated them so that I could build up my army. Indeed, three of her spawn are with me now." And Mallolwch pointed out the window to three monstrous creatures who were as tall as trees and as broad as walls and looked exactly alike. The king went on to tell Bran that only when his subjects threatened to revolt and topple him from his throne did he get rid of Llassar and Kymidei.

Mallolwch had ordered that an enormous house be built out of iron plates and the metal covered with wood so that the structure resembled a feast hall. He had then invited the two monsters to a grand feast, and when they were both thoroughly satiated with food and besotted with beer, the other feasters sneaked away, the doors were barred, and the servants kindled a great fire around the base of the structure so that it was soon an oven and the two unwelcome guests were the bread. Llassar and his wife began to bellow like bulls and throw themselves against the walls, trying to break them down. At first the walls were too strong, but then, as they grew white-hot and became weakened, Llassar seized the great cauldron, placed it on top of his head, and ran like a battering ram against the wall. He crashed through and Kymidei followed him. Both emerged singed and smoking, and they ran straight to the

Irish Sea to cool themselves off. Then, using the cauldron as a boat, they paddled across the sea to Wales.

King Bran laughed and took up the tale. "I remember their arrival well. They were impressed with my great size and also seemed subdued by their harsh treatment in Ireland. They agreed to live quietly in the hills behind Harlech and produce a new soldier for my army every six weeks if I would supply them with food and shelter." And Bran summoned six monstrous soldiers who were the result of this arrangement and sent them out to visit with their Irish brothers.

The promise of new horses, King Bran's personal gifts of silver and gold to King Mallolwch, and the pleasant and humorous conversation about their similar experiences with Llassar Llaes Gyngwyd and Kymidei Kymeinvoll had a good effect on the Irish king,

The armor worn by this mounted knight is a classic example of mid-fifteenth-century armor. By this time, armor had evolved as a result of the advent of the longbow and the development of firearms.

and he agreed to forget about the insult of Evissyen. However, while their king was willing to forget, many Irish nobles were not, and they continued, whenever they could, to urge their king to take vengeance in some way. King Mallolwch, however, was influenced by Branwen's great beauty and, by the time he had returned to Ireland, was much in love with her. In no time at all, Branwen had become pregnant, and she soon gave birth to a beautiful boy who was named Gwern.

But Mallowch's ardor cooled in three years, and the manipulations of those Irish who still sought vengeance on the Welsh fi-

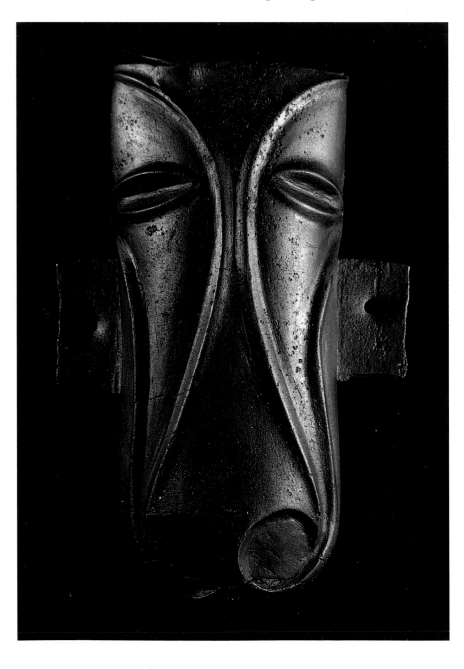

nally had its effect. The king began to take other women into his bed, and finally banished the lovely Branwen to the royal kitchens as a pot scrubber. Yet he feared the anger of Bran should the Welsh king find out about this insult to his sister, so he forbade ships to sail from Ireland to any port in Britain, lest word of Branwen's disgrace get out.

Branwen, however, was not the type of woman to accept this situation. She had befriended a young starling that had fallen from its nest and, partially out of loneliness but also with a goal of getting word to her brother, had taught the bird to speak. When she could communicate with the animal, she told it the whole story and begged it to fly across the sea and tell her brother. The bird, out of love, agreed to go, and it flew straight to King Bran. He was angry beyond words and ordered an immediate attack on the Irish for this great insult. For once, both Nissyen and Evissyen agreed that this was the right thing to do. The Welsh fleet set sail in such force that it covered the water. King Bran himself was too large to fit in a boat, so he waded along beside his ships, bearing his harpists and skilled workmen on his shoulders.

As the fleet neared the coast of Ireland, one of King Mallolwch's soldiers caught sight of it in the twilight. The size of the fleet and the near-darkness prevented the man from identifying it exactly, and he reported only that he had seen something monstrous coming toward the coast. When the king questioned him closely, the man said it seemed that a whole forest was moving toward the coast, and that it appeared that in the midst of that forest there was a high ridge with a large pool of water on either side of it. King Mallolwch realized that this could not be, and asked his wise men to try to figure out what the soldier had really seen. They could not, but one of them remembered Branwen down in the kitchen and told the king to send for his exiled wife, "for if this thing is coming from Wales, she might know what it is."

Branwen was dragged, sweaty and disheveled, from her station at the cooking fires. Although she was covered in grime, it was clear that a year in the kitchens had not diminished her beauty in the slightest. She drew herself up— every inch the queen—and demanded why she had been so unceremoniously summoned from her work. When Mallolwch described the stange phenomenon off the coast, Branwen clapped her hands and laughed. "Now, woman beater, you will see the might of the Welsh come to avenge my treatment, for the forest your man thought he saw was really the many masts of my brother's fleet gathered so thickly together on the water that they seem like a forest. The ridge with the lakes on either side was merely my brother's huge face, for the ridge is his nose and the lakes his giant blue eyes. Poor Mallolwch, you should fear for your kingdom."

Mallolwch called his warriors together and asked for advice. They were proud of their fighting ability, but they also feared the numbers of the Welsh and the great size of Bran. After hours of discussion and argument, they decided to withdraw across the River Liffy, destroy the bridge, and attempt to hold the Welsh at the river. The strategy seemed to work at first, for when the Welsh attempted to cross the river, their boats were swept out to sea by the swift current.

When Bran saw that his troops were having problems, he donned a thick helmet, slung a shield across his back, and threw himself face-down across the river so that his feet were resting on one side and his helmeted

head on the other. In this way, he formed a bridge over which his troops swarmed to fight the Irish. To this day the site of this amazing event is called Baile Atha Cliath—Toward the Hurdle Ford—for it was there that Bran helped his men hurdle the ford. This spot is now known as Dublin.

When King Mallolwch saw that his army was in danger of being defeated, he decided to try trickery. He tempted Bran with an offer to negotiate in a house large enough for Bran to sit in. In all his life Bran had never sat under a roof, and it was an experience he dearly craved; so when the Irish made the offer, Bran jumped at the chance. King Mallolwch put his workmen to building a huge house, lavishing great care and sparing no expense on its decorations. But he also determined to use the house to get the better of King Bran. His workmen hung a bag from each of the hundred posts that held up the roof. Inside each bag was a fully armed warrior who, on signal, was to jump out and attack the Welsh when they

had drunk too much beer. But Mallolwch fig-ured without the suspicions of Evissyen, who was as bitter and distrustful as ever.

Before Bran entered the hall, Evissyen went to inspect it. Carefully looking over the arrangements, he saw one of the bags move. He felt one and realized that each bag held a man. He did not make public his discovery, but instead asked one of the Irish workers what was in them. "Nothing, Lord," replied the man, "save flour."

Evissyen nodded, stuck his hand in the bag, felt for a head, and crushed it so that the man in the bag died quickly and without a sound. Then Evissyen went to the next bag and did the same, repeating this action until he had killed the inhabitant of each bag. What were the Irish workers to do? To shout a warning would only get them killed, so they stood quietly by while Evissyen did his work.

Shortly after Evissyen finished, the two kings arrived. There followed a feast during which the two expressed the greatest love for each other and swore to maintain eternal friendship. Mallolwch even brought Branwen from the kitchen, dressed in the finest clothing, to assure Bran that all was well. But lest Bran be fooled, Evissyen whis-pered into his ear, telling him about the men in the bags and showing the king how treacherous the Irish were. However, Nissyen, the brother who always spoke for for-giveness, encouraged Bran to ac-cept peace. So convincing was Nissyen that Bran finally relented. Evissyen seemed to accept this and said, "King, let us cement this friendship by agreeing to allow Gwern, the son of Branwen and Mallolwch, to be designated king of Ireland when Mallolwch dies. Call the boy forth to invest him."

Mallolwch accepted this offer and called Gwern forth. But as Gwern passed by Evissyen, the royal advisor suddenly grabbed the boy by the feet, swinging him up and around his head, and threw the lad head-first into the fire. The child landed on a stone, his head cracked open, and his brains spilled out and were cooked on the hot stones.

Amazed at this treachery, the Irish sprang to arms and began to fight, thinking that their countrymen in the bags would come to their aid. But they soon realized the "bag men" were not coming and that they were greatly outnumbered. The battle in the huge house swayed back and forth, and the Irish sent for reinforcements. Outside, they kindled a fire under their magic cauldron, filled it with wa-ter, and prepared to use its magical properties to restore their casualties. The British killed many more of the Irish than they lost, but the Irish used their magic cauldron to keep re-turning the recently killed to battle. When Evissyen noted that he had just killed a man for the second time, he realized what the Irish were doing. He fought his way to the cauldron, jumped in, and, bracing his feet against one side, pushed with all his strength against the sides of the vessel. The vessel cracked and broke into two parts, ruined. Unfortunately for Evissyen, the exertion broke his heart and he finally paid for the duplicity that had led to this situation in the first place.

With their reanimated reinforcements gone, the Irish army dwindled until all were killed. On the British side, however, the losses were also great, and by the end of the battle only seven Welsh soldiers remained of the great invasion force that had entered Ireland. Even Bran died, after he was wounded with a poisoned arrow. He realized he was dying and called the seven survivors to his side to extract a promise from them. They were to cut off his head and carry it to London, where they were to bury it on the White Hill, with the face toward France. With the foresight that was common to Welsh kings, he predicted it would take his seven friends eighty-seven years to accomplish this task, for there would be various delays on the way.

The seven immediately set out with the severed head, but stopped at Harlech, where they stayed for seven years feasting, drinking, and bragging about their adventures in Ireland. Next they went to Pembroke in Cornwall, England, where they spent eighty years at the castle of a hospitable king. Miraculously, the head remained uncorrupted all this time and spoke to its companions several times to add to the tales they told of the great battle in Ireland and to remind them to get on with their task. At the end of eighty years the head convinced them, and they finally took it all the way to London and buried it in a great ceremony. As long as the head remained buried, London was free of the plague; however, when William the Conqueror had the foundations dug for his great tower in

London, his workers dug up the head, and London has suffered intermittently from terrible plagues and diseases ever since.

In Ireland, at the end of the battle only five pregnant women had survived the slaughter, by hiding in a cave. All five bore sons. When they grew up, each of the sons took another man's mother as wife and so produced yet another set of children, so that today everyone in Ireland is descended from these five women.

GEREINT
AND ENID

Once, when Arthur, king of Britain, held court at Caer Llion ar Wysg (modern Cardiff), his forester, Madawg mac Twrgadarn, who was responsible for guarding the king's lands in the Forest of Dean, came to Arthur with an announcement. Madawg had seen a wondrous deer, pure white, proud, and fleeter than any animal he had ever seen. Arthur decided that he and his whole court would go on a hunt the next morning. His wife, Gwenhwyvar, and all her court ladies would accompany him.

The next morning, however, Gwenhwyvar was in such a deep sleep and looked so peaceful that Arthur could not bear to wake her, so he went on the hunt without her. When the beautiful queen awoke she was angry, for she loved the thrill of the hunt more than anyone else did. She summoned her ladies-in-waiting and sent one of them to get horses for them all. But the woman returned with the news that the grooms, thinking no one else was going hunting that morning, had let all but two of the horses out into the fields. Gwenhwyvar feared that if they waited for the horses to be gathered from the pasture they would never catch the hunters, so she ordered the two available horses saddled and set out.

An idealized King Arthur in late-medieval armor. The figure of Arthur extends back into the fifth century A.D., when he was depicted as a hero of the Britons. When these myths were written down, he was changed from a valiant hero to a great and celebrated king. In reality, Arthur was probably not a king, but a successful Celtic warrior who won critical battles at a time when victory was essential to the fortunes of the Celts in Britain.

Cardiff Castle, Cardiff, Wales. There has always been some kind of fortification at Cardiff to protect the natural harbor where the Taff River flows into Bristol Channel. The current castle was begun in the eleventh century, but has been modified numerous times since then. The front part of the castle dates from the eighteenth century, while the towers behind it were built in the thirteenth century.

The two women rode through the woods following the distant sound of the hunt's horns. They set a fast pace but, try as they might, could not catch the hunting party. As they rested beside a brook, a young nobleman came upon them. Gwenhwyvar clapped her hands joyfully, for the young man was Gereint, the most handsome man at court and a clever and interesting conversationalist. At least the ride through the forest would not be boring. She asked Gereint to accompany her and her companion, and the three set out to find Arthur.

No sooner had they started off, however, than they suddenly came upon an unknown knight in full armor armed with a lance and accompanied by a dwarf and a maiden. As was customary, Gwenhwyvar sent her lady-in-waiting forward to ask the name of the knight, but no sooner had the lady asked her question than the dwarf sneered, "Such a lowly person as yourself is not fit to know the name of so noble a knight." And with that, he struck the poor woman across the face with his riding crop, leaving her with a wicked red welt. She returned in tears. Gereint, angry at this treatment, rode up and demanded the meaning of such an act; the dwarf, however, did not answer but struck him across the face as well. Then the strange knight and his party rode quickly off.

Drawing his sword, Gereint moved to attack the knight, but Gwenhwyvar, as practical as she was beautiful, ordered him to sheathe his sword. "Sir knight," she said, "you are without armor. To attack that knight, who is in full battle dress, would be foolhardy. I beg you to reconsider, and wait until you are likewise armed." Gereint realized Gwenhwyvar's wisdom and put up his sword. He asked the queen and her lady to return to court to dress the poor lady's wound, while he followed the knight to learn his name.

All day Gereint followed the knight through the woods, until he arrived at a town. The strange knight entered the gates of the town and was welcomed by the guard. Gereint also entered the town, thinking that here was an opportunity to search for information. He wandered the streets making discreet inquiries until he came to a ruined building in front of which there sat an old man dressed in the most ragged clothes Gereint had ever seen. Despite his dress, though, the fellow had a dignified bearing, and Gereint asked him if he knew the strange knight who had entered the town. "Indeed I do, warrior," said the old man, whose name was Niwl. "Come home with me and I will tell you all you need to know."

So Gereint followed the man home, and there the knight met Niwl's daughter, Enid, who was as ragged as her father but was a beautiful woman nonetheless. She was also quite cheerful and full of information about the town and the people in it—she knew all about the mysterious knight. His name was Edern son of Nudd and he was a famous and skilled knight, if a little arrogant. "He has come, sir knight," said Enid, "to be in the tournament tomorrow. Every year, the local earl holds a joust. Edern has entered for the last two years and has always won. If he wins again this year, he will keep forever the great trophy cup that is the prize."

"How may I enter that tournament?" asked Gereint. "And how may I get some armor, lady?"

"No knight may enter the tournament unless he has a lady in whose honor he fights. He must dedicate the prize to her and swear to serve her forever," replied Enid.

"Then, maiden, if you will be my lady and let me enter the tournament on your behalf tomorrow, I promise that if I win you will be my wife."

Enid accepted and Niwl lent Gereint his old and rusted armor, for the old man had once been a young and restless knight. Indeed, he had been lord of all the land around—as Gereint heard that night at dinner—but had lost it to the present earl by force of arms.

The next morning, Gereint, Niwl, and Enid went to the tournament field. Gereint looked ridiculous in his rusted armor, and everybody laughed at the rusty knight, the

An array of swords and armor, including (at upper left) an upper arm protector called a pauldron. To facilitate easy movement of the arm, pauldrons had overlapping layers of metal called epaulieres. The spiked elbow piece was called a coudiere, and was designed so that a knight could deliver a lethal backward blow with his arm.

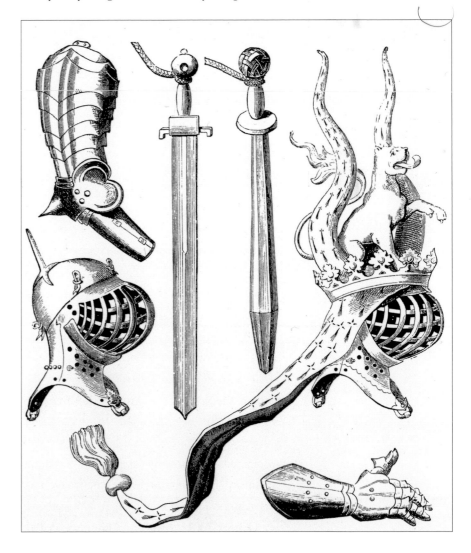

OPPOSITE: In this artist's interpretation of the battle between Gereint and Edern, both knights wear formal tournament armor, highly specialized sports equipment that was much different from and much heavier than battle armor. A suit of tournament armor could weigh up to 120 pounds (54.4kg); a man dressed in this kind of armor needed a stepladder to mount his horse. Each knight also carries a blunt lance and a small shield called a tournament targe.

ragged old man, and the young and equally ragged girl. But once Gereint began to joust, people forgot to laugh and instead were thrilled by his skill. Gereint unhorsed six knights in a row, and then, after a short rest, six more. Finally, the only knight left on the field was the mysterious warrior who had insulted Gereint and Gwenhwyvar's lady-in-waiting. The two went to opposite ends of the field and rode toward each other furiously. Twice, each splintered his lance on the other's shield. Finally, Niwl handed Gereint a lance that had been his as a youth and that had never splintered, no matter how hard he had ridden at an enemy. Armed with this lance, Gereint hit the other knight's shield right in the center, breaking it in half. Edern tumbled from the saddle. Gereint jumped off his mount, and the two men began to hack and slash at each other until their armor was bent and broken in a hundred places. Finally, Gereint succeeded in battering Edern to the ground, and Edern begged for mercy. Gereint granted mercy on the condition that Edern travel to Caer Llion ar Wysg and beg the forgiveness of Gwenhwyvar for the blow his dwarf had given her lady-in-waiting.

Within minutes of Gereint's victory, the local earl came onto the field. He congratulated Gereint on his victory and begged him to come to dinner. Remembering the hospitality of Niwl, however, Gereint replied that he already had an invitation to dinner. Yet when Niwl, Enid, and Gereint returned to Niwl's humble house, they were surprised to see servants and slaves bringing food, tables, chairs, and rich wine to Niwl's house. The earl had decided that if Gereint would not come to dinner with him, he would bring dinner to Gereint. Over dinner that night, the earl, still impressed with Gereint's skill at arms, asked if he could give him anything. "I will give you anything that is in my power to give, knight, up to half my lands." Then Gereint said to

him, "If that is true, and I do not doubt it, for you seem a man of honor, then return half of your lands to Niwl, the man from whom you took them, and give him a retinue of men-at-arms to defend them." The earl, a good-natured fellow at heart, laughed at his own foolish generosity and granted Gereint his wish. That taken care of, Gereint and Enid left the next morning for Caer Llion ar Wysg and the court of Arthur.

His arrival was expected, for Edern had taken Gereint's injunction literally and had made as rapid a journey as possible to the court of King Arthur. In fact, at the very moment that Gereint was demanding that the earl give part of his land to Niwl, Edern was begging Gwenhwyvar to forgive him. She, kind woman that she was, granted forgiveness on the condition of a year's good service to herself and her ladies.

The next morning, Arthur, having heard Edern's story, laid out the best spread he could in anticipation of Gereint's arrival, and the young knight received a hero's welcome. Arthur then "married" Gereint and Enid (there was no formal marriage in Celtic society), and Queen Gwenhwyvar and her ladies immediately took Enid under their collective wing and whisked her away to dress her in finery and prepare her for court. Enid's pleasant nature and her husband's military skills soon made them the most popular young couple at Caer Llion ar Wysg.

For the next year, Gereint fought in tournaments all over Britain, and he always won. All the while, his love and admiration for Enid grew and grew. But by the beginning of the next year, his love of Enid had begun to bring him trouble.

Because he won every tournament he fought, Gereint started to become bored with fighting altogether, and turned to the other great love of his life—Enid—with whom he never became bored. Gradually, he began to

spend much more time with her than with the other warriors at court. In the intensely male-dominated world of Arthur's court, forsaking the company of men for that of a woman, no matter how charming and beautiful, was sure to bring criticism. Edern, who was still at court, heard these criticisms and spoke to Enid about it. She was, of course, concerned, for no woman likes to see her man lose face with his peers. Yet she was afraid to

mention her concern to Gereint for fear of his anger, and her anxiety increased until one morning, as Gereint slept, she began to cry.

Her sobbing awakened Gereint and she was forced to tell him what she had heard. Uncharacteristically and illogically, Gereint became angry with Enid. He roared at the trembling woman that his fighting ability was as sharp as ever and that he would prove it that day. "We will go into the forest together, but you will ride ahead of me. On no account are you to warn me of danger. I am equal to whatever I may meet, and you will soon see that I have not lost my fighting prowess." And so the two left Caer Llion ar Wysg and went into the deepest part of the woods.

In no time at all Enid saw four strange knights approaching. Because she had never seen them before, she knew they were not the king's men, but young, unattached knights eager to build a reputation—the most dangerous and aggressive kind. She saw the danger of four against one, weighed what Gereint had said about not warning him of danger, and, deciding that there was a good chance that these four might kill Gereint if they attacked without warning, rode back to tell him of their approach. Gereint was angry and began to curse the poor girl, but had to break off quickly and defend himself, for suddenly the four knights appeared, riding down the hillside at full gallop.

In short order, and seemingly without effort, he knocked two of the knights off their horses with such force that they were dead before they hit the ground. The next two war-riors renewed their attack with extra vigor, but Gereint also knocked them off their horses. These two still had fight left in them, and Gereint had to dismount and finish them off with sword strokes. Once he had vanquished them, Gereint turned his anger on Enid, threatening her with a beating if she warned him of danger again. He then loaded all the armor of the four knights onto one of the dead men's horses, and instructed Enid to lead this horse, as well as the other three, after her. Gereint hoped that the horses and the armor would serve as a lure, tempting other knights to try and take them so that he would again have an opportunity to prove that he was still a virile man and a valiant warrior.

Within a few miles, Enid saw three more knights approaching. "Here are some easy pickings," said one of the strange knights loudly, "four suits of armor, four horses, and a young girl for our pleasure." All three knights spurred their mounts toward Enid. The poor girl now suffered quite a dilemma: the man she loved was in danger, for he was already exhausted from his previous fight and could not, she thought, possibly take on another three knights, especially if they surprised him. Still, she had been promised a beating if she warned him again. Nonetheless, so great was her love that she decided she would rather be beaten by the man she loved than see him killed, so she turned her horse around and rode back to warn him.

Instead of thanking her, Gereint glared angrily at her and rode forward to do battle. As he charged forward, he knocked the lance of the first knight aside and, without stopping, hit the second knight squarely in the chest—the knight was dead before he touched the ground. Gereint did not pause but went straight on for the third knight, knocking him off his horse as well. Jumping down off his horse, Gereint slew that knight with his sword and then coolly killed the first knight, who

Two knights fighting on foot. Both knights wear a helmet called a salade. The salade was not attached to the suit of armor, but was designed to cover the top two-thirds of the head. Being un-attached, it allowed wider freedom of movement and was much cooler. The jaw and lower face of a knight wearing a salade was generally protected by a metal attachment called a mentonniere.

was still groggy from Gereint's first blow. Poor Enid now sat silently and fearfully on her horse, expecting to be beaten. But Gereint only abused her with words and ordered her back to her position far in front of him with three more horses and three more suits of armor as a temptation for the next group of wandering knights. "Heed my words and say nothing to me even if all hell come against me, for I am equal to them in battle."

Soon the little cavalcade of two people, eight suits of armor, and nine horses was spotted by a group of five knights. Enid, far in advance, heard one of them say, "This is surely a rich prize for us! All that armor and horseflesh plus a girl to share; and guarded by only one sorry-looking knight." Enid, still willing to accept blows to save the man she loved, turned back toward Gereint and told him what she had heard. Gereint said only that she would live to hate the fact that she had broken silence, and then rode off to confront the five knights. Despite her greatest fears, he quickly and expertly killed them all.

These rounds of battles, threats, and the accumulation of additional suits of armor continued through nine more conflicts. Even though he was always outnumbered, Gereint always won, and his physical ability and stamina amazed Enid, who realized the truly astonishing ability of her lover and finally realized that he had no need of warnings from her or anyone else. But even Gereint overreached himself. Late in the day, he encountered a man sitting by the side of the road whose lord had been slain by three eighteen-foot (5.4m) giants armed with clubs the size of full-grown oak trees. Gereint questioned

the man and promised to exact vengeance for this murder. He pursued the beasts and, after a fierce fight, slew all three. But the effort was too much for him. He rode back to Enid, fell from his horse, and died in her arms.

Overcome with grief, Enid cried, moaned, and tore her hair until the noise attracted a passing knight, Earl Limwris, who upon seeing Enid decided to rape her. Oblivious to her screams and unsuccessful attempts to defend herself, he began to tear the clothes from the poor girl; he was just about to have his way with her when Gereint awoke from the dead. Enid's plight and her pure, unadulterated, all-sacrificing love had brought him back to life. He jumped up, drew his sword, and made short work of Limwris.

And it was only then that Gereint realized the overwhelming love that Enid had for him—so powerful that it raised him from the dead to defend her. He finally forgave her, and from that day forward he never again doubted her love for him.

Enid comforts the dying Gereint, who, through the power of love, would soon live again. Note the boar crest on the helmet. Boars were a sign of high rank in Celtic society, probably derived from the tradition of the hero's portion at Celtic feasts.

CHAPTER
IV

FROM
CELTIC HEROES
TO CHRISTIAN SAINTS

W hile Christianity helped preserve Celtic mythology—albeit in an altered form—it also incorporated or adapted mythological stories as miraculous events in the lives of Celtic saints. Certainly, Christian saints could not excel in battle, but they could carry on the mythological genre within a framework of miracles performed to propagate the faith.

Saint Patrick (A.D. 390–461), the most important Irish saint, not surprisingly had the greatest numbers of miracles associated with him. Many of these

St. Patrick, the patron saint of Ireland, was born to an
aristocratic family in Strathclyde, an early Celtic kingdom
that consisted of portions of modern-day southern
Scotland and northwestern England.

321

have to do with Patrick's struggle with the Druids, for these religious leaders had a great deal to lose if Christianity took root.

When Patrick first came to the court of King Loeguire, the High King of Ireland, two Druids, Lochru and Lucetmail, disputed his preaching. After Patrick endured their insults for a time, he prayed to God for help and begged that Lochru, the most obnoxious of the two, might die. No sooner had the last syllable left Patrick's mouth than a mysterious force lifted poor Lochru high into the air and dropped him head-first to the ground, where his skull burst open on a rock and his brains dripped out. The description of this mortal wound calls to mind some of the injuries inflicted by Cuchulainn on his Connacht enemies during the Tain Bo Cuailnge.

Later, Patrick performed less lethal deeds. When the Druid Lucetmail challenged Patrick to make it snow, Patrick refused, saying that he could not do what was contrary to nature. With a sneer, Lucetmail created a heavy snow that piled up to the hubs of the chariot wheels. Now Patrick showed his mettle; he raised his hand and, with a mere wave, caused all the snow to vanish. It might have been contrary to nature for it to snow in Ireland in April, Patrick explained to the king, but it was in concert with nature to clear snow away.

Next, Lucetmail brought darkness over the area at noontime. But Patrick swept this away, again with a wave of the hand, explaining to the amazed court that the Druids could work only evil, but the greatness of Christianity was that it worked magic only for good.

Finally, Patrick proposed a test of the relative power of the Druids and the Christians. He had a group of workmen construct a house, one half of which they built out of green wood and the other half out of dry wood. Then he told one of his disciples to exchange clothing with one of Lucetmail's followers. Patrick's disciple, dressed as a Druid, went and stood in the part of the house built of dry wood, while Lucetmail's disciple, dressed as a Christian, stood in the green-wood part of the house. When all was ready, Lucetmail himself set the house on fire. To the amazement of all, the Druid burned up, while Patrick's disciple emerged unharmed from the fire. Turning to the court, Patrick said, "You have seen the power of the Lord at work. I ask you to believe in the Lord Christ, or God will

destroy you all." Not surprisingly, King Loeguire and his entire court asked Patrick to baptize them right then and there.

Many of the myths of the early Celtic saints involved their power over animals. Saint Ciaran of Clonmacnoise (515–545) trained a fox to carry his copy of the Psalms, and when the fox yielded to its hunger and ate the book for its leather binding, Ciaran forgave the animal and saved it from his angry followers. Because Ciaran had been merciful, God restored the partially eaten Psalter to its original condition.

Saint Kevin of Glendalough once dropped his copy of the Psalms into a deep lake. He asked an otter to dive for the book, and the otter did so. Later, Kevin trained the animal to catch salmon each day and bring the fish to the monastic kitchen.

The most famous example of the Celtic saints' power over animals involved Saint Columba of Iona (521–597) and the Loch Ness monster. In 586, Columba went to Scotland to try to convert the fierce Picts under King Brud. On the way, he and his followers came to the southern shore of Loch Ness and wanted to cross at a point where a rope was set to draw a small boat across the loch. Unfortunately, they arrived just in time to see a huge monster surface near the boat as it came across the loch, frighten the poor boatman

LEFT: Stonehenge, Wiltshire, England. Although Stonehenge is associated in the popular mind with the Celts and their Druid priesthood, neither the Celts nor their Druids had much to do with the place. The first part of Stonehenge was built between 1900 and 1600 B.C.—long before the Celts arrived in Britain. Nevertheless, the practices of modern Druids (which have nothing to do with the Celtic religion), and their yearly meetings at Stonehenge to celebrate the summer solstice, have focused popular attention on the historic Celts.

BELOW LEFT: Most Irish saints were fond of animals, and legend has it that they could entice the creatures to do their will. Birds were especially important—they often carried messages from one person to another. Here St. Keiven (Kevin) whispers a message to a bird.

ABOVE: St. Kevin's Church and Round Tower, County Wicklow, Ireland. During the Viking raids on Ireland, the Irish monks built protective structures in the form of high, round towers that were difficult for the Vikings to take without siege equipment.

RIGHT: Loch Ailsh, Durnie, Scotland. The dark and mysterious waters of the Scottich lochs, colored black by the peat that constantly seeps into them from the surrounding soil, naturally give rise to legends and tales of monsters. The castle in the foreground is Eilean Donan.

out of the boat, and swallow the man. Without the least hesitation, Columba ordered one of his disciples to swim across the loch to get the small boat and bring it back so that he and his followers could cross. The man jumped into the water and started to swim for the boat. The monster, attracted by the swimmer, turned to attack him, but Columba, with a mere wave of his hand, caused the creature to submerge and leave the man alone. Columba's disciple then brought the boat back, and the future saint and his whole group crossed the loch in perfect safety. When word of this encounter with the monster reached King Brud and his court, the king ordered all his people to accept baptism from the saint's hand. This, by the way, is the first written reference to the monster that has fascinated both saints and sinners ever since.

PART 4
DEITIES & DEMONS OF
THE FAR EAST

INDIAN
MYTHOLOGY

Between the years 1500 and 1200 B.C. the Indus valley was invaded from the northwest by Indo-Aryan tribes. These invaders brought with them a number of sophisticated texts, called *Vedas*. The Vedas were collections of works that ranged over such subjects as theology, social institutions, legal systems, ethics, cosmology, philosophy, and science. The most important of the Vedas is the *Rig Veda*, compiled around 1000 B.C. and written in an archaic form of Sanskrit. The *Rig Veda* is the oldest Vedic work and the basis for much

Vishnu, one of the most important Hindu
deities, is depicted riding the great sunbird
Garuda with his wife Lakshmi in this
magnificent eighteenth-century painting.

329

This eleventh-century bronze statue of Shiva, another incarnation of Brahma, is from India. Under his right foot Shiva is crushing the demon of ignorance as two of his hands beat the drum of creation and the other two hands complete a gesture of benediction. Around Shiva burns the flame of destruction.

OPPOSITE: Brahma, believed by many Hindu sects to be the supreme and original being, was widely depicted. This bas-relief of Brahma and his two primary incarnations is from the Karlash Temple in India.

Hindu thought. In fact, although Hinduism remains a religion with no standardized form of worship, the *Rig Veda* is regarded as an authoritative text that is divine in origin.

Over time, the diverse stock of information contained in the Vedas was woven into the fabric of Indian life. Sometimes Vedas were adopted wholesale and sometimes changed and incorporated into the belief systems of the peoples of the Indus valley that already existed. Gradually, the Vedic influence was spread throughout the region, generally in the custody of the wealthy and learned class of men called *Brahmans*. As a result, Hinduism is sometimes referred to as Brahmanism. But there are a multitude of other forms of Hinduism as well, sometimes referred to as "village" Hinduism. These alternate forms of Hinduism are more firmly rooted in the pre-Vedic history of the Indus valley, and therefore make reference to many ancient and regional mystical beliefs and mythologies. One indication of the profound and lasting nature of Hinduism in general is the fact that the many different forms of Hinduism—from the animist to the monist—coexist peacefully in India.

Although the *Rig Veda* is the oldest accepted sacred work, Hindu mythology and theology are mostly derived from the Sanskrit masterpieces the *Mahabharata* and the *Ramayana*. These epics, which were developed gradually from around 400 B.C. to A.D. 400, relate the exploits of many deities, especially Brahma and his two main avatars, Vishnu and Shiva. Another important source for Hindu mystical beliefs and mythology is the *Puranas*, which are later Sanskrit treatises that deal with legends, religious practices, holy places, and so on.

The central Hindu deity is Brahma, the god of creation and birth. Brahma's two godly avatars—Vishnu, the god of preservation, and Shiva, the god of destruction—round out what is known as the Hindu trinity (called the *trimurti*). This triad dealt with the salvation of the human soul. Hindu worship incorporates a fundamental belief in reincarnation. Brahma created a universe that functioned in continuous cycles. Everything, even the gods, is believed to be subject to this cyclical pattern.

The early Hindus also developed a rigid caste system, which was derived in part from the concept of reincarnation. It was believed that man was born to fulfill certain predestined positions in society; he had specific duties to perform. According to the mythology, the first members of these castes originated from Brahma's own body. Brahmans and *Kshatriyas* were the top two castes. The Brahmans were the priests and teachers. They spoke and listened to the gods and performed

religious acts and sacrifices. Kshatriyas were usually members of the royal families, the ruling class, and were trained to be warriors. Their duty was to protect the people by using their military powers justly and wisely. The third caste, *Vaisyas*, comprised the merchants and farmers. The members of the fourth and lowest caste, *Sudras*, were born to serve the other castes. Aside from this strict system of hierarchy, there were those known as the Untouchables. These people carried out the tasks that were considered unclean. They were the hunters, fishermen, and builders, as well as the undertakers, who dealt with the cremation of corpses. (Mahatma Gandhi, the visionary civil rights leader, abolished the connotation of "untouchability" in the Constitution of India, written in 1950.)

According to the law of reincarnation, the manner in which one conducts one's life determines whether one rises or falls in the caste system when reborn. (It was believed that one was reincarnated approximately 82,000 times.) Someone who leads a virtuous life may eventually become a Brahman. Finally, the virtuous Brahman will be released from the cycle of earthly life and ushered into the heavenly world of eternal peace and knowledge known as *Brahmalok*, or "the domain of Brahma." On the Hindu map, Brahmalok was believed to exist at the apex of Mount Meru, north of the Himalayas.

The early Hindus believed that India was a universe unto itself, that its physical being was shaped and controlled by the gods. Because of this perspective, the world at large was considered to be an illusion that had been created by the gods. Accordingly, there were many mythological lands such as Brahmalok. For example, below the surface of India was a hell, called *Patala*, ruled by Yama, the king of the dead, and populated by the serpentine Nagas. By contrast, there also existed a paradise, *Vaikuntha*, that was the traditional dwelling place of Krishna. There were also many other realms that were associated with the gods.

Although in practice traditional Hindu rituals and legends are passed on from one generation to the next, the roots of India's rich mythological and religious heritage are to be found in the ancient Sanskrit texts. The *Rig Veda*, a composite of 1,028 hymns, contains tales of the elemental Vedic gods, including the three chief deities—Indra, Vivasvat, and Agni—and many other inferior gods. Indra, the king of the gods, was subject only to Brahma. Storms, thunder, lightning, and rain were at Indra's command. Vivasvat, the god of the sun, rode throughout the day sky in a shimmering chariot of gold drawn by seven ruddy horses. Agni, god of fire, was the mediator between the gods and humankind.

The Puranas were sacred poems that described the lives and exploits of the gods. For the most part, these texts contained stories told in verse, each section titled with the name of the god or avatar in question. In later times, *Tantras*, also in verse form, were written. The Tantras were religious poems that

This rendering of an episode from the *Bhagavata Purana*, sacred Sanskrit poems (the most important of which were written during the period between A.D. 300 and 1200), depicts Krishna during the "hour of cowdust." The painting is part of the considerable collection of Hindu art at the National Museum in New Delhi.

supplemented the older Puranas and instructed worshipers in how to perform modern ceremonies. The Tantras were written around the Middle Ages, when worship of the mother goddess Devi (Devi was the personification of the union of Shiva and his wife) increased. The "Devi-Mahatmya" was the Sanskrit poem written in her honor.

One of the greatest Sanskrit epics, and the longest single poem in world literature, is the *Mahabharata*. This eighteen-book work is the foundation of Hindu mythology and the major source of knowledge of classical Indian civilization. The *Mahabharata* contains approximately 200,000 lines compiled by many authors over hundreds of years. The

great text deals primarily with dynastic struggle and civil war, and recounts stories about mystical events and great battles. It includes the *Bhagavad-Gita*, or "Song of God," which is the most widely read and studied gospel in Hindu ritual. The *Mahabharata* also has a firm moral and philosophical base that dictates many religious and political laws.

The *Ramayana*, of epic size (but much smaller than the *Mahabharata)*, was composed by the master poet Valmiki. It tells the story of Rama, the seventh incarnation of Vishnu.

The religious and philosophical tracts known as the *Upanishads* are yet another source of Indian thought. Composed by various authors beginning in the seventh century B.C., the Upanishads are prose treatises that deal with (among other issues) the individual's soul (*atman*) and its relationship with the collective universal soul (*brahman*).

There are many other sources for the rich mythological and religious traditions of India, not the least of which is the living body of lore passed on from one generation to the next. The result of having so many sources—not to mention the many sects—is that there are innumerable variations of the same stories. The canon is rife with conflicting details, which serves only to enrich further a stock of tales that, after all, features many entities whose natures likewise encompass certain polarities (Shiva, for instance, is known as both creator and destroyer).

The philosophies of Buddhism and Jainism also contributed to and were influenced by Hinduism. Although both Buddhism and Jainism are atheistic at their cores, and embrace all people despite their castes, they nonetheless borrow from the vast palette of Hindu mythology to paint metaphorical and allegorical tales. Similarly, many of the tenets of Buddhism and Jainism (e.g., purification through leading a "good" life) are expressed in ancient Hindu texts and in the living religion.

Although India has remained mostly Hindu, around A.D. 600 the Islamic faith began to take hold. The regions known as Pakistan and Bangladesh separated from India because Islam (which is monotheistic) could not coexist with Hinduism (which is polytheistic), Buddhism, or Jainism.

OPPOSITE: This scene from the *Ramayana*, a 50,000-line poem about Vishnu's most popular avatar, Rama Chandra, depicts Rama, Lakshmana, and Visvamitra. Rendered in 1750, this painting is in the National Museum in New Delhi.

This sandstone carving of the Hindu triad (called the *trimurti*) depicts Shiva, Vishnu, and Brahma. It is part of the Temple of Shiva, on the island Elephanta, and dates from the seventh or eighth century A.D.

THE SUPREME GODS

BRAHMA

Brahma, being one with Vishnu and Shiva, represented the creative force. According to legend, Brahma was born from the seed of his will. He was the primeval essence, the collective soul of the universe and the personification of everything in the universe. Brahma created the first egg, *hiranyagarbha*, the first object of creation and life. Having emerged from the egg without cracking it, Brahma, now physical, divided the egg. One quarter became man and one quarter became woman. A third piece became heaven and the fourth became earth. His first male incarnation was known as Purusha, the cosmic man, and his first female incarnation was Prakriti, nature. (According to other versions, Brahma himself split into a female and a male who together created the earth's people.)

In the continuous cycle, when Brahma breathed out (*sa*) the universe was created; when Brahma breathed in (*ham*), the universe was destroyed. Between breaths, the world existed for two billion years, a cycle within the cycle. After souls were reborn 82,000 times they entered an exalted state, where they received eternal wisdom and knowledge.

Brahma had four faces (a fifth was burned off by Shiva when Brahma spoke in a condescending manner to him). Brahma is depicted carrying in his four arms a vase, a bow, a rosary for prayer, and a copy of the *Rig Veda*. His wife was Sarasvati, also called Brahmi, the goddess of learning and music. Brahma was responsible for creating the elements—sun, moon, wind, water, and fire—and the gods who rule them.

VISHNU

Vishnu was the preserver, the restorer, and god of the sun. He may have been the most important figure in Hindu mythology. Many of Vishnu's followers claim that it was he who created the universe and not Brahma. (Although it may seem irrelevant whether the universe was created by Brahma or one of his incarnations, it is not: Hindu deities, despite the fact that they are all avatars [to some degree] of Brahma, are distinct entities, each capable of independent and even conflicting activity. Furthermore, different sects of worshipers attribute certain actions [like the creation of the universe] to the deity they favor.)

Of course, Brahma and Vishnu are also very closely linked—they are both part of *sat*, "that which is." Along with Shiva, they comprised the *trimurti* (the "three in one"); this triumvirate is responsible for creating the world. The prefix *vish* means "to pervade." His pervading powers have been recognized in each of his ten incarnations, which were usually in human or animal form. In some incarnations he was born from woman, while in others he arose by supernatural means. The avatars of Vishnu always appeared in the world to right wrongs and to save humanity from disaster.

Depictions of Vishnu often show him with blue skin, holding in his four hands a conch, a discus, a club, and a lotus. He rode the great sunbird, Garuda, who was also his trusted messenger.

As Matsya, his first incarnation, Vishnu took the form of a fish to save man from a deluge. As Kurma, his second incarnation, he took the form of a turtle and assisted in the churning of the ocean (from which activity several divine beings, not to mention an ambrosia of immortality, arose). In the form of a boar, Varaha, he again saved earth from a devastating flood. Narasimha, his fourth avatar, was half man and half lion. In this mythical form, Vishnu fought and defeated Hiranyakashipu, a demon-king strong enough to force Indra, the sky god, from his throne.

As Vamana, his fifth incarnation, Vishnu assumed the guise of a dwarf. His task was to regain control over the three worlds that were then ruled by the demon-king Bali. One day when Bali was offering a sacrifice, Vamana—also a Brahman priest—asked the demon-king for a boon.

"I ask you for a little patch of earth, as much as I can measure with three of my strides."

Bali agreed. The dwarf then grew into a cosmic giant and in two strides crossed the universe. With the third stride he stepped on the demon's head, defeating him. Not being a vengeful God, Vishnu banished the demon to rule a part of Patala.

In his sixth incarnation, Vishnu took the form of a Brahman, Parashu-Rama, who was both a holy man and a warrior. He came to earth, on the gods' behalf, to lessen the power of the Kshatriyas, the ruling class. He used his advanced knowledge of weaponry and his supreme mind to complete his task.

In the epic *Ramayana*, Vishnu was incarnated as Rama Chandra, the son of King Dasa-ratha of Oudh, Sri Lanka. King Dasa-ratha was very devoted to Brahma and had acquired extraordi-

This exquisite eighth-century bronze statue of Vishnu shows the deity holding various sacred items and making a gesture of benediction with one of his right hands.

nary supernatural powers. The gods felt that the king had too much power and they appealed to Vishnu for help. Vishnu, as always, heeded the words of the gods and appeared before the king bearing a gift: a pot of nectar for the king's wives to drink. Dasa-ratha gave half the drink to his wife Kausalya, and she gave birth to Rama Chandra, who had half the divine essence of Vishnu. A quarter of the nectar was given to the king's second wife, Kaikey, and she gave birth to Rama's brother Bharata. Finally, the last quarter of the nectar was given to his wife Su-mitra, who gave birth to Lakshmana and Batru-ghna. Each of these children was instilled with some portion of Vishnu's essence and thus each was more powerful than the king.

Sage Visvamitra took Rama, at this point a young man, to perform two tasks. The first was to defeat a female demon who had been plaguing the countryside. For the second, Vishvamitra brought Rama to the court of Janaka, king of Videha. Rama instantly fell in love with the king's daughter, Sita. The king had decided that he would marry off his daughter to the winner of a contest of strength. The king had a sacred bow that belonged to Shiva. Offering up the bow to the contestants, the king announced that the man who could bend the bow would win his daughter's hand.

Not surprisingly, none of the suitors could bend the bow except for Rama, who not only bent it but broke it in half. Rama and Sita were married, and were very happy until Sita was abducted by Ravana, the most powerful demon in the universe. Rama, along with his faithful brother Lakshmana and the resourceful monkey god, Hanuman, relentlessly pursued his wife's captor. Many heroic adventures ensued until Rama was finally reunited with his wife.

Whenever Vishnu was incarnated on earth, he was always reunited with his heavenly wife, Lakshmi. In the story from the *Ramayana*, Lakshmi was Sita. Together, Vishnu and Lakshmi represent the ideal marriage of one man to one woman.

The eighth and most popular incarnation of Vishnu was Krishna, the hero of the *Mahabharata* (and more notably the *Bhagavad-Gita*, which attests to his divinity). Krishna was born the eighth child of Devaki, wife of Vasudeva. Devaki had been impris-

ABOVE: This eighteenth-century painting depicts the birth of Krishna to Devaki.

RIGHT: Krishna, one of the most popular incarnations of Vishnu, ravishes a Gopi, or cowherd's wife, in this nineteenth-century painting.

OPPOSITE: Krishna, who was revered for his talents as a musician and dancer as much as for his martial skill, plays the flute and leads four dancers in this painting from the National Museum in New Delhi.

oned by the powerful demon-king Kansa because it had been foretold that a son born to Devaki would defeat the evil ruler. When Krishna was born, Vasudeva smuggled the infant out with Vishnu's help. To conceal Krishna's identity from the horrible Kansa, Vasudeva exchanged babies with Yasoda, a country woman who had given birth at the same time as Devaki had. When Kansa found that Krishna had survived, he sent six demons to find and kill the child. Every one of these dark minions failed in the task.

As Krishna grew into a man, he had many adventures and destroyed many demons, but one of the most important stories associated with this incarnation of Vishnu was the tale of the Gopis. Krishna was a gifted flute player,

and every time he began to play, the Gopis (the cowherds' wives) dropped their work and came running. For as long as he played, the women would dance. Some believed that

Many cosmologies
purport that the
universe began as
an egg, usually the
divine creation of
one of the members
of the *trimurti*
(depending on the
particular sect).
This arresting
nineteenth-century
painting, which
is part of the
collection at the
Victoria and Albert
Museum, shows
Krishna in cosmic
form, embodying
the substance of
the universe.

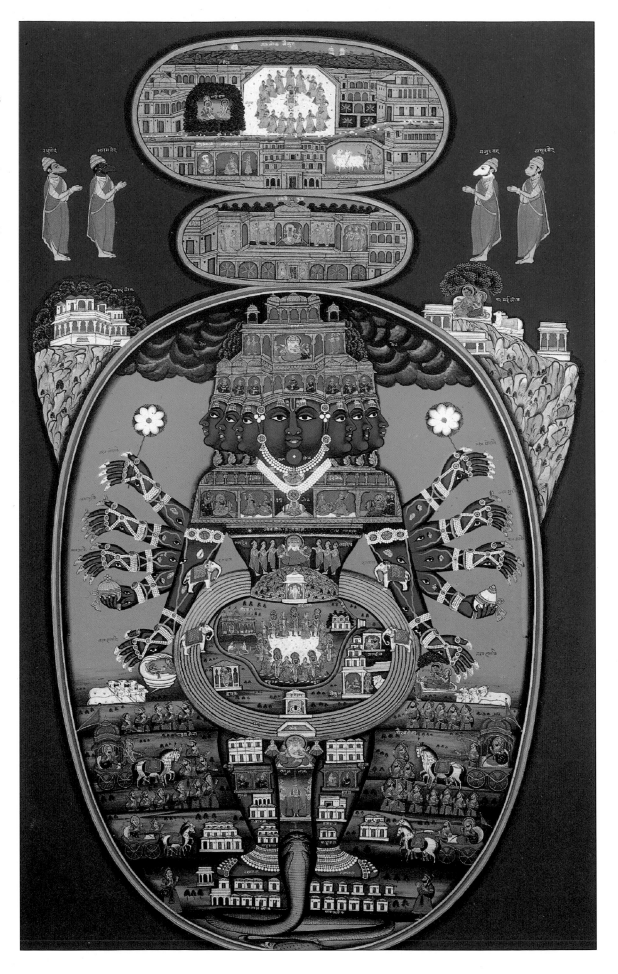

many orgiastic affairs occurred between the god and these married women, but others believed it was a very innocent—and indeed, symbolic—association. In fact, the relationship Krishna had with the Gopis is sometimes thought to be representative in Hinduism of the soul's relationship to the divine. By playing the flute, Krishna expressed his divinity. The women, in turn, expressed their selfless devotion (one of the two paths, in addition to self-knowledge, to self-realization) by dropping whatever they were doing and dancing to the music, which was an extension of the god. Appropriately, Krishna the demon-slayer is also the god of dance and music.

According to the beliefs of both Hinduism and Buddhism the ninth incarnation of Vishnu was the sage Buddha. The tenth and final avatar of Vishnu is Kalki. This, the final appearance of Vishnu during this cycle of the universe, has yet to come, but when this avatar arises he will appear in the form of a white horse.

SHIVA

Shiva, the third god of the *trimurti*, was the god of destruction. According to many beliefs he was also the god of the moon and the Himalayas. Shiva is often depicted (encircled by flames representing his divine powers) dancing the cosmic dance, moving to the rhythm of the universe. He is portrayed with blue skin (like his counterpart Vishnu), four arms, and four faces with three eyes each. The third eye, located in the middle of each forehead, possessed the supernatural power both to destroy and create. He wore the fur of a tiger and a scarf of snakeskin.

Shiva sat alone on the top of Mount Kailasa in the Himalayas, contemplating and meditating. Shiva was an ascetic and the god of the yogis (religious men who practice the power of mind over body). He was also known as Rudra, the howling one, the god of storms.

Rudra was the Vedic antecedent to Shiva, whose identity is intertwined with that of his Vedic forerunner.

The golden lines that radiated from Shiva's third eye symbolize destruction—not complete annihilation, but a waning, such as the end of the day or the coming of autumn—death for the sake of rebirth. Once, Shiva's wife Shakti (or Parvati) playfully covered his eyes. Everything in the universe went black, like a void. He opened his third eye, and order returned.

This painting, which was completed between 1760 and 1770, shows Shiva and Krishna attended by a bull, a tiger, and jackals. It is also housed in the Victoria and Albert Museum.

FAR LEFT: Bordering on Pakistan, the Rajasthan region of India is the home of many famous Hindu temples of worship. This beautiful and isolated temple is in the middle of Holy Lake.

LEFT: This stone lingam (a stylized phallic symbol associated with Shiva) illustrates the masculine principle of the universe. The female parallel of this type of representation is called a *yoni*.

Besides being the god of destruction, Shiva was also the god of the forest, the god of hunting and fishing, and therefore ruler of the Untouchables.

Shiva and his wife, Parvati, symbolize the ideal union—he is meditative, she is creative. They are two in one, calm and chaos, like life itself. Parvati's creative powers are evident in the tale of Ganesha, her son.

Once, when Shiva went away, Parvati created a boy from clay because she was lonely. She ordered him to stand guard while she bathed. It was at this time that Shiva returned home. He went to see his wife but was stopped by the boy. Enraged, Shiva cut the boy's head off. Parvati was stricken with grief. Upon seeing his wife weep, Shiva sent out his beasts to find a head that could replace the missing one. They came back with the head of a young elephant. He put the new head onto the boy's body and presented the ele-

phant-headed boy to his wife. She was overjoyed. The boy became Shiva's son. In Hindu mythology, the elephant was a character of great wisdom and knowledge. Ganesha became the god of wisdom.

One of the best-known tales about Shiva is also one of the creation myths. Meeting upon a sacred mountain, the gods decided to churn the ocean in order to refine from it the ambrosia of immortality. At this time the demons and gods were not yet enemies, so they worked together to stir up the ocean using a giant turtle mounted on the tip of an uprooted mountain. They spun this gargantuan churning device by using the enormous serpent Vasuki as the spinning cord. Various divine objects and entities were generated by this activity, as were many features of the world. Finally, the ambrosia was created, at which point Vasuki began to suffer from all the wear on his body, spewing poison everywhere from his one thousand mouths. Implored by Vishnu to save the universe, Shiva took the poison into his throat, which consequently turned blue. (The gods kept the ambrosia, which infuriated the demons, giv-

ing rise to an immense battle and the undying conflict between god and demon.) Because of his swallowing the poison, Shiva is sometimes known as Nilakantha, "blue throat." Shiva was also the patron of the demons.

OTHER
HINDU GODS

There are many other deities in the Hindu pantheon, some of whom were native to the Indus valley and some of whom arrived with the Aryan invaders; many of course became composites of the indigenous and the foreign traditions. These gods were, like the universe, subject to the eternal cycle. They died and were reborn with the universe. They were seen as part of creation, part of the universe, but not creators themselves. Below are described several of the most important remaining Hindu gods and goddesses.

INDRA

Indra was the supreme Vedic god, and tales about him fill the pages of the *Rig Veda*. He was the king of the gods and the most powerful of the three primary elemental deities. He controlled the

OPPOSITE: Flanked by his faithful mount, the sacred bull Nandi, Shiva sits in meditation. This seventeenth-century painting shows how the substance of the universe is believed by some Hindus to flow from Shiva's person.

LEFT: This intricate stone carving of Ganesha dates from the twelfth century. Ganesha is worshiped as the god of wisdom, good fortune, and prudence; he is also known as "the remover of obstacles."

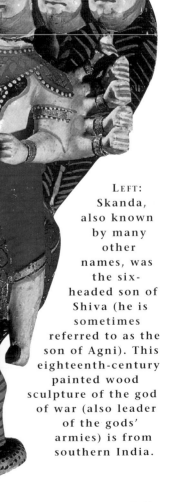

LEFT: Skanda, also known by many other names, was the six-headed son of Shiva (he is sometimes referred to as the son of Agni). This eighteenth-century painted wood sculpture of the god of war (also leader of the gods' armies) is from southern India.

rains and storms, dispensing them according to his whim. The lightning bolt was his weapon. He rode an elephant, a symbol of his wisdom and knowledge. His skin shone gold and his huge arms encompassed the skies. When Indra became the king of gods he created a heavenly domain known as Svarga.

Indra was the son of Dyaus-Pitri (Sky Father) and Prithvi-Matri (Earth Mother). Dyaus-Pitri and Prithvi-Matri were the parents of all the older Vedic gods as well as of the first humans. In Greek mythology, Indra's counterpart is Zeus. Both Indra and Zeus were the progeny of a union between earth and sky.

Indra's wife was Indrani, the goddess of the sky. Although he had many illicit affairs, Indra shared his rule only with Indrani. One of Indra's most noted love affairs was with sage Gautama's daughter Ahalya. Indra, who had the power to change into any form, transformed himself into the likeness of the sage

LEFT: Located on the shores of Lake Garisar in Jaisalmer, Rajasthan, India, this magnificent temple of worship reflects in its splendor and construction the rich Hindu heritage of religion, philosophy, and science.

and seduced the all-too-willing Ahalya. Gautama caught the god as the latter was sneaking away after the tryst. The sage was so enraged with Indra for using his daughter that he visited a curse of impotence upon the god. As soon as the words of the curse were spoken, Indra's testicles dropped off and fell to the ground. Terrified, Indras asked his fellow deities to help him restore his virility. The gods replaced Indra's departed privates with the testicles of a ram.

Vritra (or Ahi), the serpent of drought, was Indra's archenemy. The two battled long and hard (and often), but Indra was always victorious (often winning battles in underhanded fashion). According to the *Rig Veda*, many other fights ensued between Indra and other demons bent on destroying the earth and the rule of the gods. These fights were symbolic of the eternal conflict between good and evil. The defeat of Vritra by Indra is one of the central episodes of the *Rig Veda*.

AGNI

Indra's brother, Agni, the god of fire, was the second of the three chief Vedic gods. He was omnipresent. A friend of humankind, Agni was the mediator be-

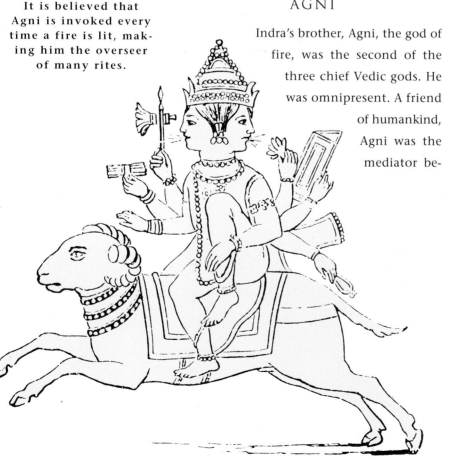

Agni, the Vedic god of fire and Indra's brother, was another of the elemental gods. It is believed that Agni is invoked every time a fire is lit, making him the overseer of many rites.

tween human and god. Agni had red skin, with two faces and seven tongues. His mount was a ram, another symbol of fire.

As the god of fire, Agni was essential to the practice of ritual sacrifice. When an offering was made to the gods, Agni, with all seven of his tongues, would lick the butter from the altar and then bring the essence of the burnt sacrifice to the heavens. All altars honoring the fire god were built to face the southeast, the direction of the sunrise, which was associated with Agni.

Agni created fire for cooking and for clearing the fields for farming. As the god of purification, he was responsible for cleansing corpses on the funeral pyre and taking their souls to heaven. He also united the bride and groom in the Hindu marriage ceremony when they encircled the sacred flame seven times. All uses of fire, beneficial or destructive, were associated with Agni.

The *Rig Veda* cites Agni as the father of Skanda, the general of the god's armies. In later Hindu myths, especially those related in the Puranas, Skanda is the son of Shiva.

VIVASVAT

Vivasvat, the third chief Vedic deity, was the god of the sun. Although many gods were associated with the sun (including Vivasvat's brother Agni, whose fire made up the sun, and the great Vishnu), Vivasvat was the central solar deity. He had a copper-colored body and rode through the sky on his chariot, which was drawn by seven ruddy horses. When he was not traveling across the heavens, Vivasvat resided in the golden city of Vivasvati. He was a nurturing deity and was often called upon for successful crops. Whenever Vivasvat was unhappy, he created the oppressive heat that caused the fields to become barren and the riverbeds to dry up.

Sanjana, Vivasvat's wife, married him despite the fact that he was made of fire and in-

tense heat. One day when Vivasvat was at his brightest, Sanjana came to him; he leaned over to kiss her, but she held up her arms and stepped away in fear—he was radiating too much heat. Vivasvat was so insulted and hurt by her response to his amorous overture that he cursed their children, Manu, Yama, and Yamuna. Manu was forced to leave the heavens and wait until the next age of men (that is, the current age), when he would become the father of humankind. Yama was banished to the underworld, where he became the king of the dead, and their daughter, Yamuna, was turned into a river.

Some tales say the Ashvins, the heavenly twins, were also Vivasvat's sons. They were the first to ride the morning sky, preceding their sister, Ushas, the dawn, and their father, the sun. The twins were bearers of medicine and could grant the gift of eternal youth.

YAMA

Yama, the god of death, was the least popular of the Vedic gods. He is depicted with green skin, mounted on a buffalo. In one of his four hands he carries a mace, in another a noose.

Most importantly, Yama is the judge of the dead. According to some tales, he may have been the first man, and hence the first to die. Being the first man to reach the afterlife, he founded the City of the Dead, Yamapua. Yama's sister, Yamuna, was also his wife. All inferior gods feared Yama, because they too could die.

At the gate to Yama's domain two vicious dogs, with four eyes each, guarded against any attack. Past these terrifying sentries, souls were met by Chitragupta, the registrar of the dead. He notified Yama of the soul and its mortal deeds. Yama then passed judgment on the soul, deciding whether it would be reborn, go to heaven, or enter into one of the twenty-one hells.

VAYU

Vayu, the god of storms, was often associated with Indra. Vayu alone made up the air and wind. He was without substance and at all

places at all times. Although the deer was his mount he often shared Indra's chariot as they rode through the sky. Vayu was also worshiped as the god of breath. According to legend, in a fit of rage he blew off the top of Mount Meru and hurled it into the ocean, creating what is now known as Sri Lanka.

Vayu also fathered Hanuman, the monkey god. Hanuman was the great assistant to Rama Chandra in the Ramayana. For instance, Hanuman located the captured Sita and reported her whereabouts to Rama. Hanuman was also instrumental in Sita's rescue. For all his help, Hanuman was granted eternal youth by Rama.

Although Hanuman was depicted as a monkey with human characteristics, he was capable of changing his shape and size. Being the son of the wind, he could fly. Hanuman was also known as a healer, and it was he who found the medicinal herbs that healed wounded soldiers. He was also a master of poetry and science.

VARUNA

Varuna, the god of night skies and the oceans, was responsible for the shape and brightness of the moon. Varuna helped ships find their way in the night, and it was he who put the stars in their places. Like his Greek counterpart, Poseidon, Varuna was usually depicted riding a dolphin across the ocean surface.

Varuna was also the Vedic god of honesty. He detested falsehood and generally inflicted disease, especially dropsy, upon offenders. In the Vedic pantheon Varuna was also the god of the West.

PUSHAN

Pushan, the god of nourishment, gave man cattle. Since he was a toothless god, offerings of gruel were made to him. (It was said that he insulted the great Shiva and was hit in the mouth, thereby losing his teeth.) Pushan's chariot was drawn by male goats. He was the guide for travelers and protected them on their journeys.

SOMA

Soma, the god of the moon, was also known as Chandra. He sent the morning dew. "Soma" was also the name of the ambrosia of the gods, the elixir that sustained immortality. Since the ambrosia was considered an intoxicant, Soma himself was associated with drunkenness, as was his Greek counterpart, Dionysus. He rode through the night sky in a chariot drawn by ten pure white horses. Some said the moon was inhabited by a hare and thus all hares were looked upon as incarnations of Soma.

KAMA

Kama, the god of love, was similar to the Greek Eros. He was the son of Lakshmi, the goddess of good fortune. Once Parvati sent Kama to arouse her husband, Shiva, from a deep meditation. Shiva was startled by the little god and opened his third eye. Kama was caught in the devastating beam that was emitted from the eye, and his form was destroyed. He was henceforth without physical form. His invisibility was suited to the emotion he represented, love—also a force unseen. When two people came together in union, Kama was there. He rode a wise parrot and carried a sugarcane bow with a string of bees and flower-tipped shafts.

Soma, the god of the moon (and the deity associated with an ancient rite known by the same name that involved an intoxicating drink also of the same name), rides a chariot drawn by an antelope.

THE
GODDESSES

Many sects worshiped the powerful goddesses of the Hindu pantheon. Many sects believe that these female deities were, in fact, stronger than the gods. The most often worshiped (and the most powerful) goddesses were the wives of the gods Brahma, Vishnu, and Shiva. The other goddesses, usually the wives of the Vedic gods, were not stronger but were nonetheless influential. Besides, the goddesses could ask their husbands for favors—which were rarely denied.

It is impossible to overstress the importance of the goddesses. Many sects regarded these deities as more approachable and more connected to the human experience than their male counterparts.

SHAKTI

Shakti, the mother goddess, was also commonly referred to as Sati, Parvati, Devi, Kali, and Durga. Shakti was the wife of Shiva and the goddess of wisdom. She helped guide Shiva in his sacred tasks and decisions.

As her incarnation Sati, she was the daughter of the demigod Daksha, who was Brahma's son and the personification of eternal rebirth (he died with every generation, and was reborn with each new one). Daksha was unhappy when Sati married Shiva, and slandered the god and berated his daughter. Sati could not take the incessant ridiculing, so she threw herself upon a funeral pyre. Sati's suicide was viewed as an act performed by the perfect wife, who died for her husband's honor. Without the presence of Sati, Shiva fell into a great depression and the universe became disordered.

Sati was reborn into a fishing community. She was named Parvati at birth and was fully aware, as are all incarnate gods, that her right-

OPPOSITE: Kali, one of the incarnations of Shakti, is feared as the goddess of death and vengeance. This fifteenth-century painted wood sculpture from Trivandrum, India, is a particularly gruesome depiction (notice the vicious clawed hand in the foreground).

LEFT: This early nineteenth-century painting depicts the rock-solid union between Shiva and Parvati; around them is the holy family, including Ganesha, Skanda, and Nandi. In the foreground are most of the other major deities in the Hindu pantheon as well as several worshipers.

ful place was in the heavens. Shiva, unaware of her birth, had a vision of his wife that instilled confidence that she would return. He resumed his meditation. Parvati tried to gain the attention of her husband, but he was too deep in thought. She prayed intensely and eventually acquired the help of Kama (the god of love). With Kama's help, she succeeded in getting his attention, and she and Shiva were reunited.

When Shiva and his wife are a single being, they are together called Devi. Devi is the male and female united in one form, representing the ideal union. Devi was the name

RIGHT: This magnificent bronze sculpture represents Devi, the unified conception of Shiva and Shakti, who are considered to have a perfect union. Understandably, Devi features both male and female characteristics. This thirteenth-century artifact is housed in the National Museum in New Delhi.

FAR RIGHT: This vibrant Punjabi watercolor depicts Durga, the warrior avatar of Shakti, slaying a demon. Typically, she is riding her lion mount and wielding several weapons. This painting is part of the collection at the Victoria and Albert Museum.

usually used in praise of the goddess. A great poem that was composed for the goddess (and some say written by the goddess) was known as "Devi-Mahatmya."

Another, fiercer incarnation of Sati was Kali. Shiva, the patron god of the demons, was usually depicted in his meditative state, calm and serene. By contrast, Shiva's wife Kali took

on characteristics of the demon, and was both fierce and vengeful. Kali was a dark and sinister incarnation. She was black as night and had a long red tongue. A truly frightening avatar, she wore a necklace of skulls and was praised as the goddess of death. Kali was capable of the same fury as the demon Rudra, the howling one.

Durga, Sati's warrior incarnation, closely associated with Kali, was known as a supreme goddess who held the universe in her womb. She radiated a yellow aura that glowed like the sun. Once when the gods were threatened by the giants Sumbha and Nisumbha, the deities turned to Shakti for help. As Durga she rode her lion into battle to protect the gods.

Shakti, of all the deities, demanded the most respect. She was the goddess of physical illusion; the goddess of life and death; the perfect wife; and a deadly warrior. Her supremacy could not be denied. Shakti was the most versatile goddess.

LAKSHMI

Lakshmi was the goddess of love, luck, and wealth. She was probably one of the most beloved of the gods because she had compassion for everyone, regardless of their caste. She could be easily flattered with praises and

gifts. When worshipers went out of their way to gain her attention, Lakshmi almost always acknowledged the supplicants by granting them their wishes.

Lakshmi, the eternal wife of Vishnu, was incarnated every time her husband was. In

FAR LEFT: This Hindu painting from 1649 is an illustration of a scene from the *Ramayana*. It shows the wedding procession from Rama's marriage to Sita, one of the incarnations of Lakshmi, goddess of love and good fortune.

LEFT: Born from a lotus, Lakshmi sits in the meditative position that takes its name from the flower.

legend, they always meet and marry. When Vishnu was reincarnated as Rama, she was reincarnated as Sita; when he was Krishna, she was Rukmini.

Lakshmi was born from a lotus flower floating on the ocean; in fact, she was brought forth from the ocean during the great churning undertaken to obtain the ambrosia of immortality. No god could deny her magnificent beauty; she was forever young and had shining gold skin laced with pearls. All the gods and demons fell in love with her, but her love was given only to Vishnu, to the despair of all the others.

Some tales portray Lakshmi as a ceaseless wanderer, roaming all lands in search of gifts and sacrifices to her. She was associated with good crops and thus good fortune. Her fellowship with the land made her the goddess of agriculture, and when one had a good crop, it was partly her doing.

Yakshini, goddess of
the woods, eighth
to tenth century,
Gyaraspur, India.

SARASVATI

Sarasvati was the goddess of learning. She was associated with the arts and sciences. As Vak, she was acknowledged as the creator of speech, including the holy Sanskrit language. All the poets and musicians praised her name, for she was responsible for giving them the fundamentals of their craft. As the wife of Brahma, Sarasvati was known as Brahmi and resided with the supreme deity in the heavenly Brahmalok.

Sarasvati—depicted as eternally young and beautiful, with four arms—had great power over her husband. When Brahma took a second wife, Brahmi (Sarasvati) was furious. Brahmi cursed Brahma as well as Vishnu, Shiva, and Indra. She said to her husband that he would fall out of man's favor, and would thus not be worshiped as widely or as often as he was accustomed. To Vishnu she said he would be reincarnated ten times. Finally, Sarasvati cursed Shiva with impotency, and foretold of Indra's defeat and the eventual loss of his kingdom.

Sarasvati favored the world of mortals and often walked among them. The mythical Sarasvati River was named for her. The swan was her favorite bird and she often rode upon an enormous swan.

OTHER IMPORTANT GODDESSES

There are many other significant goddesses in the Hindu pantheon. All of these deities seem to have direct correlations with the workings of nature. Earth itself was personified by the goddess Prithvi. She was the mother of all the gods, and was kind, loving, and gentle. Prithvi's daughter, Ushas, was the goddess of dawn as well as of poetry. Maya, the goddess of physical reality and illusion, had characteristics associated with many different gods. Maya shared her traits of versatility with the goddess Shakti. Yakshini was the playful goddess of the forest, and she frequently tried to trick travelers into losing their way. Finally, looming above the earth was the queen of the sky, Indrani. She was Indra's radiant and everlastingly happy wife.

HINDU SERPENTS AND DEMONS

There were two forms of serpents, the Anantas and the Nagas. Both had important roles in the functions of the universe. The Anantas, referred to as the Endless Ones, were the world serpents. They made up the mythological islands to the south of India. The Anantas also aided the gods in the churning of the ocean, at which time the universe was created and many things assumed their roles in the cosmic order.

The king of the Anantas, Shesha, was the floating island upon which the great Vishnu rested. Shesha's thousand heads sheltered the god when he slept, representing a mutual respect. Shesha's venom was very poisonous:

the slightest drop from his mouth could cause mass destruction. It was believed that when one of his heads yawned, an earthquake rattled the earth.

The Nagas, closely associated with the Anantas, were also snakelike in form, but had human faces. They inhabited Patala (one of the many hells), where they answered only to Yama and Shiva. Other tales portrayed the Nagas as completely different from the Anantas; they were depicted as water deities that inhabited rivers, oceans, and lakes. It was believed that their daughters were very beautiful and often mistaken for divine humans.

ABOVE: This tenth-century carving, a detail from the Gatashrama Temple in Mathura, shows Vishnu in the meditative position. He sometimes made his home on the back of one of the Anantas.

LEFT: This seventeenth-century painting from Rajasthan is a miniature depicting Vishnu and Lakshmi riding on the back of an Ananta between two periods of cosmic evolution, destruction and creation. Many of the other deities in the Hindu pantheon are depicted, also waiting for the genesis of the new order.

The Nagas also had the duty of guarding shrines. Their forms were usually engraved in the pillars.

Demons were usually symbols of evil, or at least maliciousness. They were a nuisance to man, often causing conflict or disease. They were depicted as horrible in form, some with beastlike and some with human characteristics. The gods were involved in many conflicts with demons, and were sometimes defeated by them. Demons could be very powerful, and always had to be watched. They were ruled by Shiva, who had compassion for them

despite their evil dispositions. Demons played a vital role in the storytelling of Hindu mythology by providing dramatic tension.

There are many demons who affected man and god. The breed of Asura, the "anti-gods," were renowned for the trouble they caused the gods. The vicious Rakshasas, ruled by Ravana, were responsible for kidnapping Vishnu's wife. Ravana, who had ten heads, twenty arms, and huge fangs, was finally defeated by Vishnu's incarnation as Rama Chandra. Vishnu had been incarnated many times for the purpose of defeating demons. Another archenemy of Vishnu, Bana, had one thousand arms and was a very skillful warrior. The intervention of Shiva saved Bana from Vishnu's wrath.

The race of cannibalistic demons known as Dakini served the goddess Kali. They were savage and were often depicted with blood dripping from their mouths. Daitya, the race

of giant demons, challenged the gods many times and would have succeeded in defeating them if it hadn't been for the might of Durga, the warrior goddess.

Other demons interfered directly with the lives of mortals. The Bhuta were ghosts who misled people by mysteriously changing recognizable things in the night. It was believed that the Bhuta were once humans who died violently and consequently came to resent the living. The forest dwellers, Yakshas, also deceived men, usually by taking the form of beautiful women. Mortal men would pursue these delicious visions, but once the men had been lured deep into the forest, the Yakshas would turn into trees and leave the men lost and hopeless.

HOLY
MEN

India was the birthplace of several important religions and philosophies besides Hinduism, including Buddhism and Jainism. These belief systems are similar in that they promote self-awareness and self-betterment through specific actions. They are also similar in that each was institutionalized because of the determination of a visionary individual. Naturally, there were other important thinkers besides Buddha and Mahavira, but they were two of the most influential.

BUDDHA

Gautama Siddhartha was born in northern India in the year 566 B.C. His mother, Queen Maya of Kapilavastu, had a dream in which a white elephant floated down from the heavens on a rain cloud. The elephant circled her three times and then entered her womb on the right side of her body. Before Siddhartha was born, the sages predicted that Maya's son

would be a great holy man and not a ruler. When it was time for birth, Siddhartha emerged from Maya's right side without causing her pain. Seven days later, Maya died. When the boy took his first step, a lotus sprang where his foot touched the ground, a symbol of his holiness. Throughout Siddhartha's youth, his father sheltered him in luxury, fearful that his son would deny his royalty. At age sixteen, Siddhartha competed successfully in a contest, winning the hand of Princess Yasodhara. They had only one son, Rahula, before Gautama Siddhartha began his life's work.

On four occasions, the prince escaped the palace and explored the city. On each occasion he encountered a man whose experience was new to Siddhartha: the first was an old man, the second a sick man, the third a dead

This majestic statue of Buddha seated in a meditative stance atop a lotus flower is a fifth-century artifact that came from the northern region of India. Its discovery at a major Viking trading center in Helgo, Sweden, is a fascinating demonstration of how widespread the influence of Buddhism was.

man, and the fourth a religious man. Siddhartha was deeply moved by the human condition. As a result, he began to ponder humankind's condition. Seeing that earthly pleasures were temporal at best, he began to search for philosophical satisfaction with regard to humankind's plight. For six years Siddhartha sought enlightenment, experimenting with Brahmanic, Yogic, and ascetic religious practices.

Then in 531 B.C., the *bodhisattva* ("he who will undergo enlightenment") began to meditate under a pipal tree. Mara, the demon of death, feared that Siddhartha might achieve a state of salvation and pass on the information to humankind, ending suffering. Thus, Mara sent his seductive daughters to try to tempt the bodhisattva. Despite these diversions, Gautama remained in perfect peace and felt no sexual desire.

At the end of a period of seven days, Gautama Siddhartha had experienced his "awakening," which involved his appreciation of the Four Noble Truths. The first of these (and the kernel of Buddhist doctrine) is that all existence is suffering; the second is that the suffering has a cause; the third is that the suffering can come to an end; and the fourth is knowledge of the way in which the suffering can end. He had become Buddha, "the enlightened one."

Although Buddha had achieved the ability to look beyond his earthly self (enlightenment), he returned to the world and shared his wisdom instead of leaving his earthly form. He became a guru, teaching for forty-five years, and finally left his body at age eighty. His followers became known as Buddhists and brought his teachings to all of India. Eventually Buddhism spread to southeast Asia, where it firmly took root.

According to some Buddhist and Hindu legends, Buddha was the ninth incarnation of Vishnu (and many accounts of the sage's birth and life include references to the Vedic pantheon). The Buddhists believed that he was, in addition, one of a long line of Buddhas. The *Jataka* depicted these incarnations, of which there are 547 in all.

MAHAVIRA

Mahavira was born from semidivine means around the same time as Buddha. He was born the child of a Kshatriya family sometime in the early sixth century B.C. His mother, Trisala, after having divinely conceived, saw fourteen omens in her dreams. They were images of a white elephant, a white lion, and a white bull; the Jain goddess of good fortune, Sri; a garland of flowers; the moon and then

A canyon in Gwalior, India, is home to this dramatic set of twenty-two sculptures representing the first twenty-two of the twenty-four Jinas, or Jainist teachers. Rendered in the fifteenth century, these depictions were unique to northern India. They suffered mutilation in the early sixteenth century at imperial command, but were restored in later generations by loyal followers of Jainist doctrine.

the sun; a golden banner and then a vase; a lotus flower floating on a lake; the expansive ocean of milk; a palace; jewelry; and finally the sanctifying fire. Trisala's husband was blessed with good fortune after the embryo appeared in his wife's womb.

As a child, Mahavira saved his friends from an attacking serpent, and this noble feat earned him his name, which means "great hero." As the young hero grew to manhood, Mahavira denounced the pleasurable life and subsequently became an ascetic. For twelve years he meditated, until, like Buddha, he reached enlightenment. He was considered the twenty-fourth (and last) in a series of both legendary and real teachers of Jainism. Each of these teachers was known as Jina, or "conqueror" (that is, of the woes of existence). Mahavira then shared his wisdom and his principles with the people, and updated and consolidated the existing Jainist doctrine. Among other things, Mahavira taught that one could escape the eternal cycle of rebirth if one achieved enlightenment.

The Jainists did not acknowledge one supreme god, but did recognize a large company of lesser deities. Like human beings, these deities were subject to the principle of *karma*, which teaches that the effect of an action will be experienced by the person who performs that action either in a current or future incarnation. The gods, subject to the same requirement as humans, had to escape the karmic cycle by living in a virtuous fashion, thereby progressing toward salvation (the release of a soul that has no further karmic obligations).

The Jains believed that Mahavira, in life, was omniscient and of divine stature. During his final sermon, when everyone went to sleep, Mahavira died in the night, unseen by his followers. He had been meditating on a throne made of diamonds when he left his body, a mere shell, behind.

This magnificent Jain temple is nestled in the hilly region of Ranakpur, located in Rajasthan, India's largest state. Rajasthan houses many of India's ancient religious sites, including Bihar, the modern name for Magadha, which was the birthplace of both Buddhism and Jainism. Mahavira was born in Magadha and spent the majority of his life preaching in and around the region.

JAPANESE
MYTHOLOGY

Shinto, the "way of the gods," was the ancient native religion of Japan. A modified form of Shinto that is less a religion than a set of traditional customs is still in practice today. Shintoism emerged around 300 B.C., during a time of peace after many years of war among the clans. At this time, farming, and rice growing in particular, became the mainstay of Japanese life, so it is not surprising that in its early form, Shintoism dealt solely with agriculture. At its most basic level, Shintoism was a system of rituals and prayers for successful

Daibutsu ("great Buddha") are huge statues of the great sage, the largest of which is in Nara, near Tokyo. This daibutsu in Kamakura is over 42 feet (12.8m) high and weighs 103 tons (93t). It was rendered by Ono Goroemon, a famous sculptor of the Kamakura period.

BELOW: This thirteenth-century sculpture depicts a deity of hell holding a scroll. The Shinto underworld was believed to be a place of impurity and uncleanliness.

RIGHT: Shinto shrines, such as this one in Ise, are usually simple wooden structures that are believed to house the local *kami*, or spirits. Rituals of varying degrees of complexity, involving food, song, and dance, are performed in these shrines.

crops and, specifically, good rice harvests. Every town prayed to its own nature spirits and every family paid respect to the spirits of its ancestors. Eventually, when Japan was united under one ruling house, a common pantheon of gods was worshiped.

Like many early religions, Shintoism originated as worship of the forces of nature. Its rituals paid respect to nature for its nourishing effect and bowed to it for its destructive force. Eventually, this worship of nature evolved into a kind of pantheism, in which nature was seen to feature a host of spiritual beings, or *kami*, which controlled the elements, the terrain, the sky, and all the things below it, including the rice fields that were essential for survival.

As Shinto spread throughout the Japanese islands, it became more complex. Until the fifth century, however, when Chinese writing was introduced to Japan, the myths and practices of Shinto were transmitted orally.

The earliest text of recorded Shinto belief was the *Kojiki*, or *Record of Ancient Matters*. This text, completed in A.D. 712, upon the emperor's request, was divided into three chapters: "Life with the Gods,"

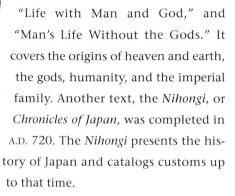

"Life with Man and God," and "Man's Life Without the Gods." It covers the origins of heaven and earth, the gods, humanity, and the imperial family. Another text, the *Nihongi*, or *Chronicles of Japan*, was completed in A.D. 720. The *Nihongi* presents the history of Japan and catalogs customs up to that time.

The *Kojiki* begins with the emergence of heaven and earth from the primeval chaos. It tells of the Heavenly Plain, where the kami first came into existence, and of the creation of the many islands of Japan.

Many of the tales told in the *Kojiki* focus on the twofold state of the spirit as being a mixture of pure and impure; one must struggle to overcome impurities in order to exist in harmony with the world. By living a pious life, humans could hope to achieve harmony with nature.

It is clear from the *Kojiki* that the kami, loosely translated as "spirit deities," were not considered gods in the Western sense. The great eighteenth-century scholar Motoori Norinaga described the kami as "anything whatsoever that was outside of the ordinary, which possessed superior power or was awe-inspiring." Thus the kami included the spirits of heaven and earth and of all the forms of nature, ancestors, nobles past and present, and, of course, the emperor and his family. Not necessarily immortal, Kami were sometimes recorded

as deceased. In addition, these spirits often were believed to have mothers and fathers—indeed, entire families.

As Shintoism became more formalized, shrines were built in praise of the kami. It was believed that within each shrine, the actual essence of the kami existed; the shrines were houses for the spirits. The most important city of Shinto worship was Ise, the "Mecca" of Japan. The three shrines of Ise, said to have been built in 4 B.C., are stunning examples of shrine architecture that can still be seen today. The holy shrine of Amaterasu, the sun goddess, still houses the Sacred Mirror, one of the three treasures of the imperial regalia.

In A.D. 522, Buddhism made its way to Japan from Korea. The Korean king sent the icon of the golden image of Buddha to the Japanese Emperor Kimmei. At first, the Japanese people looked upon the idol with great doubt and suspicion. It wasn't until Chinese Buddhism (which was laced with concepts taken from both Confucianism and Taoism) was introduced that the Japanese were willing to explore its precepts. After a period of experimental worship, the golden idol was accepted by a small part of society. By the early seventh century, Emperor Shotoku introduced Buddha to all of Japan. The Japanese Buddhists, or Zen Buddhists, later honored Shotoku as a bodhisattva (a Buddha-to-be).

Buddhism, originally exported from India, changed as it developed within each new region. In Japan, the Chinese form of Buddhism converged with Shintoism to become Zen Buddhism, a very extensive system of beliefs. Shinto deities were sometimes looked upon as avatars of Buddha and protectors of sacred temples. As Buddhism became the religion of the masses, shrines were still erected in Buddhist temples to honor the Shinto spirits. In the nineteenth century, after the Imperial Restoration, the state made a vigorous effort to restore Shintoism as the religion of the nation. After Japan's defeat in World War II, however, state-supported Shinto was officially discontinued. Today, sectarian Shinto thrives as a system of traditional customs and rituals.

Following are descriptions of the more important Shinto deities who were widely worshiped before the introduction of Buddhism. This information is derived from the *Kojiki* and the *Nihongi*, as well as from popular legend.

IZANAGI AND IZANAMI

According to the *Kojiki* and the *Nihongi*, two kami, the brother and sister Izanagi and Izanami, created the islands of Japan. They stood upon the heavenly Floating Bridge (or rainbow) and lowered the Jewelled Spear into the primeval substance below. When they re-

OPPOSITE PAGE: This slender bronze figurine of a bodhisattva was made during the Kamakura period. It is now part of the collection of the Museum of Oriental Art in Rome.

LEFT: Izanagi and Izanami, the first early spirits, stir the primeval substance to create land. The spear is called *Ame no tamaboko*, which means "celestial jewel spear."

BELOW: The Wedded Rocks at Futamigaura in Ise Bay are believed to have sheltered Izanagi and Izanami.

moved the spear, the brine dripped down off the spear's tip and formed an island. Izanagi, the "male who invites," and Izanami, the "female who invites," descended to the land, conjoined, and gave birth to the eight islands of Japan. They went on to create thirty spirits of earth, sea, seasons, winds, mountains, trees, moors, and fire. But as Her Augustness, the "female who invites," gave birth to fire, she was scorched and grew very ill.

In her sickness she gave birth to the Metal Mountain Prince and Princess, the Viscid Clay Prince and Princess, the Spirit Princess Water, and Young Wondrous Producing Spirit. Her Augustness, the mother deity, then retired from existence.

Izanagi was so stricken with grief over the loss of his sister that he wept and danced, thereby expressing his tremendous sorrow.

The strength of his emotion was such that through his grieving he created the Weeping Spirit. His Augustness then sliced off the head of his son, the Fire Spirit, Kazu-tsuchi. From the blood of Kazu-tsuchi that dripped through Izanagi's fingers arose the dragon gods Kora-okami, "dragon god of the valleys," and Kura-mitsu-ha, "dark water snake." From the lifeless limbs of the Fire Spirit emerged many other spirits.

Izanagi, wishing to reunite with Izanami, descended into the "land of the night" to find her. When he came upon the entrance to the underworld, he called for his sister. Izanami came but refused to be seen. He pleaded for her to come back with him, for they had not yet finished creating the world. But she could not; she had eaten the fruit from Yami, the land of the dead. The fruit, once inside

OPPOSITE PAGE: Rice is not only a major source of sustenance to the Japanese; it is also a very important part of many rituals and customs. Because Japan has so little level land area, the Japanese developed an ingenious method of staggering rice paddies on the sides of mountains and hills.

ABOVE: The Izumo shrine, located in Matsue, is the oldest existing Shinto shrine.

This view of
Inari Sanctuary on
Honshu Island, Kyoto,
reveals the Japanese
flair for simple
architectural designs
that subtly guide
the eye and evoke
an appreciation for
line and texture.
Inari is the goddess
of rice, and thus
an important
Japanese deity.

Prince Shotoku in the seventh century. One of the main Buddhist tenets explained in that text was that everything past, present, and future coexisted—that the concept of linear time was an illusion.

The Chinese developed a school of Buddhism known as *Ch'an*. In Japan, the Ch'an school became the Zen school—the most influential of the many forms of Buddhism.

Buddhism developed in Japan during four distinguishable periods. The first period was inaugurated by a great statue of Buddha erected in the Todaiji Temple at Nara, circa A.D. 752. This icon, influenced by Chinese art, made Nara the first Buddhist capital. The bronze Buddha was seated on a sacred lotus flower and measured sixty-eight feet (20.7m) in height. It was the Buddha of no time, no place, and no race, and evolved into one of the five guardian Buddhas of meditation. The Japanese praised it as the "great sun Buddha," Dainichi-nyorai.

The second period in the development of Japanese Buddhist thought occurred in Kyoto between the years 794 and 835. Dengyo Daishi and Kobo Daishi were two Japanese monks who developed a completely Japanese form of Buddhism. Kobo Daishi wrote one of the most important texts of the time, the *Ryobu*, or *Shinto with Two Faces*. He taught that Buddhism and Shintoism could coexist. One important belief introduced by the *Ryobu* was that the Shinto kami were bodhisattvas, or spiritual guardians of the Buddhist temple. Dengyo founded the Tendai sect, which later became associated with the imperial family. Dengyo and Kobo's impact lasted until the year 894, when the third period began. The sect formed by their combined teachings became known as the Shingon.

The third period came about as Japanese Buddhism matured and established uniquely Japanese traditions. This important period is

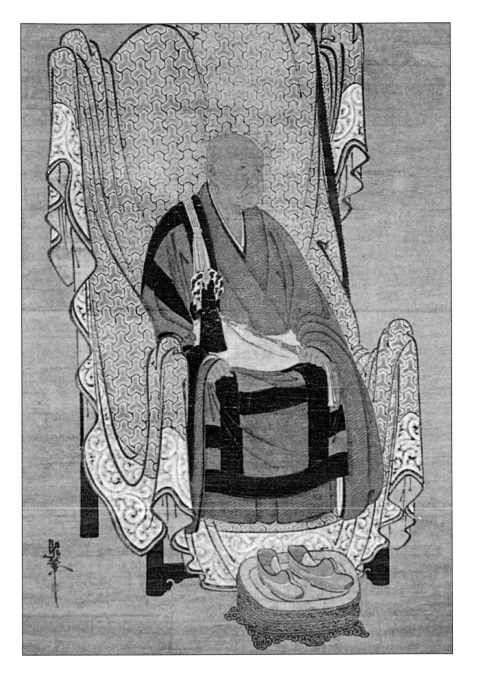

also symbolized by one of Japan's greatest works of literature, *The Tale of Genji*, written by Lady Murasaki.

The fourth period, the Kamakura, reflected the development of four distinct schools of Japanese Buddhism. They were, first and second, the Jodo and the Shinshu, which eventually converged and became known as the Amida sect. Jodo was founded by Honen and Shinran; together they taught the word and worship of the Amida Buddha as well as the seven Gods of Fortune. The third and fourth sects were Nichiren and Zen.

OPPOSITE: **The Zen garden at Daitokuji Temple, Kyoto, is typically serene, featuring rocks, statuary, and coarse sand carefully raked into a soothing pattern. Zen expression is always characterized by an overriding simplicity.**

ABOVE: **This painting of a Zen monk highlights the characteristically simple garb worn by such men by contrasting it with a luxurious wing chair.**

This torii, or gate, is located off the island Itsukushima, just southwest of Hiroshima. Built in 1875, the torii shares the island with an ancient Shinto shrine, a ninth-century Buddhist temple, a fifteenth-century pagoda, and a famous hall built by Hideyoshi in the sixteenth century. This island is also known as Miyajima, or Shrine Island.

Nichiren, the founder of the Nichiren sect, was opposed to all other forms of Buddhism, claiming that his version alone was the only true version of Buddhism. Eisai was believed to have been the first to introduce Zen, the most influential of the sects, into Japan. (There is a Japanese saying, "The Tendai is for the royal family, the Shingon for the nobility, the Zen for the warrior classes, and the Jodo for the masses.")

Most of the mythological tales not pertaining directly to the Buddha revolve around the exploits of Japanese heroes. These legends are usually associated with the samurai and thus reflect Zen beliefs.

Zen had a significant influence on Japanese culture. This philosophy explored life from within as well as from without and bloomed in a society built on the performance of rituals. The Zen influence is felt in many important Japanese art forms: archery, swordsmanship, painting, gardening (stone gardens), ceramics, architecture (teahouses), poetry (the haiku), diet, and Noh theater. (In Noh drama, masked spirits represent demons, ghosts, or witches. They enter over a wooden bridge as if coming from another world. A single step signifies a journey. Noh drama is an exercise in the economy of gesture, movement, and symbolism. The audience experiences *yugen*, a feeling of deep contemplation of beauty.)

In the quest for enlightenment, Zen dismisses traditional patterns of thought along with the language of reason that expresses such thought. Reaching true awareness, a state of conciousness known as the "Buddha mind," requires the freeing of the mind from reason. It cannot be taught but must rather be attained, through *zazen*, "seated meditation," and the use of *koans*, mental puzzles of which perhaps the most famous is "What is the sound of one hand clapping?" Only when the mind is free of the prison of rational thought can true insight be attained. This break-

though—which takes the form of a sudden flash of insight referred to as *satori*—generally takes years to achieve, and represents the first step on the even longer road to true enlightenment.

In Japan, Zen's disciplined and practical approach appealed to members of the warrior class, the samurai. Why would something so peaceful and harmonious appeal to a warrior? The answer lies in Zen's reliance on intuition as opposed to intellect. It was only through transcending thought (*mushen*, "no mind") that one achieved enlightenment. Zen helped the warrior overcome mental restrictions in order to find the transcendent in ordinary experience. The way of the Zen warrior became known as *bushido*.

There is a story about Menechika, who was asked by Emperor Ichijo (986–1011) to forge a sword. This was a great honor and Menechika would not even think about disappointing the emperor. Menechika called upon the bodhisattva Inari, the Shinto goddess of rice, to help support his endeavor. The goddess came and whispered instructions to him, and the sword he made was magnificent. Thus, the sacred sword—two of them are worn by the samurai, with one smaller than the other—is not an object of destruction, but rather a symbol of inspiration.

ZEN HEROES AND DEITIES

In Zen Buddhism, historical figures often attained a state of deification. This is a prime example of the historical and mythical uniting. For example, the regent Hojo Tokimune was praised as a "Buddha to be" because he defeated the invading Mongolian forces. Many tales such as this exist about Zen warriors and their accomplishments.

Early Shinto worship generally focused on objects of nature. The impressive Kinkakuji Temple, overlooking a lake in Kyoto, seems an ideal spot for such meditation, as it combines solitude and a stunning natural vista.

RIGHT: The Seven Gods
of Fortune are the
patrons of spiritual
beneficence.

BELOW: Emmo-o was
the god of death and
the enemy of Amida,
his polar opposite.

EMMO-O

Emmo-o, the black-faced, morbid god of
death, was Amida's archenemy. He resided in
his own land, which was the complete opposite of Gokuraku Jodo, the Pure Land. He was
a merciless and fierce judge of the dead. Those
unfortunate souls who were condemned to
spend eternity in Emmo-o's domain were consoled by the gentle-faced Jizo-bosatsu. Jizo-
bosatsu wandered the land of Emmo-o
comforting the suffering souls. The kind and
merciful Jizo-bosatsu is depicted as having a
shaved head, wearing a long robe, and carrying a staff that rings when it touches the
ground. It was believed that his staff had the
power to ward off evil.

THE SEVEN GODS OF FORTUNE

Also associated with Honen's teachings are
the Seven Gods of Fortune. These gods did
not advocate physical riches or wealth, but
richness of spirit.

Hotei had a huge protruding potbelly. His
large belly symbolized his satisfaction, for it
was filled with serenity.

Jurojin was the god of longevity. He is depicted with a long white beard and in the
company of either a crane, tortoise, or deer—
animals that symbolized long spiritual lives.
Jurojin carried a scroll that contained the wisdom of the world.

Fukurokuju had a long, narrow head, a
squat torso, and short legs. Like Jurojin, he
was associated with long life and was known
for his deep wisdom.

Daikoku, the patron of farmers, is often
depicted sitting on a mound of rice. He carried a hammer and used it to grant special re-
quests to favored supplicants.

Ebisu, the god of fishermen and traders, is depicted sporting a rod and his catch.

Bishamon-tenno is depicted as a powerful military monarch, clad in full armor, with spear in hand. He was prepared to battle those who opposed Buddhism. Prince Shotoku, the first of the imperial family to welcome Buddhism, called upon Bishamon to help convey Buddhist thought to the Japanese clans—noble families that were unwilling to accept Buddhism. Thus, Bishamon was a missionary as well as a warrior.

Benton was a goddess who was the bearer of wealth, patron of musicians, and guardian of speech. Benton married a sea dragon king. At first she was reluctant to marry him but after careful contemplation warmed to the idea. Their union symbolized Benton's association with the sea, and she was eventually worshiped as the goddess of the sea. Benton is often depicted riding on a serpent's, or her husband's, back. Other depictions show her playing a *biwa*, a mandolinlike instrument. She is usually found in tales about sea serpents and dragons.

OTHER JAPANESE BUDDHIST GODS

DAINICHI-NYORAI

Dainichi-nyorai, the "great sun Buddha," or "great illuminator," was associated with the Shingon sect founded by Kukai, also known as Kobo Daishi (774–835). Some say that Kukai was born with his hands clasped together in prayer. Kukai brought Dainichi-nyorai to Japan after traveling to China, where he studied *chen yen*, or "true word school." In his later years, Kukai instructed his students to bury him alive, whereupon he would wait for the coming of Miroku-bosatsu, the Buddha who has yet to come.

Dainichi is often depicted seated on a white lotus and in deep contemplation. Kukai taught that it was possible to tap into magical and spiritual powers and call upon Dainichi so that his presence could be felt on earth. It was also believed that Kukai used mystical powers—powers instilled in him by his firm belief in Dainichi—to drive away many evil dragons from Japan.

NICHIREN

Like many masters of Buddhism—including Honen, Shiron, and Eisa—Nichiren is the subject of many legends. He labeled himself a bodhisattva with "distinguished action," a protector of truth. His name means "sun lotus." Even his birth was legendary: it is said that his mother dreamed of the sun falling from a lotus flower and thus conceived Nichiren. In his teachings, Nichiren condemned all other forms of Buddhism, proclaiming his the only true one.

HAKUTAKU

Hakutaku was a strange creature who had a body resembling a hand with a human head. It was believed that Hakutaku ate humanity's bad dreams and evil experiences, freeing humans from anxiety. Hakutaku was a welcomed guest in most homes. When a family member was sick, a picture of Hakutaku was placed in the entrance of the infected person's room.

FUGEN-BOSATSU

Fugen-bosatsu is the final Buddha who has yet to come. He is the Buddha with "divine compassion" for all men. He now spreads his enlightening wisdom throughout the people. Fugen-bosatsu is depicted as a young man sitting atop a white elephant with six tusks; when he is not carrying a lotus flower, his hands are shown clasped together in prayer.

CHAPTER

III

CHINESE
MYTHOLOGY

China is an ancient land of many myths and legends. The two major belief

systems based on original Chinese thought are Confucianism and Taoism,

which were founded by Confucius, or Kung Fu-tzu (c. 551–479? B.C.),

and Lao Tzu (604 B.C.), respectively. The other important doctrine,

Buddhism, was introduced into China during the Han dynasty, around A.D. 67,

by traders traveling the Silk Road from India to China. With its remarkable abil-

ity to absorb and integrate outside influences, Chinese society was able to sup-

This seventeenth-century painting depicts events in the lives of certain Tang
dynasty emperors. The Tang dynasty ruled for almost three centuries. In that
time China experienced rapid cultural and territorial growth, with great
advances in artistic output, especially in sculpture, painting, and poetry.

port all three schools, which shared some basic thought and eventually combined to give rise to a number of unique practices and traditions. Thus, the ancient spirits and gods coexisted with the ethical imperatives of Confucianism, the universal power of the Tao, and the meditative search for enlightenment of Zen Buddhism. Indeed, it is often noted that the Chinese follow Confucius in public life, Lao Tzu in private life, Buddha at the end of life, and the ancient traditions in daily life.

Well before these philosophies took hold, however, the people of China practiced a primitive form of worship. An early Chinese culture, the Shang people, built a complex society at the basin of the great Yellow River during the twelfth century B.C. The practices of this and earlier Chinese cultures were thought to be shamanistic, and like many such cultures often featured a belief in spirit powers, which were appeased with magic and ritual. A shaman, a respected person who could com-

municate with the spirit world, would call for rain by dancing a furious rain dance. As the shaman danced, sweat fell from his body, symbolizing the coming of rain. The shaman was also the medicine man, who healed the sick with certain potions and herbs. (These ancient herbal remedies formed the basis of traditional Chinese medicine, which still uses herbs in a holistic approach to health that has received significant attention from the Western medical establishment in recent years.) The reign of the shamanistic leader waned with the introduction of organized religion.

One enduring concept of ancient Chinese thought is the principle of opposition—light/dark, male/female, active/passive—that is part of all life. These opposing principles balance and complement one another, creating the circle of life. This concept is known as yin-yang and is central to Chinese culture. Yang is the active, positive principle, and yin is the reactive, negative principle. Yin and yang are believed to maintain the precarious balance of the universe, existing together and creating harmony. If one principle were to operate independently from the other, chaos would prevail.

The ancient Chinese traced their history from the creation of the world straight through the earliest emperors and the building of the Chinese empire with no significant distinction between the historical and the mythical. There are many periods in the development of this great culture, the histories of which are recounted through symbolic tales. The earliest ages are depicted as follows:

The earliest humans lived in trees to avoid the predatory hazards that prevailed on the ground. Then there was the period of the fire drillers, when sages first introduced fire to man so that he could cook his food— the raw food was destroying his stomach. Finally, in the earliest period of man, there were great floods; tales recount how Kung Kung, the god of water, banged his head on a mountain and tilted the earth.

Next was the period of highest virtue. During this era Jung Ch'eng, the creator of the calendar, and Chu Jung, the god of fire, came into existence.

There followed the period of the Great Ten Legendary Rulers. Fu Hsi was the first ruler and the creator of the written symbols upon which the I Ching, *or* Book of Changes, *was based. The great Yu, the champion of the great flood and founder of the Hsia dynasty, was the last.*

This magnificent Buddhist statue is from the Hsiangkuo monastery in Kaifeng, a city that has been the center of Chinese culture at several different times over the centuries. Founded in the third century B.C., Kaifeng was the capital of the Five Dynasties (A.D. 906–959) and the Sung dynasty (A.D. 960–1127).

Most of the great Chinese emperors gained deification. When an emperor died, he was buried with all his belongings: jewels, chariots, servants, and so on. Many great sages were also worshiped as gods. The most revered of these teachers were Confucius, Lao Tzu, and Bodhidharma.

The writings of most of the great sages have been permanently lost. During the Ch'in dynasty (221–206 B.C.) the Great Wall of China was built to keep the empire safe from invading forces. In contradistinction to the humanistic spirit of this architectural feat was the Burning of the Books: almost all the literature of the Ch'in and earlier eras was destroyed. Included among the burned books may have been most of the written works of Confucius. Shih Huang-Ti was the emperor whose intent was to erase the entire history of China so as to assert himself as the first em-

peror. Scholars caught meeting secretly to discuss the written word—as well as those who outwardly protested the burning—were burned to death alongside their books. This event is the cause of the gap in China's recorded history. What we know as Confucius' lessons were retold many times by his disciples and may have lost their original meaning. A text of Confucius that did survive was the *Ch'un Ch'iu* (*The Spring and Autumn*)—the history of his hometown, Lu. It is believed that some of Lao Tzu's philosophical and moral writings—collected and called the *Tao Te Ching*—also survived this devastating event.

Perhaps the most important of the surviving ancient Chinese texts is the *I Ching*. A book of prophecy and wisdom told through brief and eloquent sayings, the *I Ching* contains eight trigrams (sets of three lines, broken and unbroken) that were believed to have

The Lungmen Grottoes (numbering around 2,100), near Loyang, contain an estimated 100,000 images of Buddha, including these colossal carvings. According to legend, the Buddhist sutras were first introduced to China in Loyang by two monks (traveling from India on a white horse) sometime in the first century A.D. Loyang was the capital of a number of ancient dynasties, including the Tang, during which period the Lungmen carvings (begun at the end of the fifth or beginning of the sixth century A.D.) were embellished.

Shao Hao ruled for only seven years. His life remains something of a mystery.

Kao Yang had eight sons, one of whom was Kun, the father of the "Great Yu."

K'u was the husband to Chiang Yuan and Chien Ti. Both of his wives were known for having conceived sons through the miraculous powers of the gods.

Yao Ti, the "Divine Yao," lived from 2357 to 2255 B.C. He was a virtuous monarch and the ultimate example of a great sage. He is responsible for employing Kun to stop the great floods, although Kun was unsuccessful; the task was eventually completed by Yu. Legend tells that the supreme god in heaven was disappointed with humanity and decided to rid the earth of man. He sent torrential rains to flood the land. Kun took pity on the people and stole some of the supreme god's enchanted soil, brought it to earth, and succeeding in damming the floods. The supreme god was angered by Kun's interference and had him destroyed. But Kun's spirit would not die. The supreme god then had Kun's limbs severed from his body. From Kun's remains, a dragon burst forth. The dragon was the Great Yu, Kun's son, who finally stopped the floods and drained the floodwaters. Yao Ti had taken an interest in a peasant boy, Shun, and offered him his two daughters to marry. Yao Ti then asked Shun to complete several tasks, one of which tested Shun's strength against the elements of fierce rain, wind, and thunder. Shun succeeded and was deemed to be strong, honorable, and pious. These distinguished qualities earned him Yao Ti's respect. Yao Ti bequeathed the throne to his son-in-law, favoring Shun over his own son.

Shun ruled from 2317 to 2208 B.C. He was a just and humane sovereign. Shun's father had remarried (after leaving his first wife) and fathered a second son. His father was a very evil and corrupt man and attempted to murder Shun. But Shun was patient with his father and never held a grudge. Shun honored his father no matter how disrespectfully the old man acted toward him. Shun is placed at the head of the Twenty-four Examples of Filial Piety (examples of great rulers who revered both their families and the governed).

Yu, the Great Yu, ruled from 2205 to 2197 B.C. Yu was the son of Kun and the grandson of Kao Yang. Kun had failed to drain the floodwaters and thus the task fell upon Yu's shoulders. For nine years Yu labored until he succeeded.

Yu was responsible for dividing China's great land into nine provinces. He also had a meeting with the ancient sovereign-sage Fu Hsi, who gave him an instrument made of jade (the sacred stone) with which he could measure heaven and earth.

Yu is depicted as having a long neck with an ugly face and a mouth like a raven's beak. He is considered the Confucian model of virtue.

YI THE GREAT ARCHER AND CHANG E THE MOON LADY

Ten suns appeared in the sky and the intense heat that radiated from them was destroying the land and drying up the riverbeds. People across the land were suffering. Yi, or Hou I, came down from heaven with his enchanted bow and shot down nine of the suns; Yi's bravery restored order over the land and sky. He later shot the celestial dog, Tien Kou, for trying to eat the moon.

Yi then set out to visit Hsi Wang Mu, the goddess of the West. Here, he obtained the precious Immortal Elixir. He was told that there was enough for his wife, Chang E, and himself. Returning home, he put it aside for the right moment and went out hunting. In the meantime, Chang E took the elixir and started to consume it. The more she had, the lighter she felt, and she began to float into the sky. For fear that she wouldn't make it to heaven, she finished it all. Chang E kept on ascending until she reached the moon. Once on the moon, Chang E was distraught because it was barren except for the company of a certain rabbit. Yi was miserable over the loss of his wife.

Yi later took on a disciple, Peng Meng, who murdered Yi out of jealousy of his master's skill. Yi had taught Peng Meng well, and thus Peng Meng became the greatest archer alive after Yi's death.

LEGENDARY CREATURES

The dragon and the phoenix were a pair of mythical creatures that were treasured and respected by the Chinese people. Among other

a frog; the scales of a carp; the talons of an eagle; and the paws of a tiger. Dragons were believed to have been deaf. Most dragons were not winged, but had fins for swimming that were (understandably) mistaken for wings.

The scales on the dragon's body signified universal harmony. In all, the dragon had 117 scales. Eighty-one scales were under the yang influence, good fortune; and thirty-six were under the yin influence, bad fortune. The dragon was a creature of both active and reactive powers, part preserver and part eliminator.

Dragons inhabited bodies of water—the larger the body of water, the more powerful the dragon. They controlled the dispensing of rains, and created thunder by rolling huge pearls in the heavens. They were seen as both water gods and the guardians of pearls. Dragons were also the bearers of wealth and good fortune. Each town believed in its own local dragon.

The Chinese believed that there were heavenly dragons as well as earthly dragons. Those in heaven resided in the part of the sky known as the Palace of the Green Dragon. (It was given this title by the Chinese astronomers who studied the constellation of the dragon.)

Some dragons pulled the chariots of many emperors, as well as the chariot of the sun. There were also many dragon kings, known as *lung wang*, throughout China's mythological history.

This fierce warrior's head belonged to a Tang dynasty tomb guardian. His helmet is crested with a phoenix, the mythical fire bird associated with the empress. Most likely the protector of an imperial tomb, this glazed pottery figure dates from the late seventh or early eighth century.

things, the dragon represented the male characteristic, yang; and the phoenix represented the female, yin. Together these complementary creatures symbolized emperor and empress, marital harmony.

THE DRAGON

According to legend, the dragon had the head of a camel; the horns of a deer; the eyes of a demon; the ears of a cow; the long whiskers of a cat; the long neck of a snake; the belly of

THE PHOENIX

The phoenix, *feng huang*, was the sacred fire bird. It was truly a magnificent creature to behold, and it had the features of several different animals. It had the head of a swan; the throat of a swallow; the beak of a chicken; the neck of a snake; the legs of a unicorn; the arched back of a turtle; and the stripes of a dragon. Its feathers were made up of the five sacred colors: black, white, red, green, and yellow.

THE CHINESE GODDESSES

HSI WANG MU

The great Taoist philosopher Lieh-tzu tells the story of the enormous peach tree of immortality that grew on top of the highest peak in the Kwun-lun Mountains. This apex was known as the Chinese paradise. Here, Hsi Wang Mu, the goddess of the West and the empress of immortals, lived in the Jade Mountain Palace, where she tended to her magnificent gardens. Hsi Wang Mu was described as fairylike with messy hair, the teeth of a tiger, and a tail like a panther's. Sparrows—the symbol of gentleness— brought her food whenever she was out patrolling her garden. The beasts closely associated with Hsi Wang Mu were a blue stork, an albino tiger, a deer, and a huge tortoise— all gods of longevity. She also dispensed the cures for diseases.

Wu Ti, the fourth emperor of the Han dynasty, watched an uncommon-looking sparrow fly into his chamber. Tung-fang Shuo, the emperor's magician, said that the sparrow was the sign of a good omen. Indeed it was, because soon Hsi Wang Mu came to the emperor. The goddess rode in on the back of a white dragon with a procession of creatures behind her. The sight was magnificent to behold. She carried a tray with seven peaches from her immortality tree. When Hsi Wang Mu presented the peaches to Wu Ti, a few of them had been secretly eaten by Tung-fang Shuo. Wu Ti ate the remaining peaches and became immortal. (In another version of this tale, the gift was a wine elixir.)

CHUN T'I

Chun T'i is the Tao goddess of light, who radiated an enigmatic light. She had eight hands, with two holding the sun and the moon. Celestial knowledge was hers, and she rode through the heavens in her chariot drawn by seven pigs.

Chun T'i, a mythical personage in the Taoist canon, is the mother of the seven stars of the Great Bear constellation (also referred to as the Ladle), where she resides.

Dragon Hall, a pagoda in Kaifeng, China, is a magnificent example of this architectural style, which traces back to Indian Buddhism. The pagoda in all its many manifestations in Asian countries is based on the *stupa*, an ancient Indian Buddhist reliquary with a three-tiered umbrella finial.

PATRON GODS AND OTHER DEITIES

There were many patron gods in China who were called upon for help by persons in the many professions and trades. These deities, usually historical figures, often held jobs pertaining to their worship. Because there were so many trades, there were likewise a huge number of patron gods. Some of the more popular or more commonly invoked patron gods are discussed below.

LU PAN

The patron deity of carpenters and builders, Lu Pan is honored on the twelfth day of the sixth moon. His father was falsely accused of a crime, and in protest, Lu Pan built a huge statue of the emperor. When he finished the statue, an awful drought befell the land. The people attributed it to the statue and pleaded with Lu

Pan to do something. Honoring the people's request, he cut off a hand on the statue and the rain immediately began to fall. It was also believed that he was the creator of many tools, including the ball and socket. When a builder was stumped or needed advice, Lu Pan was always there to help.

WEN CH'ANG

Wen Ch'ang was a god of literature and patron to librarians and booksellers. As a man, he was an impoverished scholar who passed his imperial exams with the highest honors. He was to receive an award from the emperor but when the emperor gazed upon Wen Ch'ang, the award was revoked. Too ugly to be given the honor, Wen Ch'ang threw himself into the ocean in despair. But before he could drown, the ocean dragon saved him and brought him to heaven. In heaven he was made the expert of all literature. Wen Ch'ang is depicted as a small demon.

PA CH'A

Pa Ch'a, god of the grasshopper, was the protector of the crops. It was his duty to prevent pests from destroying the fields. He was depicted in human form with a bird's beak for a mouth and claws instead of feet.

T'AI SUI

T'ai Sui, the god of astronomy, historically was the minister of time. He was the son of Emperor Chou Wang.

OPPOSITE: The Wild Goose pagoda in Xian dates back to the Tang dynasty, when Xian became the western capital of China and a great center of both Buddhist and Muslim activity.

ABOVE: This flag bearer was a minor deity whose role was significant mainly to soldiers or to military mandarins.

BELOW, LEFT: This is a depiction of the goddess of midwifery seated upon a tiger; she is another minor deity, perhaps associated with Kwan Yin, the goddess of fertility.

The Great Wall of China (of which the Mu Tian Yu section is pictured here) is one of the largest and most ambitious constructions ever undertaken by human beings. Its many separate sections were unified into one wall during the reign of Shih Huang-ti and once extended for some 6,200 miles (9,920km), from the Yalu River in the northeast to Xinjiang in the northwest.

BELOW, RIGHT: Ti Yu, a version of the underworld, was not an original idea of the Chinese. The concept came from the Buddhists, who also introduced the god of the underworld, Yama. In China, Yama was known as Yen-lo.

OPPOSITE: The Iren Pagoda, located in Kaifeng, was built in A.D. 1049. Kaifeng is one of the six famous capital cities of imperial China. In the eleventh century, when this pagoda was built, Kaifeng was the hub of the northern Sung dynasty.

When T'ai Sui was born, he had the appearance of a shapeless blob of skin. Due to his unsightly features, associates of the emperor said he was a demon, and that both mother and child should be put to death. They were to be thrown from the palace tower, but the child was saved and was raised by Ho Hsien-ku, an immortal woman. When he was older, T'ai Sui joined the emperor's army, unbeknownst to his father. He rose to prominence in the military and then revealed himself to his father, and together they sought vengeance against those who had originally discredited T'ai Sui.

DOOR GODS

Door gods were evoked as protectors of the sick. Their likenesses were posted on both sides of a door to ward off evil spirits bent on inflicting harm.

TI YU,
EARTH PRISON

The concept of a hell—an underworld where evil spirits go after death—did not exist for the Chinese until the introduction of Buddhism. Before the idea of hell was proposed, humans sought immortality, which allowed them to reside in paradise. The introduction of the notion of hell—Ti Yu, "earth prison"—was accompanied by a new pantheon of gods. Some were directly associated with the Indian gods and some were original to China—an example of the ability of the Chinese to incorporate and expand an imported mythological canon.

The Hindu Yama, king of the underworld, became Yen-lo in China. Yen-lo's domain was not solely for evil spirits; in fact, all spirits entered through the gates of hell before proceeding to their destiny.

There were various stages that a soul had to go through. First, souls were met at the gate by demons demanding money for admission. Second, the souls were weighed on a huge scale—the good were light and the bad were heavy. Third, the souls were ushered into the Bad Dog Village, where the unblemished souls were weeded out from the corrupt souls. Fourth, they were paraded in front of the reincarnation mirror, which reflected images of their future forms. Fifth, they were brought to a terrace where they could glimpse the family they had left behind. Sixth, they were led across bridges—the evil walked over narrow bridges and the good were paraded over elaborately decorated and sturdy bridges. Seventh, they came to the wheel of law, where a drink was offered to erase all previous memories.

There were several different messengers from hell who catered to Yen-lo. Two were Mu Mien and Niu T'ou; Mu Mien had a horse's head and Niu T'ou had an ox's head. Another two were the ghostly messengers *wu-ch'ang*

Seers, 81, 82, 99, *99*, 266

Seisrech Bresligi, 273, *273*

Semele, 68, *68*

Sequona, 246

Serpents, 53, 92, 107,
    136, 157, 168, 211,
    212, 216, *216*, 333,
    347, 361, 362

Sessrymnir, 178, 190

Shakti, 343, 354, *354*,
    355, 356, *356*, 358, 360

Shamans, 398

Shang Ti, 419

Shao Hao, 411

Shen Nung, 407

Shesha, 361

Shih Huang-Ti, 401

Shintoism, 371, 372, 374,
    378, 380, 384, 387

Shiva, 12, 330, *330*, 335,
    336, *336*, 343, *343*,
    345, *346*, 347, 350,
    353, 354, 355, *355*,

356, *356*, 361, 362

Shoten, 391

Siculius, Diodorus, 240

Siddhartha, 364

Sidhs, 262, 263, *263*, 287,
    287

Sif, 152, 160, 161, 164,
    177, 202

Sigurd's Helmet, *208*, 209

Sigyn, 164, 165, *165*

Sinon, 106

Sirens, 114, 115, *115*

Sita, 338, 339, 352, 359

Siva, 13

Sixfold Slaughter, 273,
    273

Skadi, 173

Skanda, 347, *347*, 350,
    355, *355*

Skidbladnir, 161, 174

Skirnir, 174, 175, 216

Skoll, 134, 210, 219

Skrymir, 154, 155, *155*,

157

Skuld, 11, 136, *200*, 201,
    207

Sleipnir, 139, *139*, 142,
    196, 199, 209

Sol, 11, 12, 134, 219

Soma, 353, *353*

Son, 183

Sons of Mil, 261, 262

Souconna, 246

Sparta, 97

Sri, 365

Sthenelus, 86

Stone of Fah, 256, *256*

Strabo, 231, 240

Sturluson, Snorri, 122

Stymphalian Birds, 89,
    90, *90*

Sualdam the Smith, 270,
    273, 274

Sukuna-Biko, 380

Sulevia, 10, 12, 244, 246,
    247

Sulis, 10, 244

Sumbha, 357

Su-mitra, 338

Sun Hou-Tzu, 428, *428*,
    429

Surtr, 130, 214, 216, 220

Susanowo, 378, 379, *379*,
    380

Suttung, 183, 184, 185

Svadilfari, 138, *138*, 139,
    142

Svalin, 134

Svarga, 348

Svartalfheim, 134, *135*,
    160, 161, 183

Sweden, *132*, 133

Symplegades, 82, *82*

Syn, 149

T

T, 270

Tain Bo Cuailnge,
    265–275, 279, 322

T'ai Sui, 423, 426

Tale of Genji, The, 387

Tanngniostr, *150*, 151,
    152, 154

Tanngrisnt, *150*, 151,
    152, 154

Tantras, 333, 334
Tao Chun, 419
Taoism, 374, 397,
    402–403, 419
Tao Te Ching, 401, 403
Tara, 10, 254, 255, 256,
    256, 262, 281, 286
Tara Brooch, 237
Tartarus, 23, 36, 40, 42,
    43
Tartessus, 91, 92
Tath, 250
Tech Midchuarta, 275
Teeth-Men, 82, 83
Teirnon, 305, 307
Telemachus, 116, 117
Tenedos, 99
Tengu, 384
Terpsichore, 75
Tethis, 23
Tethys, 18, 32
Teucer, 99
Teutates, 243, 244
Thalia, 72, *73,* 75
Thanatos, 39
Thebes, 68, 78, 86
Theia, 18
Themis, 18
Themiscyra, 91
Theseus (King of Greece),
    86, 87, *87,* 258, 259
Thetis, 61, 95, 96, *96,*
    101, 102, 104
Thialfi, 154, 156, 157,
    160
Thiazi, *158,* 159, 185,
    186, 187
Thok, 199
Thor, 10, 139, 142, *150,*
    151, 152, *152,* 153,
    153, 154, 155, *155,*
    157, 162, 164, 186,

194, 198, 214, 216,
    220, *220*
Thorwald Cross, 214, *215*
Thrace, 81, 91
Thrud, 152, 153
Thrudgelmir, 131
Thrudheim, 152, 157
Thrymheim, 186, 187
T'ien Hou Niang Niang,
    418
Tiresias, 113, *113,* 114
Titans, 18, 23, 25, 40, 48,
    53, 65, 68, 72, 92
Ti Yu, 13, 426, 428
Tjasse, 173
Toward the Hurdle Ford,
    311
Tricksters, 10, 33, 65, 138,
    139, 142, 154, 155,
    157, *158,* 159, 160,
    161, 162, 163, 164,
    165, *165,* 186, 187,
    190, 191, *191,* 195,
    195, 196, 199, 209,
    210, 211, 212, 214,
    216, *216*
Trimurti, 330, 336, *336,*
    343
Trisala, 365, 366
Trojan War, 61, 94–107
Troy, *94,* 95, 96, 97
Tsukiyomi, 13, 378, 380
Tuan, 251
Tuatha de Danu, 10, 253,
    254, *254–255,* 255,
    256, 257, 261, 262,
    263, 270
Tureinn, 257, 261
Turkey, 99, 239
Twelve Labors of
    Heracles, 84–93
Twins of Macha, 265

Tyndareus, 98
Tyr, 154, 163, *166,* 167,
    169, 216

U

Uath, 279, *279,* 280
Uller, 142, 201, 202
Ulysses, 110, *110,* 112,
    112, 115, *115,* 116, *116*
Underworld, 67, 113
    Celtic, 244
    Chinese, 426
    geography of, 40–43
    Greco-Roman, 13
    Greek, 23, 39, 40–43
    Indian, 333, 351
    Irish, 262

Japanese, 9, 13, 372,
    377, 378
    Chinese, 13
    Norse, 163
    Roman, 40–43
    Welsh, 299, 303
Upanishads, 335
Urania, 48, 75
Uranus, 18, *18,* 19, 48
Urd, 11, 136, *200,* 201,
    207
Ushas, 351, 360
Utgard, 153, 154, 155
Utgard-Loki, 10, 155, 156,
    157, 160
Uther Pendragon, 12
Uzume, 378

V

Vaikuntha, 333
Vak, 360
Valaskialf, 143
Valfreya, 178
Valhala, 11, 126, 142,
  143, 144, 148, 152,
  178, 182, 190, 207, 212
Vali, 142, 164, 199, 201,
  206, 220
Valkyrs, 136, 139, *139,*
  144, *144,* 178, 207
Valmiki, 335
Vamana, 337
Vanaheim, 136, 202
Vandals, 149
Vanir, 12, 136, 173, 177,
  182, 202, 214
Vara, 149
Varaha, 337
Varuna, 353
Vasudeva, 12, 340
Vasuki, 347
Vayu, 352
Ve, 9, 131, 133, 134, 220
Vedas, 329, 330
Venus, *46,* 47, 51, *51*

Verdandi, 11, 136, *200,*
  201, 207
Vidar, 201, 204, 216, 220
Vigrid, 212, 214, 216
Vili, 9, 131, 133, 134,
  136, 185, 202, 220
Vingnir, 152
Vishni, 361, *361*
Vishnu, 11, 13, *328,* 329,
  330, 336, *336,* 337,
  337, 339, 340, 343,
  350, 354, 359, 364
Visvamitra, *334,* 335, 338
Vivasvat, 11, 12, 13, 333,
  350, 351, *351*
Vjofn, 149
Vritra, 350

W

Wen Ch'ang, 423
*White Book of Rhydderch,
  The,* 290
Winilers, 149
Witham Shield, 236, 281,
  281
Woden, 141
World Tree, 12
Wotan, 141, 243

Y

Yakshas, 363
Yakshina, 12
Yakshini, 11, 360, *360*
Yama, 13, 333, 351, 352,
  352, 361
Yamapua, 13
Yamato-Take, 381
Yami, 377
Yamuna, 351, 352
Yao Ti, 411, 412
Yasoda, 340
Yellow Book of Lecan, 265
Yen-lo, 13
Yen Ti, 407
Yggdrasil, 136, *140,* 141,
  143, 145, *200,* 201,
  207, 211, 214, 220
Yi, 413, *413*
Yin and yang, 391, 398
Ymir, 9, 131, 133, 134,
  143, 220
Yomi, 13
Yu, 412
Yu Huang, 419

Z

Zetes, 81
Zeus, 11, *20,* 21, 22, 23,
  26, 28, 29, 31–33, 35,
  37, 43, 48, 49, 53, 59,
  60, 63, 65, 68, 69, 72,
  74, 81, 85, 86, 96, 98,
  101, 102, 114
Zhurong, 406
Zocho, 384

Tantras, 333, 334

Tao Chun, 419

Taoism, 374, 397, 402–403, 419

Tao Te Ching, 401, 403

Tara, 10, 254, 255, 256, *256*, 262, 281, 286

Tara Brooch, 237

Tartarus, 23, 36, 40, 42, 43

Tartessus, 91, 92

Tath, 250

Tech Midchuarta, 275

Teeth-Men, 82, 83

Teirnon, 305, 307

Telemachus, 116, 117

Tenedos, 99

Tengu, 384

Terpsichore, 75

Tethis, 23

Tethys, 18, 32

Teucer, 99

Teutates, 243, 244

Thalia, 72, *73*, 75

Thanatos, 39

Thebes, 68, 78, 86

Theia, 18

Themis, 18

Themiscyra, 91

Theseus (King of Greece), 86, 87, *87*, 258, 259

Thetis, 61, 95, 96, *96*, 101, 102, 104

Thialfi, 154, 156, 157, 160

Thiazi, *158*, 159, 185, 186, 187

Thok, 199

Thor, 10, 139, 142, *150*, 151, 152, *152*, 153, *153*, 154, 155, *155*, 157, 162, 164, 186,

194, 198, 214, 216, 220, *220*

Thorwald Cross, 214, *215*

Thrace, 81, 91

Thrud, 152, 153

Thrudgelmir, 131

Thrudheim, 152, 157

Thrymheim, 186, 187

T'ien Hou Niang Niang, 418

Tiresias, 113, *113*, 114

Titans, 18, 23, 25, 40, 48, 53, 65, 68, 72, 92

Ti Yu, 13, 426, 428

Tjasse, 173

Toward the Hurdle Ford, 311

Tricksters, 10, 33, 65, 138, 139, 142, 154, 155, 157, *158*, 159, 160, 161, 162, 163, 164, 165, *165*, 186, 187, 190, 191, *191*, 195, *195*, 196, 199, 209, 210, 211, 212, 214, 216, *216*

Trimurti, 330, 336, *336*, 343

Trisala, 365, 366

Trojan War, 61, 94–107

Troy, *94*, 95, 96, 97

Tsukiyomi, 13, 378, 380

Tuan, 251

Tuatha de Danu, 10, 253, 254, *254–255*, 255, 256, 257, 261, 262, 263, 270

Tureinn, 257, 261

Turkey, 99, 239

Twelve Labors of Heracles, 84–93

Twins of Macha, 265

Tyndareus, 98

Tyr, 154, 163, *166*, 167, 169, 216

U

Uath, 279, *279*, 280

Uller, 142, 201, 202

Ulysses, 110, *110*, 112, *112*, 115, *115*, 116, *116*

Underworld, 67, 113

   Celtic, 244

   Chinese, 426

   geography of, 40–43

   Greco-Roman, 13

   Greek, 23, 39, 40–43

   Indian, 333, 351

   Irish, 262

   Japanese, 9, 13, 372, 377, 378

      Chinese, 13

   Norse, 163

   Roman, 40–43

   Welsh, 299, 303

Upanishads, 335

Urania, 48, 75

Uranus, 18, *18*, 19, 48

Urd, 11, 136, *200*, 201, 207

Ushas, 351, 360

Utgard, 153, 154, 155

Utgard-Loki, 10, 155, 156, 157, 160

Uther Pendragon, 12

Uzume, 378

V

Vaikuntha, 333
Vak, 360
Valaskialf, 143
Valfreya, 178
Valhala, 11, 126, 142,
    143, 144, 148, 152,
    178, 182, 190, 207, 212
Vali, 142, 164, 199, 201,
    206, 220
Valkyrs, 136, 139, *139*,
    144, *144*, 178, 207
Valmiki, 335
Vamana, 337
Vanaheim, 136, 202
Vandals, 149
Vanir, 12, 136, 173, 177,
    182, 202, 214
Vara, 149
Varaha, 337
Varuna, 353
Vasudeva, 12, 340
Vasuki, 347
Vayu, 352
Ve, 9, 131, 133, 134, 220
Vedas, 329, 330
Venus, *46*, 47, 51, *51*

Verdandi, 11, 136, *200*,
    201, 207
Vidar, 201, 204, 216, 220
Vigrid, 212, 214, 216
Vili, 9, 131, 133, 134,
    136, 185, 202, 220
Vingnir, 152
Vishni, 361, *361*
Vishnu, 11, 13, *328*, 329,
    330, 336, *336*, 337,
    337, 339, 340, 343,
    350, 354, 359, 364
Visvamitra, *334*, 335, 338
Vivasvat, 11, 12, 13, 333,
    350, 351, *351*
Vjofn, 149
Vritra, 350

W

Wen Ch'ang, 423
*White Book of Rhydderch,
    The*, 290
Winilers, 149
Witham Shield, 236, 281,
    281
Woden, 141
World Tree, 12
Wotan, 141, 243

Y

Yakshas, 363
Yakshina, 12
Yakshini, 11, 360, *360*
Yama, 13, 333, 351, 352,
    352, 361
Yamapua, 13
Yamato-Take, 381
Yami, 377
Yamuna, 351, 352
Yao Ti, 411, 412
Yasoda, 340
Yellow Book of Lecan, 265
Yen-lo, 13
Yen Ti, 407
Yggdrasil, 136, *140*, 141,
    143, 145, *200*, 201,
    207, 211, 214, 220
Yi, 413, *413*
Yin and yang, 391, 398
Ymir, 9, 131, 133, 134,
    143, 220
Yomi, 13
Yu, 412
Yu Huang, 419

Z

Zetes, 81
Zeus, 11, *20*, 21, 22, 23,
    26, 28, 29, 31–33, 35,
    37, 43, 48, 49, 53, 59,
    60, 63, 65, 68, 69, 72,
    74, 81, 85, 86, 96, 98,
    101, 102, 114
Zhurong, 406
Zocho, 384